Fear and Temptation

Fear and Temptation,

The Image of the Indigene in Canadian, Australian, and New Zealand Literatures

TERRY GOLDIE

McGill-Queen's University Press
Kingston, Montreal, London

©McGill-Queen's University Press 1989
ISBN 0–7735–0691–8

Legal deposit first quarter 1989
Bibliothèque nationale du Québec

Printed in Canada on acid-free paper

This book has been published with the help of a grant from the Canadian Federation for the Humanities, using funds provided by the Social Sciences and Humanities Research Council of Canada.

Canadian Cataloguing in Publication Data

Goldie, Terry
  Fear and temptation: the image of the indigene in Canadian, Australian, and New Zealand literatures
  Includes index.
  Bibliography: p.
  ISBN 0–7735–0691–8
  1. Indians of North America in literature.
  2. Australian aborigines in literature. 3. Maoris in literature. 4. Canadian literature (English) – History and criticism. 5. Australian literature – History and criticism. 6. New Zealand literature – History and criticism. I. Title.
  PN3426.I64G64 1989   C810'.9'3520397   C88-090369-4

Contents

Foreword   vii

Acknowledgments   xi

1 Fear and Temptation   3

2 The Natural   19

3 Form   41

4 Sexuality   63

5 Violence   85

6 Orality   107

7 Mysticism   127

8 Historicity   148

9 Theatre   170

10 Rudy Wiebe and Patrick White   191

11 A Polemical Conclusion   215

Works Cited   225

Index   245

Foreword

This book began many years ago with an interest in doing a comparative study between Australian and Canadian literatures. I had spent all of my time as a graduate student delving into Canadian subjects, and I felt much might be learned by a comparison with a literature of similar roots and similar international stature (or lack of it). Comparisons with African literature, for instance, involve cultural differences which seemed to me overwhelming. Those with American literature lead to a compulsive need to reject the inferiority of the "smaller partner."

The next step was a search for a subject. I recognized that the best one would in some sense draw on the similarity of the colonial experience. Having spent some time looking at the role of the Indian in Canadian literature, I thought that indigenous peoples might provide such an example. I realized from the beginning the difficulty presented by the enormous differences between the cultures of the various Aboriginal groups and those of Canadian Indians. I hoped that what seem to me obvious similarities between the two white cultures might provide sufficient common ground.

As I examined the material I became convinced that the similarities were much greater than one might have expected and that such similarities suggested major ideological questions. A subject that seemed simply one of many possible became one that for me has its own driving force, almost its own inevitability. As I recognized this, I began to turn outside once more to New Zealand. Through examining Australian material I had learned that many of the issues we tend to deem innately Canadian are also Australian. And I had gained interpretations of Canadian material which were only possible through the reshaped vision provided by the Australian. Still, while very useful in furthering this reshaping, the New Zealand material in the following study is limited by the depth of my research and by available space. New Zealand became, as I am afraid it so often becomes in such studies, primarily a control or a series of addenda, although the apparently significant variable of the enormous ethnographic differences between the Maori and the indigenous peoples of Canada and Australia does not appear a major factor. My experience of New Zealand culture, both literary and other, leaves me with no reason to exclude it from the majority of my remarks in this study.

The obvious American analogies present a different issue. The extent of material is daunting but so is the amount of analysis which has been applied to that material. Also, as suggested above, there is an inherent difficulty in making any comparisons between big US and teeny-tiny Canada and Australia, even if that is only a result of superficial perceptions. As well, there are some significant variations between cultures which openly evolve from the British empire and one which hides such an evolution through a myth of Revolution and a different form of government. But, as any student of American literature will discern from the present study, these variations do not make the American image of the indigene essentially different but rather contribute to certain variants.

My general acknowledgments follow, but I must first note that my perception of the political ramifications of the semiotic process began through reading Edward Said, Gayatri Chakravorty Spivak, and Michel Foucault, although they are not precisely semioticians and Foucault in particular might have recoiled at such a reference. But their work led to my recognition that semiosis is neither an individual psychological experience nor an abstruse philosophical game but a basic, perhaps the most basic, part of the power relationships in all cultures. Thus my own episteme, and my justification for the theoretical base of my analysis. Thus my hesitation at words such as "essential" and "inevitable," although I believe, from my centre, through my own episteme, that these interpretations are essential, are inevitable. It is the purpose of my writing here to convince you to search for the same episteme, and thus to perceive the same semiosis, and the same political value of that semiosis. But I realize that I can claim with assurance no essence beyond that of my own perception.

Throughout the study a date is given at the first reference to a text. This is the date of the earliest edition, or in the case of a play, when such information is available, of the first performance. For some early works, such as Joseph Howe's "Acadia," published long after writing, an approximate date of composition is given. The publication data for the actual texts examined are given at the end of the study, under "Works Cited." I provide the dates in the text primarily to suggest the diachronic subtext to my synchronic approach. Unfortunately dates may not always be precise: I may have overlooked earlier editions of obscure publications, and the dates of nineteenth-century poems, which usually represent book publication, might be misleading since many were published in book form only long after their appearance in periodicals.

Acknowledgments

The major part of my research was done at the Fryer Library of the University of Queensland, and I owe a great debt to Margaret O'Hagan, the Fryer Librarian, and her staff. I owe a lesser but similar thanks to the Mitchell Library, Sydney, the Hocken Library, Dunedin, the Turnbull Library, Wellington, and the National Library and National Archives of Canada.

For funding and administrative support I would like to thank the Social Sciences and Humanities Research Council of Canada, the University of Queensland, and Memorial University of Newfoundland.

A different version of chapter eight was published in *Australasian Drama Studies*.

The remaining notes of gratitude, some personal and some academic, most both, I give in alphabetical order: Barry Andrews, Sue Bell, Patrick Evans, Jack Healy, Laurie Hergenhan, Witi Ihimaera, Dorothy Jones, Veronica Kelly, Alan Lawson, Carol Lawson, Annie Liénard, Ron Marks, Robin Mathews, John Matthews, Margaret Maynard, Les Monkman, Craig Munro, Malcolm Page, Janice Price, Peter Simpson, Alrene Sykes, and Elizabeth Webby.

The greatest thanks, as always, are to Robyn Goldie.

Fear and Temptation

CHAPTER ONE

Fear and Temptation

"Lo, the poor Indian." This short phrase from Alexander Pope's *An Essay on Man* (1734) soon became a part of popular culture. By the mid-nineteenth century caricatures had appeared in which a dejected-looking Indian was labelled as "Lo." In Pope, "lo" was a directive interjection in a serious comment on the position of the Indian in the universal order. In the caricatures it became a proper name, a silly name for the silly literary obsession with the dying Indian culture and, presumably, dying Indian race. Pope's words had been subjected to a conscious mis-reading to suit parodic needs. A simplistic description of the process might be from reality to Pope to caricature. And yet one must remember that the first step of transformation, while apparently the more subtle, is, in fact, the larger. The movement from life to art is always greater than from art to art.

A very different form of art is the television commercial. Some time ago on Australian television there was an advertisement for the Metropolitan Building Society. A couple dressed as American pioneers are captured by Indians and tied to a stake. Just when their situation seems hopeless, the "loan arranger" comes to save them with a loan from Metropolitan. Australian cultural history offers a number of similar examples of an indigenous people reacting against white invaders in what later came to be called an "Aboriginal massacre," but when the advertisers did their creating they turned to the American context or, more precisely, to no context, at least in terms of what might be called historical fact. The Indians of the advertisement are almost completely separated from the ethnic groups which provided their origins. Like their predecessor, "Lo," they have become only image. To explain the process in semiotic terms, the signifier, the image here presented, does not lead back to the implied signified, the racial group usually termed Indian or

Amerindian, but rather to other images. The process might be called
the Quaker Oats box view of the sign. You begin with the picture
of the person on the box, who is holding a box with a picture of the
same person holding a box with a picture of the same person holding
a box, etc. An originary image cannot exist for there must always
be another image on the box being held, no matter how small it
gets. In the same way, each signifier can refer only to another signifier. There might be an implied signified but it is unreachable.

All of the terms in any analysis are of course themselves "loaded,"
significantly so in a discussion of the image of the indigene. For
example, "image" might seem too reductive, reminiscent of image
analysis, that gently thematic means of dissecting a text. A more
precise term might be "representations," as it occurs in Edward
Said's *Orientalism* (1978): "In any instance of at least written language, there is no such thing as a delivered presence, but a *re-
presence*, or a representation" (21). While "representation" is indeed
used in this sense throughout this study, the term might also suggest
a general, perhaps somewhat unshaped, portrait, a signifier which
if it cannot re-produce at least re-presents the referent. For the indigene, "image," with its implication of hard-edge packaging, has the
right aura. John Berger's *Ways of Seeing* (1972) describes an image as
"a sight which has been recreated or reproduced. It is an appearance,
or a set of appearances, which has been detached from the place
and time in which it first made its appearance and preserved – for
a few moments or a few centuries" (9–10). A literary representation
might seem less absolute but, as this study shows, the indigene in
literature is such a reified preservation, and not just as it appears
in such obvious manipulations as "Lo" and the opposition to the
"loan arranger." Each representation of the indigene is a signifier
for which the signified is the Image. The referent has little purpose
in the equation.

A comment on a similar process is found in Tzvetan Todorov's
exploration of "Art According to Artaud" (1971): "We must not confuse the relation between signifier and signified with the relation
between sign and referent. Whereas the former must be reinforced
by analogy, the latter must, on the contrary, be denaturalized; we
must break down the automatism which makes us take the word
for the thing, makes us consider one as the natural product of the
other" (*Poetics of Prose*, 213). There is no suggestion here that the
various writers on the indigene have intended, as did Artaud, to
deny the referent, but this is the effect of their creations. If examined
in this context, the semiotic process becomes a more useful tool in
understanding the image of the indigene. The truism of poststruc-
turalist theory that the distance between signifier and signified is an

alterity never to be surmounted becomes not an abstruse philosophical concept with nihilist tendencies but a means of understanding various limitations. The valorization of the image is determined
by a process in which the signified is only a signifier, which is not
to claim that there is no connection between text and "reality." What
is important, Said suggests in *Orientalism,* is not the approximation
of presence which seems to be the intention of western discussions
of eastern culture, but rather the conformity of the works to an
ideology that Said and others have called orientalism. Thus, he is
studying not the reality the works seem to represent, the truths they
claim to depict, but the reality of the texts and their ideology, and
of the ideology of the authors and their culture. Creative literature
is but one of the more visible examples of the reification of the
indigene, something which permeates our cultures, even those
aspects of it that seem most removed from native peoples. I am
"writing" this line on a computer purchased from Beothuk Data
Systems, named for the now-extinct indigenes of Newfoundland.

Behind this reality of an ideology lies another reality, of a history
of invasion and oppression. In all three countries, indigenous peoples were forced to succumb to the needs of British imperial expansion. In Australia, the Aborigines at first had little purpose in the
white economy except as guides in exploration. By the mid-nineteenth century, however, they became important, perhaps vital,
labourers on stations in the interior. The situation in Canada was
reversed, with the Indians essential as fur traders to the early economy and of less value thereafter. The Maori, because of differences
in topography, and in both white and indigenous economy, seemed
of limited "use" at the beginning and remained so.

All this may seem at best facile, pot-boiled history, unnecessary
for a consideration of the subject at hand – although not unnecessary
because untrue or irrelevant. The history of invasion and oppression
is essential to the present study, truly of the essence, although the
details and even the central events of the conquest are not major
factors in the image of the indigene. The overwhelming fact of the
oppression awarded semiotic control to the invaders, and since then
the image of "them" has been "ours," a point Wolf underscores in
Europe and the People Without History (1982): "Racial designations,
such as 'Indian' or 'Negro,' are the outcome of the subjugation of
populations in the course of European mercantile expansion. The
term *Indian* stands for the conquered populations of the New World,
in disregard of any cultural or physical differences among native
Americans" (380).

This study finds its synchronic character both in its intent and in
the object of its discussion. It would certainly be possible to dem-

onstrate how historical change, the diachronic, has affected the image of the indigene, but the focus of this examination is to show the uniformity of that ongoing semiotic control and the power of that image. Because the study is about the image rather than the people the image claims to represent, I use that synchronic designation of conquest, "Indian," throughout in reference to Canadian native peoples. The historical error which the term represents becomes a comment – and a useful comment – on all aspects of this study. It is also an unavoidable comment in that no appropriate alternatives are available. The word "Amerindian," itself a rather superficial disguise, has too many resonances of the United States. "Inuit," "Aborigine," and "Maori" create problems but, unlike "Indian," all are accepted by at least a large part of the groups which they represent. "Native peoples," the generic term usually preferred, is used sometimes when no distinction is required between Canada, Australia, and New Zealand, but "indigene" is employed most often.

Our image of the indigene has functioned then as a constant source for semiotic reproduction in which each textual image refers back to those offered before. Said devotes much of *Orientalism* to an examination of this process: "Most important, such texts can *create* not only knowledge but also the very reality they appear to describe. In time such knowledge and reality produce a tradition, or what Michel Foucault calls a discourse, whose material presence or weight, not the originality of a given author, is really responsible for the texts produced out of it" (94). The image of the indigene has been textually defined and, through an extended intertextuality, national and international, diachronic and synchronic, which embraces the implied discourse of such apparently *hors texte* items as visual art, it constantly reproduces itself, a pervasive autogenesis.

A word that is seldom used in this study is "racist." It is avoided for many reasons, not the least that it is generally employed in simplistic fashion as a diatribe not unlike "communist" or "fascist." If there is a text which can claim to be beyond racism, I have not read it. If there is a person who can claim to be beyond racism, I have not met him/her/me. But questions of racism, like those of imperial history, lie behind each line of this analysis, perhaps *sous rature*. In "Racism's Last Word" (1985), Jacques Derrida reacts to the word, "apartheid": "Surely an idiom should never incline toward racism. It often does, however, and this is not altogether fortuitous: there's no racism without a language. The point is not that acts of racial violence are only words but rather that they have to have a word. Even though it offers the excuse of blood, color, birth – or, rather, *because* it uses this naturalist and sometimes creationist discourse – racism always betrays the perversion of a man, the 'talking animal.' It institutes, declares, writes, inscribes, prescribes. A system of marks, it outlines space in order to assign forced residence or to close off borders. It does not discern, it discriminates" (292).

Yet regardless of such assertions of the constant danger of discursive closure, few texts avoid simplistic assumptions about the non-racist reality of their image of the indigene. Even those critics who depend on words such as "verisimilitude" eventually slip into the assurance that they can assess whether or not a certain work is "realistic" or, more to the point, an accurate representation of reality. One commentator on Canadian radio suggested that while early images of Indians in Canadian literature were often racist stereotypes, now some authors are beginning to get it right. Any thinker with a sense of history should be able to recognize the danger in judging contemporary material successful in contrast to past failures. Michel Foucault asserts in "Prison Talk" (1975): "I adopt the methodical precaution and the radical but unagressive scepticism which makes it a principle not to regard the point in time where we are now standing as the outcome of a teleological progression which it would be one's business to reconstruct historically: that scepticism regarding ourselves and what we are, our here and now, which prevents one from assuming that what we have is better than – or more than – in the past" (*Power*, 49).

Foucault opposes this complacent teleology with a recognition of the "systems of power" which control the "Truth" of a culture, in the past, present, and future ("Truth and Power," *Power*, 133). The most useful source of analysis is thus not chronological but ideological distance. Historical perspective might provide a shift sufficient to re-examine a past text, but a determined displacement must be adopted as the approach to deciphering the subtle unconsidered elements which shape a contemporary text. Rosalind Coward and John Ellis, in *Language and Materialism* (1977), call for an awareness of "the political purpose of semiology" to "produce a knowledge of sign systems and their naturalisation which can be a basis for a constant demystification of established systems of meaning: showing that what appears to be unchangeable is humanly created and can be recreated in certain directions" (31–2).

I realize that my own reading has a certain very specific centre, as a white Canadian male of a certain age. I write as an "insider" of only one culture, the white Canadian. I am a foreign observer of New Zealand and Australia. A much larger limitation is that I can make no claims to know any of the indigenous cultures from within. I would find much surer ground from which to attack white images if this study itself were not very much a white text in its authorial perspective. But perhaps my very precarious position is itself an asset. As Said posits in "Orientalism Reconsidered" (1985): "The Orient and the Occident are facts produced by human beings, and as such must be studied as integral components of the social, and not the divine or natural, world. And because the social world includes the person or subject doing the studying as well as the object or realm being studied, it is imperative to include them both in any consideration of Orientalism for, obviously enough, there could be no Orientalism without, on the one hand, the Orientalists, and on the other, the Orientals" (15). Yet Said seems not to see himself as a position in this equation, as the human being studying the Orientalists. As the white student of the white texts I am constantly aware of this position, as I hope is the text of this study. While I might appear to be claiming that I should be excused from the chain of semiotic manipulation because of my sensitivity to all these problems of distance, this study shows throughout that sensitivity has failed to erase the circumscriptions of the image of the indigene. My claim is not for the perfection of my centre but for the decentring process that I have applied. My criticism is based on a constant attempt to attack the apparent centre of the works under consideration, particularly to show the semiotic limitations of texts which have been said to provide "positive" or "realistic" views of indigenous peoples. I seek what Pierre Macherey's *A Theory of Literary Production* calls the "ideological horizon" (132), the concealed but omnipresent ideology controlling the text. Yet in identifying that horizon, in deconstructing that centre of control, I must recognize that I cannot avoid asserting my own centre, my own "truth," no matter how carefully I might try to hide it. As in any such critical stance I must recognize that, in Yeats's words, "the centre cannot hold" ("The Second Coming" 211).

I hope that my work is not Procrustean, the obvious attack which might be made, but my recognition of my centre leaves me unable to reject this accusation. Part of the centring for any reader is that reader's participation in the episteme, or method of knowing, of his or her culture. Although some theorists treat epistemology as objective, a scientifically understandable process, even a limited analysis will show that the episteme is culturally determined and the sponsor of many shifts of centre. As Claude Lévi-Strauss suggests in *The Savage Mind* (1962), some basic anthropological errors have been made because of failures to recognize such epistemic variations. His example of such a failure is totemic classification: "The mistake of classical ethnologists was to try to reify this form and to tie it to a determinate content when in fact what it provides is a method for assimilating any kind of content" (75). Even so, "like the rest of us," Jack Goody points out in *The Domestication of the Savage Mind* (1977), Lévi-Strauss is "a victim of the ethnocentric binarism enshrined in our own categories" (8). Each episteme makes inevitable approaches which another will deem Procrustean.

The limitations of such centres, of such epistemes, create a constant question for any representation of the indigene in a white text. It is a commonplace in creative writing classes to direct students to "write about what you know," but in a very obvious sense any white writing about the indigene is writing "about what you do not know." In his introduction to *The Feast of the Bunya* (1901) Cornelius Moynihan reflects: "I remember a modern philosopher, discoursing on the subject of 'Intellect in Dogs,' confesses the chief difficulty with which he finds himself confronted is to 'think dog.' In like manner, though not, to be sure, to the same extent, the difficulty one encounters with all savage races is to 'think blackfellow.' Did ever civilized white man dare pretend to a full acquaintance with the mind and heart of the savage; in other words, 'think blackfellow' so surely as to enable him to appreciate the feelings and passions of 'God's image in ebony?'" (14). Moynihan's dehumanizing analogy, use of the term "blackfellow" for Aborigine, and general aura of superiority make it difficult to accept his comment, perhaps doubly difficult because these words are followed by Moynihan's own attempt, even more deficient than most, at writing something representing this "full acquaintance." But the essence of his observation on the white failure to penetrate the indigene episteme remains valid.

A more useful analogy than Moynihan's canine might be the image of women in male-written texts. Feminist critics have often discussed the stereotypical literary view of women, sometimes suggesting, "men can't write about women." Male authors may reply that no writer can be absolutely limited to personal experience and that men have aptly portrayed women characters. At one time, a likely example of a well-drawn woman would have been James Joyce's Molly Bloom, but recent feminist critics have shown quite clearly the inadequacies of that portrait. The only proof of whether the male text can "think woman" or the white "think indigene" is in the readings which the text provides.

It is my perception that the shape of the signifying process as it applies to indigenous peoples is formed by a certain semiotic field, a field that provides the boundaries within which the images of the indigene function. The existence of this semiotic field constitutes an important aspect of the "subjugated knowledges" (81) to which Foucault refers in *Power/Knowledge* (1980). The indigene is a semiotic pawn on a chess board under the control of the white signmaker. And yet the individual signmaker, the individual player, the individual writer, can move these pawns only within certain prescribed areas. Whether the context is Canada, New Zealand, or Australia becomes a minor issue since the game, the signmaking, is all happening on one form of board, within one field of discourse, that of British imperialism. Terms such as "war-dance," "war-whoop," "tomahawk," and "dusky" are immediately suggestive everywhere of the indigene. To a North American, at least the first three would seem to be obvious Indianisms, but they are also common in works on the Maori and the Aborigine. Explorers like Phillip King (*Narrative* 1827) generally refer to Aborigines as Indian, and specific analogies to North American Indians are ubiquitous in nineteenth-century Australian literature. Terms misapplied in the Americas became re-misapplied in a parody of imperialist discourse. The process is quite similar to one Lévi-Strauss describes in *The Savage Mind*: "In other words, the operative value of the systems of naming and classifying commonly called totemic derives from their formal character: they are codes suitable for conveying messages which can be transposed into other codes, and for expressing messages received by means of different codes in terms of their own system" (75). Obvious extreme ethnographic differences between the different indigenous cultures did little to impede the transposition.

To extend the chessboard analogy, it would not be oversimplistic to maintain that the play between white and indigene is a replica of the black and white squares, with clearly limited oppositional moves. The basic dualism, however, is not that of good and evil, although it has often been argued to be so, as in Abdul R. Jan-Mohammed's "The Economy of Manichean Allegory" (1985): "The dominant model of power – and interest – relations in all colonial societies is the manichean opposition between the putative superiority of the European and the supposed inferiority of the native" (63). JanMohammed maintains that in apparent exceptions "any evident 'ambivalence' is in fact a product of deliberate, if at times subconscious, imperialist duplicity, operating very efficiently through the economy of its central trope, the manichean allegory" (61). Such a basic moral conflict is often implied but in contemporary texts the opposition is frequently between the "putative superiority" of the indigene and the "supposed inferiority" of the white. As Said suggests, the positive and negative sides of the image are but swings of one and the same pendulum: "Many of the earliest Oriental amateurs began by welcoming the Orient as a salutary *dérangement* of their European habits of mind and spirit. The Orient was overvalued for its pantheism, its spirituality, its stability, its longevity, its primitivism, and so forth... Yet almost without exception such overesteem was followed by a counter-response: the Orient suddenly appeared lamentably under-humanized, antidemocratic, backward, barbaric, and so forth" (*Orientalism*, 150). Almost all of these characterizations could be applied to the indigenes of Australia, New Zealand, and Canada, as positive or negative attributes.

The complications of the issue extend even beyond oppositions of race, as Sander Gilman suggests in *Difference and Pathology* (1985): "Because there is no real line between self and the Other, an imaginary line must be drawn; and so that the illusion of an absolute difference between self and Other is never troubled, this line is as dynamic in its ability to alter itself as is the self. This can be observed in the shifting relationship of antithetical stereotypes that parallel the existence of 'bad' and 'good' representations of self and Other. But the line between 'good' and 'bad' responds to stresses occurring within the psyche. Thus paradigm shifts in our mental representations of the world can and do occur. We can move from fearing to glorifying the Other. We can move from loving to hating" (18). The problem is not the negative or positive aura associated with the image but rather the image itself.

The problem is also the way the image is valorized. In his introduction to *Brown Man's Burden and Later Stories* (1973), a collection of sketches by Roderick Finlayson, Bill Pearson, who has written often on the image of the Maori in *pakeha* (white) fiction, claims, "There is no patronage in his feeling for Maoris and his admiration for their culture is not because their needs are fewer but because their sense of what is important in living strikes him as truer. The implication of Finlayson's stories is to question the worth of the values of our industrial society" (ix). "Fewer" and "truer," a "question" of "our." Perhaps patronage is the wrong word but ethnocentric might be the right one, in the assumption that the Maori exist only in a white comparative context. The Other is of interest only to the extent that it comments on the self, a judgment that could quite correctly be applied to the present study. With the exception of certain comments in the conclusion, my interest is not in the indigenes but in the image of the indigenes, a white image. Olivier Richon examines a similar problem in the visual arts in "Representation, the Despot and the Harem" (1985): "The aim of this paper is to show to what extent western representations of the Orient address the West itself, as if the Occident attempted to project itself and look at itself from an imaginary vanishing point, represented by the

Orient" (1). The focus is not as overtly reflective but the image of the indigene similarly reveals very little about the indigenes or their cultures. It reveals a great deal about the whites and their cultures. One of which is my culture.

At least since Fanon's *Black Skin White Masks* (1952) it has been a commonplace to use "Other" and "Not-self" for the white view of blacks and for the resulting black view of themselves. The implication of this assertion of a white self as subject in discourse is to leave the black Other as object. The terms are similarly applicable to the Indian, the Maori, and the Aborigine but with an important shift. They are Other and Not-self but also must become self. Thus as Richon suggests and Pearson implies, imperialist discourse valorizes the colonized according to its own needs for reflection. "The project of imperialism has always already historically refracted what might have been the absolute Other into a domesticated Other that consolidated the imperialist self," explains Gayatri Spivak in "Three Women's Texts and a Critique of Imperialism" (1985, 253). Tzvetan Todorov in *The Conquest of America: The Question of the Other* (1982) also notes how the group as Other can function. "This group in turn can be interior to society: women for men, the rich for the poor, the mad for the 'normal'; or it can be exterior to society, i.e., another society which will be near or far away, depending on the case: beings whom everything links to me on the cultural, moral, historical plane; or else unknown quantities, outsiders whose language and customs I do not understand, so foreign that in extreme instances I am reluctant to admit they belong to the same species as my own" (3).

But Spivak's area of study, the Indian sub-continent, is a different case from that of the Australian, Canadian, and New Zealand because the imperialist discourse remains admittedly non-indigenous. India is valorized by its relationship to imperialist dynamics but it "belongs" to the white realm only as part of the empire. Todorov writes as a European about the Spanish during the time of conquest, but he fails to recognize the possibility of an almost complete crossing of the interior and the exterior, in which the group is an apparently different species yet so far from "foreign," epistemologically more than "far away" yet also more than "near," here. Australians, New Zealanders, and Canadians have, and long have had, a clear agenda to erase this separation of belonging. The white Canadian looks at the Indian. The Indian is Other and therefore alien. But the Indian is indigenous and therefore cannot be alien. So the Canadian must be alien. But how can the Canadian be alien within Canada?

There are only two possible answers. The white culture can attempt to incorporate the Other, superficially, through beaded moccasins and names like Mohawk Motors, or with much more sophistication, through the novels of Rudy Wiebe. Conversely, the white culture may reject the indigene: "This country really began with the arrival of the whites." This is no longer an openly popular alternative, but its historical importance is reflected in things like the "native societies" that existed in all three countries in the late nineteenth century, societies to which no non-white, no matter how native, need have applied.

The importance of the alien within cannot be overstated. In their need to become "native," to belong here, whites in Canada, New Zealand, and Australia have adopted a process which I have termed "indigenization." A peculiar word, it suggests the impossible necessity of becoming indigenous. For many writers, the only chance for indigenization seemed to be through writing about the humans who are truly indigenous, the Indians, Inuit, Maori, and Aborigines. As J.J. Healy notes in *Literature and the Aborigine in Australia* (1978), "The Aborigine was part of the tension of an indigenous consciousness. Not the contemporary Aborigine, not even a plausible historical one, but the sort of creature that *might* persuade a white Australian to look in the direction of the surviving race" (173). Many Canadians, New Zealanders, and Australians have responded strongly to this creature and to their own need to become indigenous. The would-be indigenous are a diffuse body, with few overt connections between them. The obvious exception is the Australian Jindyworobaks, who had a clear collective agenda to "free Australian art from whatever alien influences trammel it," in the words of Rex Ingamells from *Conditional Culture* (1938). Ingamells defined Jindyworobak to mean "to annex, to join," and he asked his followers to join in:

1. A clear recognition of environmental values.
2. The debunking of much nonsense.
3. An understanding of Australia's history and traditions, primaeval, colonial, and modern (Elliott, 231).

The polemical character of these words cannot hide their lack of specificity. Brian Elliott, in his introduction to *The Jindyworobaks* (1979), suggests of Ingamells, "As he saw it, the need was to 'annex' or 'join' the white to the black, or the black to the white – it is not clear how" (xxvii). Yet this small group made a general program out of what my study and others (Healy, Jones) have shown to be a consistent concern of white culture in Australia, and, with slight variations, in Canada (Monkman), and New Zealand (Pearson).

Of course, the majority of writers in all three countries have given brief or no attention to native peoples. Perhaps then, while the image of the indigene may be a consistent concern, it is a limited one, the

Jindyworobaks notwithstanding. But the process of indigenization is complex. Each reference in *The Bulletin*, the nationalistic nineteenth-century Australian magazine, to the white Australian as "native" or "indigenous" is a comment on indigenization, regardless of the absence of Aborigines in those references. As Macherey claims, "an ideology is made of what it does not mention; it exists because there are things which must not be spoken of" (132). In other words, absence is also negative presence. Thus in a work such as Henry Handel Richardson's *The Fortunes of Richard Mahony* (1920s), a trilogy which uses the Australian gold rush as a field through which to explore the founding of a nation, the Aborigine is an essential non-participant.

Neither the racial split between self and Other nor the process of indigenization originates with Canada, Australia, or New Zealand, but neither do they have clear origins which might be seen as the source for these manifestations. Presumably the first instance in which one human perceived another as Other in racial terms came when the first recognized the second as different in colour, facial features, language, etc. And the first felt need for indigenization came when a person moved to a new place and recognized an Other as having greater roots in that place. The lack of a specific origin for these conditions is reflected in the widespread occurrence of their modern manifestations. This study is limited to the literatures of the three countries of the "white Commonwealth," because they provide a body of material which is manageable and because their relationships with indigenous peoples, both historical and contemporary, are similar in many specific ways. The majority of the assertions, however, are applicable to a number of analogous literatures which attempt to deal with the indigenous other, most obviously in American literature and in Canadian literature in French but also in South American literature. To look beyond the "Indian" context, South African literature also "fits," with J.M. Coetzee's *Waiting for the Barbarians* (1980) a perfect example of the valorization of the semiotic field of the indigene. For general comparisons, the ideological frameworks of Robert F. Berkhofer's *The White Man's Indian: Images of the American Indian from Columbus to the Present* (1978) and *Les Figures de l'Indien* (1988), edited by Gilles Thérien, are different from the present study but the conclusions are similar.

The image of the indigene is perhaps most clearly defined in association with nature. For the majority of the explorers, the first writers who attempted to make their signifying process represent real experience, the indigene as the "natural" seems to be a given, although there are ambivalences such as the attempts in John Nicholas's *Narrative of a Voyage to New Zealand* (1817) to separate a very positive portrait of "Nature" from the "barbarisms" of the Maori. Nicholas's superficial task was to document what happened, but an important part of that work was to create a suitable form for that documentation, a natural way of presenting the natural. Richard Terdiman, in "Ideological Voyages" (1985), divides such genres of heuristic process into "two symmetrical figures for representing the confrontation with the Other. These might be termed *penetration* (the forcible imposition of the dominator and his discursive system within the dominated space) and *appropriation* (the consumption enforced by the dominator of what belongs to the dominated)" (32).

Penetration might seem to lead to the absence seen in *Richard Mahony* but there are a number of genres of penetration that admit the indigene, including the explorer's narrative itself, which thrusts the gaze within the country. Most of the forms considered in this study have been employed towards appropriation, whether in the obvious manner of the Jindyworobaks or in the various attempts in fiction to capture the subjectivity of the indigene. However, regardless of the changes made in the form of the chessboard, whether dismissive histories of penetration or sensitive novels of appropriation, the semiotic field has continued, particularly in the few basic moves which the indigenous pawn has been allowed to make.

These few basic moves Said calls "standard commodities" (*Orientalism*, 190). Two such commodities which appear to be standard in the "economy" created by the semiotic field of the indigene in Australian, Canadian, and New Zealand literatures are sex and violence. They are poles of attraction and repulsion, temptation by the dusky maiden and fear of the demonic violence of the fiendish warrior. Often both are found in the same work, as in John Richardson's *Wacousta or The Prophecy* (1832), in which the warrior constantly attacks, but the maiden is an agent to avoid that attack. They are emotional signs, semiotic embodiments of primal responses. Could one create a more appropriate signifier for fear than the treacherous redskin? He incorporates, in generous quantities, the terror of the impassioned, uncontrolled spirit of evil. He is strangely joined by the Indian maiden, who tempts the being chained by civilization towards the liberation represented by free and open sexuality, not the realm of untamed evil but of unrestrained joy. "The 'bad' Other becomes the negative stereotype; the 'good' Other becomes the positive stereotype. The former is that which we fear to become; the latter, that which we fear we cannot achieve" (Gilman, *Difference*, 20). Added to this is the alien's fear of the "redskin" as hostile wilderness, the new, threatening land, and the arrivant's attraction to the maiden as restorative pastoral, this new, available land.

A third important commodity is orality, all the associations raised by the indigene's speaking, non-writing, state. The writers' sense of indigenes as having completely different systems of understanding, different epistemes, is based on an often undefined belief that cultures without writing operate within a different dimension of consciousness. This different dimension suggests a fourth commodity, mysticism, in which the indigene becomes a sign of oracular power, either malevolent, in most nineteenth-century texts, or beneficent, in most contemporary ones. In an interesting variant on the semiotic process, the inadequacies of the writer's culture, in which little knowledge is to be gained from the popular beliefs of its own traditions – in which the distancing Quaker Oats box leaves divine power completely beyond reach – is placed in contrast to an indigenous belief system (usually quite asystemic) which holds the promise of a Presence to exceed even the presence of orality.

Spivak has commented on the "soul-making" enterprise which was the agenda for imperialist missionaries ("Three"). They intended to take indigenous peoples whose lives teetered between the absolute material and the false anti-phenomenal and make new creations who would possess the reality of the Christian noumenal. But in so many of the texts in this study, the white needs not to instill spirit in the Other but to gain it from the Other. Through the indigene the white character gains soul and the potential to become of the land. A quite appropriate pun is that it is only by going native that the European arrivant can become native. Often in such narratives the Otherness of the indigene is first heightened, by the use of an indigenous language or by the defamiliarization of common aspects of white culture. For example, when Indians are presented as having an intricately metaphorical "iron horse" view of a train, it makes the Indians doubly Other. They are Other because the white perceives them as such and also because their own perception is so clearly that of other.

Orientalism does not present a question of indigenization but it has an important spatial dimension that is in many ways an inverted comment on the process. The mystical exotic element of the orient is quickly lost in simplistic racism when the oriental becomes an immigrant; the connection between Sir Richard Burton's travels and the local Bengali grocer is often lost on the descendants of imperial adventurers. In recent anti-racist demonstrations in England, women in saris carried placards that read, "We're here because you were there." In the case of indigenous peoples the contradiction between exotic image and immediate experience remains but it slips.

The Indians in the Metropolitan Building Society advertisement are not acting as indigenes because they are not the locally indigenous, the Aborigines. Had they been Aborigines, the implications arising would have been well beyond what commercial television could handle. Similarly, the one reference to indigenous peoples in *Richard Mahony*, to a book on American Indians, makes no overt comment on indigenization. When the subject is the local indigenes, however, they cannot be simply floated as exotics. Instead the spatial split usually becomes temporal and leads to a fifth commodity in the semiotic field of the indigene, the prehistoric. The historicity of the text, in which action makes a statement, whether overt or covert, on the chronology of the culture, shapes the indigene into an historical artifact, a remnant of a golden age that seems to have little connection to anything akin to contemporary life. A corollary of the temporal split between this golden age and the present degradation is a tendency to see indigenous culture as true, pure, and static. Whatever fails this test is not really a part of that culture.

The commodities – sex, violence, orality, mysticism, the prehistoric – can be seen as part of a circular economy within and without the semiotic field of the indigene. Indigene violence is only a part of the semiotic field of violence, in the same way that violence is only a part of the semiotic field of the indigene. But revelations of Foucault's subjugated knowledges can be found by considering the whole through the part. A more general study of violence could be made by a consideration of many more ramifications of violence and the indigene than are noted here. Similarly, the whole valorization of the image of the indigene within white cultures could be examined through the filter of violence, or of any other individual commodity.

A variety of factors are involved in incorporating the indigene for the page but still more are added when the genre requires that the indigene be corporally present, in the theatre. There must be presence in the theatre, although the presence is that of the actors and not of the author. If this pawn is played by a white actor in disguise, signifying processes are at play similar to those in the novel but if an indigenous actor is used the cross-cultural leap in which the white author creates the lines and the context for the indigene's speech might seem a beneficial erasing of boundaries. It might also be considered a means of hiding some very necessary distinctions.

The general approach of this study is to demonstrate the major elements of the semiosis involved in the representation of indigenous peoples. It examines these elements individually rather than providing overall analyses of individual texts. In the penultimate chapter, however, the various factors already considered form the basis for a more narrowly focused discussion of the texts of Wiebe and Patrick White. Each has devoted extensive and intensive attention to the indigene, Wiebe to the Indian and White to the Aborigine. Each has spent his life as a novelist in an attempt to reveal the inner workings of the national consciousness, Wiebe of Canada and White of Australia.

And each, in his obvious, and stated, positive intentions in the portrayal of the indigene, has created texts that are subtle and complicated and yet remain clearly rooted in the semiosis developed by the white Canadian and Australian cultures. It appears that as long as this semiotic field exists, as long as the shapes of the standard commodities change but the commodities remain the same, the chess match can appear to vary but there is still a defineable limit to the board. The necessities of indigenization can compel the players to participate but they cannot liberate the pawn.

CHAPTER TWO

The Natural

This study as a whole is an attempt to define the semiotic field of the indigene, primarily through the way it is valorized in a limited assortment of standard commodities in the economy of the image of the indigene in Canadian, Australian, and New Zealand literatures. But this is only one way in which the image can be "sliced." It might also, as suggested above, be examined as one aspect of a different semiotic field. To emphasize the point, just as mysticism is only one of the standard commodities in which the indigene takes part, the indigene is only one vehicle of the many through which mysticism might be introduced in literature.

This ambivalent balance between the indigene as whole and the commodity as part and the opposite relationship is perhaps most ambivalent in the context of nature. It would be possible to divide much of the semiosis of our society, if not all, between the semiotic fields of nature and art, that part of our environment which is not shaped by man and that which is. Or, to follow the neo-Heideggerian scheme presented by Dennis Lee in *Savage Fields: An Essay in Literature and Cosmology* (1978), between the natural earth and the artful world. The indigene is often used to present the possibility of nature in a human form. In the same way, the indigene's closeness to nature is used to justify an emphasis on the indigene as the land. In the one, nature becomes human, in the other, human becomes nature. Elements of each of the standard commodities in which the indigene participates are valorized, whether as negative or as positive, through their emphatically natural genesis.

In his division of experience into the two traditional realms, Lee recognizes the impossibility of separating the non-man from the man and vice versa. He suggests that certain texts appear to bring the two profoundly together in something which he terms "planet": "But this resolution is only partial. It evades a knife-cut dichotomization of planet. But planet not only worlds; it earths. And world and earth are largely at loggerheads" (58). Whether using the familiar nouns of nature and art or some creative verbalizations such as "worlds" and "earths," the joining seems an impossible synthesis while the separation seems an impossible dissection.

Similarly, to see any human as natural in the art-nature dichotomy is absurd. All humans "artfully" rearrange nature to suit their desires or perceived needs. But again similarly, all humans must conform to the biological processes associated with animals, no matter how much these processes are superficially manipulated by technology. In human society, art and nature are perhaps the savage fields of physics denoted by Lee's title. Art-nature is at least a continuum, not unlike the chronological one of historicity. And like that other continuum, placement on the scale is a response to various subjective valorizations. For example, their limited material culture makes it likely that the Australian Aborigine will be deemed more natural than the profoundly material-laden white European, although various anthropological studies have suggested that Aboriginal culture has developed parapsychological powers to a degree which white European culture is unable to understand.

Claude Lévi-Strauss dismisses the idea of the natural primitive quite easily: "The 'savage' has certainly never borne any resemblance either to that creature barely emerged from an animal condition and still a prey to his needs and instincts who has so often been imagined nor to that consciousness governed by emotions and lost in a maze of confusion and participation" (*Savage*, 42). Yet this is certainly what has been "imagined" or, more precisely, "imaged." The Canadian explorer Samuel Hearne refers to the need to "humanize" the Indian and Inuit (*Journey* [1795], 340). The standard commodity at play here is violence and the text uses the term in the sense of "make more humane," or less cruel, but the import of the signifier is much larger. The explorers' narratives seldom present the slightest doubt that the indigene is a part of nature, whether of nature's cruelty or of its beneficence. Their texts are similar to those noted by Tzvetan Todorov in *The Conquest of America*: "Columbus speaks about the men he sees only because they too, after all, constitute a part of the landscape. His allusions to the inhabitants of the islands always occur amid his notations concerning nature, somewhere between birds and trees" (34). These documentary accounts of personal experience, presented as information texts, became a base from which the literary images of indigenous peoples grew.

A base but not a beginning. Hoxie Fairchild's *The Noble Savage: A Study in Romantic Naturalism* (1928) links his title concept to ideas found in ancient Rome. Such primary aspects of the semiotic field of the indigene as the sense of Other and indigenization have no defineable beginning. The same can be said of the split between the civilized self and the natural Other. If the former perceives itself as the same in essence as the Other but more sophisticated, more developed, then the evolutionary continuum noted above is in play. The least artful is the least evolved and thus inevitably the most natural. If the self is in spatial terms alien to the land of the Other, an arrivant, the very process of transportation from the place of origin asserts artifice beyond that of a society which has remained where it began.

The "natural" character of the indigene is etymologically obvious in the term itself. It represents beginnings. Similar associations are provided by related words such as "roots." In John Patrick's *Inapatua* (1966), a de-indigenized Aborigine reflects on what he has done in bringing his wife to live in white society: "I killed her! What do you think would happen if you hacked the roots off this tree and threw it on a rubbish dump?" (183). An earlier Canadian example, Harriet Cheney's "Jacques Cartier and the Little Indian Girl" (1848), goes beyond metaphor when the girl, after a long absence from nature, sees some trees: "Fayawana flew to them with bounding steps; she cast herself on the ground, and twined her arms around them, as if a human heart responded to her wild caresses" (526). The sense of belonging to nature associated with the indigene creates an imme-diate organicist metaphor which is often then used, in a somewhat circular form of logic, to justify the emphatically natural indigene.

Even the most obvious aspects of the indigene's artifice are trans-formed into emanations of the natural. This process achieves its most varied exposition in a Canadian example, the canoe. Often the canoe is made to seem a simplistic evocation of nature in opposition to white technology. In Peter Such's *Riverrun* (1973), the canoe is said to be "easing" the sea unlike the "bruising" action of the white ships (3). An Indian character in Fred Bodsworth's *The Strange One* (1959) suggests the canoe's ambivalent position when she provides a neat summation of the canoe as a nature/art dichotomy in a refutation of the common argument that the Indians never invented the wheel:

We had the canoe. It was perfect for the land and people who produced it, because we had lakes and rivers leading everywhere. It was a tech-nological blind alley, so useful in its original form that there was no incentive to change or improve it. (216)

Explicit credit for production is given to nature as much as to the human manifestation of that nature. The perfection of this natural creation is a reflection of its limitations and of its "original" form.

Within this apparent concern for Indian technology hides a presentation of the canoe as autochthonous.

In Isabella Valancy Crawford's "Malcolm's Katie" (1884), the canoe, with no apparent connection to contemporary native peoples, or to any "productive" source, provides the white characters with an entry into the symbolic power of nature. This movement begins to approach a metaphysical realm when the white in the canoe is clearly "entering" the nature which belongs to the Indian. In Alan Fry's *Come a Long Journey* (1971) the white narrator's developing skill with the canoe bonds him with his Indian guide, who is the catalyst for his indigenization. The centrepiece of Hubert Evans's *Mist on the River* (1954) is the steaming of the dug-out canoe, a ritual which Evans uses to blend mysticism and nature. Emily Carr, in "Canoe" (*Klee Wyck* 1941), encapsulates the combination of personification and "re-naturalizing" which identifies many depictions of the canoe:

> As the canoe glided on, her human cargo was as silent as the cedar-life that once had filled her. She had done with the forest now; when they shoved her into the sea they had dug out her heart. Submissively she accepted the new element, going with the tide. (110–11)

The converse of this transformation of the humans when taken within an element of natural technology is found in James Houston's novel of the Inuit, *Spirit Wrestler* (1980). The white man with mystical powers, known only as "Kayaker," reawakens the spirit which lies within a legendary wrecked kayak and blends with the boat to become part of the general spiritualism of the novel. Yet most such texts, like Fry's, are oriented at some level to the larger ritual of transformation found in the journey made through the agency of the canoe. In the first sentence of *The Village of Souls* (1933), by Philip Child, the canoe feels "alive like a good horse" to the indigenizing Bertrand. At the end of the novel, having been transported to the place of the title, the repository of death and also his source of rebirth, Bertrand in his canoe encounters the mystical feminine spirit of Anne as she paddles towards him in hers, "within the infinite wilderness" (294).

No element of Maori or Aboriginal technology seems to have a similar impact within the literatures. This seems especially surprising in the Maori context in which canoes are a major part of the mythology; the carefully carved war canoes are certainly a significant part of the semiotic field of the Maori in visual arts. Keri Hulme's *The Bone People* (1983) is rather an exception in its concern for the canoe tradition, but it emphasizes history and mysticism rather than natural technology. Although the Maori had a highly developed material culture, it seems to have made less impression on the New Zealand literary mind than the equivalent Indian on Canadian. Even artifacts such as the greenstone carvings tend to be used as mystical talismen, equivalent to the alcheringa, the ritual stones of the Aborigines, although the Maori carvings clearly represent a more sophisticated material technology in white terms.

Yet such avoidance of technological issues is certainly understandable if considered in the context of another aspect of the indigene as natural, the indigene as natural freedom. Accumulation of material wealth is often considered one of the negative aspects of western civilization. Lyndon Rose's *Country of the Dead* (1959) provides a very simple view of the white as sponsor of materialism:

> A native passed him carrying a twenty-pound bag of flour on his head, and the pastor was glad that he had been the moving figure behind this gift. It did not occur to him that he was also the reason why the gift of flour was needed at all. (22)

The view of nature as alien to the physical requirements of civilization connects to nature as an image of social liberation. In *Prospero and Caliban: The Psychology of Colonization* (1950), Mannoni resorts to a Freudian analysis of this rejection of constraint: "The savage, as I have said, is identified in the unconscious with a certain image of the instincts – of the id, in analytical terminology. And civilized man is painfully divided between the desire to 'correct' the 'errors' of the savages and the desire to identify himself with them in his search for some lost paradise (a desire which at once casts doubt upon the merits of the very civilization he is trying to transmit to them) because of his unconscious and ambivalent attitude towards his memories of his own early childhood" (21). Regardless of the value of a perhaps overdetermined psychological framework, Mannoni's view of the indigene as a sign for liberation is accurate. Dugald Ferguson's "The Upper Darling" (1883) describes the Aborigines as "A simple race, devoid of cares, /Who herd in camps, like beasts in lairs" (154). Words such as "free" are ubiquitous modifiers of the indigene, and the standard commodities, particularly sexuality and violence, are often represented as products of the indigene's natural freedom.

In earlier texts, freedom may be presented as a negative aspect of the natural, as in Ralph Connor's *The Patrol of the Sundance Trail* (1914), where violent Indians are "free from all control" (257). At other times, as in the idyllic, arcadian freedom found by the British sailor among the Maori in Alfred Domett's *Ranolf and Amohia* (1883), it is given a positive value. Domett makes no attempt to define the

rigorous, profoundly "un-free" life of a common seaman in the nineteenth century, but it would have been a logical dichotomy to
explore: the freedom of the Australian Aborigine is often presented
in contrast to the life of the convict. As many critics of Australian
literature and of Australian culture in general have noted, convictism
is a major philosophical thread in the history of white Australia.
One of the central tenets of convictism is that through transportation
the working class was viciously manipulated in the service of the
empire and thus became the base for the Australian population. In
texts such as James Tucker's *Ralph Rashleigh* (1845?) the convict
escapes to enter the harsh yet free life of the "white blackfellow."
John Boyle O'Reilly's *Moondyne* (1880) presents a very philosophical
view of how the convict hero after his escape devotes his life to
prison reform, with the aid of his Aboriginal servant, who displays
his race in "an air of freedom about him" (82).

Contemporary literature usually emphasizes the attractions of a
libertarian environment, as shown by the Indians of *The Vanishing
Point* (1973) by W.O. Mitchell and the various stories by W.P. Kinsella, or by the Maori of Noel Hilliard's *A Night at Green River* (1969).
In these texts and many others of the past thirty years an anarchic,
disordered contemporary society of indigenes is shown as an extension of the "natural" "freedom" of the indigene of the past. The
naturalness is opposed to a tightly restrictive white system that, in
The Vanishing Point, is shown to be literally anal retentive. The icon-
oclastic Indian, Archie Nicotine, expresses his amazement to the
white teacher, Carlyle Sinclair, at the technology devoted to toilets:

> "Just to take care of shit," Archie said.
> "Oh, Archie!"
>   "Excuse me – I guess they can make a lot of shiny white dishes to catch
> it in, but they didn't make a nice word to put it into yet." (38)

Archie later discovers that "the Super-Arcade's Green Magic Garden
Centre," a perfect signifier for the commercial technologizing of
nature and spirituality, is selling processed human excrement: "You
people charge for that" (60).

As Carlyle's process of indigenization continues, he finds himself
drawn closer and closer to Archie and further from his very pale
and extremely civilized Aunt Pearl with whom he lived as a child.
Her body is emphatically white, as is even her excrement, which
Carlyle observes as "little white dumplings" (306). Archie's rejection
of anal-retentive technology is met by the exact opposite in Aunt
Pearl: "She was always burning string in the bathroom or in the
kitchen. Bad smells bothered her, or any smells that were not per-

fume smells" (306). Carlyle's indigenization is achieved primarily through the liberation of his sexuality (another aspect of life which Aunt Pearl attempted to deny), but the text uses a variety of references to show that excretory freedom is also an important factor. When the Reverend Dingle attempts to use the Stony language, he mistranslates and says not thank you but "Bull shit!" (175) The passage leaves no question which episteme can understand natural processes.

Mitchell's scatological text seems a logical application of Joel Kovel's claims in *White Racism: A Psychohistory* (1970). Kovel maintains that whites reject blacks out of a Manichean sense of order: "The mind, good, makes words and thoughts; the body, bad, makes shit and filth. And words are placed in the service of aggression toward the natural world, just as feces had been instruments of aggression toward the mother" (132). For Kovel and Mitchell, and for a number of other Australian, Canadian, and New Zealand texts with a similar view of indigenous body as freedom, the answer to white puritanism is to embrace the excretory and recognize the natural man. The obvious blunt answer seems to be missed, however, in the enjoyment of a Freudian liberation. The excretory indigene is once again a reified response to a white psychological need, whether the excrement is loved or hated.

To the extent that they are perceived as human, the indigenes demonstrate a potential bridge to the freedom of the non-man in nature. Thomas Bracken in "The March of Te Rauparaha" (1884) refers to the Maori as "a step beyond the brute!" (21), one example of the various similes and metaphors that relate the indigene to animals. In the nineteenth century, pejorative examples – Australian references to Aborigines "like monkeys" or Canadian to "Indian wolves" – can be opposed by idyllic images of "bird-like" indigenous maidens. Animal imagery in recent literature tends to suggest a positive view but it is still a continuation of the "natural" indigene. The subtleties of such associations can be seen in *Mist on the River*:

> The salmon were born here, the people were born here, and no matter how far they travelled they always came back up river when their natures called them home. They had to; that was the way it was. (229)

The indigenes are instinctual, with not even the possibility of deviating from the compulsion of "their natures." Their sense of belonging to place is not a human choice but animal gene-tics.

In contemporary literature, the belonging animal, the indigene, is often used to emphasize the evil powers of the invading techno-human, the white. Trish Sheppard's *Children of Blindness* (1976) compares Aborigines to mistreated kangaroos. Robert Drewe's *The Savage Crows* (1976) employs both the title figure and a mutilated pony. *The Strange One* uses a book-length comparison of an Indian woman and a Scottish man, a Canadian goose and a Scottish one.

Just as the Canadian context seems to provide the most interesting example of the natural technology, so does it of the indigene-animal analogy. Perhaps because of its exotic indigenous quality, its essential position in the economy of Plains Indians or its nobility of appearance, the American bison, better known as the buffalo, has a particularly resonant position in the de-anthropomorphic balance of the indigene. Charles Mair's "The Last Bison" (1890) suggests a more negative reason for the association between buffalo and Indian: the immense decrease in the number of buffalo is an extinction of the species analogous to the near-genocide of the Indians (*Dreamland*, 148–53). Al Purdy's poem, "Sundance" (1976), follows a similar theme in its reference to the buffalo as "shaggy people of old time" (*Sundance*, 14). A number of recent texts parody this connection. In Susan Musgrave's *The Charcoal Burners* (1980), an absurd chainsaw salesman tries to appeal to his west-coast Indian customers by carving a buffalo, an animal none of them had ever seen. In Robert Kroetsch's *Gone Indian* (1973), the hero's extravagant attempts at indigenization begin with his claims that "In a previous existence I was a buffalo" (9). He eventually reaches the stage at which he can only make love standing up, in imitation of the buffalo. His former mentor's assessment emphasizes another aspect of bison physiology: "He was a buffalo's ass from the word go" (106).

The Strange One's goose-human indigenization also provides an interesting example of what might be termed the Celtic connection. The primitive and "natural" character of the Irish, Scots, Welsh, and Cornish was a common image in the eighteenth and nineteenth centuries and even before. As Norah Carlin notes in "Ireland and Natural Man in 1649" (1985), Edmund Spenser's *A View of the Present State of Ireland* (1596) refers to Ireland as "that savage nation" (1) and even includes a common aspect of the standard commodity of violence, cannibalism: "they did eat of the dead carrions, happy were they could find them" (104). This is a response to starvation rather than simple bloodlust, but it is a direct result of their propensity for war: "the extremity of famine, which they themselves had wrought" (104).

The associations of these Celtic savages are reflected in a great many works in the three literatures. Don Watson's history, *Caledonia Australis: Scottish Highlanders on the Frontier of Australia* (1984), notes the irony that the Scottish highlanders, labelled "truly savage" (5) by other Europeans, should have been at the forefront of the removal of Aborigines in certain parts of Australia. The title character in Ralph Connor's *Corporal Cameron of the North West Mounted Police: A Tale of the Macleod Trail* (1912) turns to the Canadian west to find a land more suitable to his Scottish temper than the effete civilization of the Montreal lawyer, Mr. Denman. Cameron shouts, "'I want to get away into the open.' Mr. Denman did not, or could not, recognize this as the instinctive cry of the primitive man for a closer fellowship with Mother Nature" (139). In Richardson's *Wacousta or the Prophecy*, the Cornish heritage and Scottish experience of the title figure make it possible for him to join the Indians. He, like Clara, his love from the Scottish highlands, is asserted to be a child of nature (250), perverted by the intrigues of their sophisticated English friend, De Haldimar. Similarly, in Tarlton Rayment's *The Valley of the Sky* (1937), a Scot is able to become "bluid-brither" (5) to the Aborigines.

These works imply that the process of indigenization is easier for the Celts, because of their own association with an unstructured, free nature, but the search for indigenization is much broader and deeper than just a response to Celtic stereotypes. Perhaps the prime example of the indigenizing text, Xavier Herbert's *Poor Fellow My Country* (1975), describes the mixed race boy Prindy as he turns to the Aboriginal side of his heritage: "his being yearned for Aboriginal community with his environment, rejecting the patent empty alienness of the non-indigenous" (464). The potential level of association between indigene and land is suggested by the title of Frank Parker Day's novel, *John Paul's Rock* (1932). As John Paul pursues his life of isolation in nature, he and the rock come to have a near symbiotic relationship.

Many of the explorers' narratives assessed the land through the indigenes and vice versa. This tends to be the case throughout Captain Cook's *A Voyage to the Pacific Ocean* (1784), which touches on various cultures of what would become Canada, Australia, and New Zealand. Edward Eyre's *Journals of Expeditions of Discovery into Central Australia* (1845) records, "In the midst of these barren miserable plains I met with four natives, as impoverished and wretched looking as the country they inhabited" (1:97). Yet explorers such as Eyre were indigenizers as well as discoverers. The subtitle of the *Journals* asserts that Eyre was "*Sent by the Colonists of South Australia*," not by some far away imperial power, and thus was part of the general push for indigenization. For Eyre the land was nature but it was also beginning to be country, that new patria which caused so many early nineteenth-century poets of all three countries to hope for a new Britannia of the south or north.

Such a feeling, although quite differently phrased, is much stronger in many contemporary texts in which assertions of indigenization lead to ambivalent views of the explorers as ancestors of the indigenizers and yet also foreign invaders. George Bowering emphasizes his prenominal relationship with George Vancouver in *Burning Water* (1980), but the latter is constantly insensitive to the necessities of indigenization which the text exhibits so strongly. Patrick Lane's "For Simon Fraser" (1974) encapsulates the contemporary response:

> as you in trembling
> filled with the conqueror's blood
> discovered them
> who did not know
> they were lost. (*Beware*, 41)

John Manifold's *Six Sonnets on Human Ecology* (1974) recalls his childhood desire to embrace the Australian land:

> I couldn't eat it, kiss it, hold its hand
> Or suck its breast – I tried to turn my back;
>
> But used to dream of it at boarding-school
> And envy Pompey Austin whom the land
> Seemed to enfold and bless, since he was black.

Pompey is thus a "child of nature" in as clear a sense as is possible. As a statement on historicity, this phrase often implies a lack of evolutionary maturity, of being early on the continuum of human existence, it also suggests the immediate genesis, the begetting, of the indigene. In line with the passage from Cheney above, Joseph Howe's "Acadia" (1830s) refers to the Indian as the "forest's dusky child" (*Poems* 11). The indigene as progeny leads easily to the assumptions that the indigene has an innate understanding of the parent. In G. Firth Scott's *The Last Lemurian: A Westralian Romance* (1898), the Aborigines have uncanny abilities as trackers because "Nature's order is theirs" (139). Standish O'Grady's *The Emigrant* (1841) supplies a similar explanation for Indian handicrafts: "In toils well wrought by nature's gifts supplied, /Their ready handmaid she they best confide" (69).

The powers of the indigene weaver or tracker are represented as the powers of nature. These are but two examples of the assumption that all aspects of indigenous culture are in some sense a part of the natural. Christine Townend's *Travels With Myself* (1976) suggests that the pure Aborigine functions according to a "biology of sharing" (38), but there is a severe epistemological conflict when the innate tries to maintain control in an individual of mixed-race. The title character in Thomas Keneally's *The Chant of Jimmie Blacksmith* (1972) is, like many such literary figures, confused by the Aboriginal traits which interfere with his attempt to emphasize his acquisitive white part. Also like other texts, *Jimmie Blacksmith* shows a continuum in which the innate is rated by measurement of blood. In the opening lines of the novel, the racial power enjoyed by Jimmie's maternal uncle is given clear cause: "For Tabidgi Jackie Smolders was full-blooded." But regardless of the dilution, Jimmie's Aboriginal self exerts a genetic control which Tabidgi uses on him: "So that Jimmie Blacksmith was suddenly ashamed and overcome with a fatalism native to his blood, the fatalism that had kept him at Verona once against his will" (66). As for other literary indigenes, overdetermined by nature, the human quality of "will" can give but small opposition. Thus E.L. Grant Watson's text, *The Desert Horizon* (1923), sees the Aborigine as "entirely foreign" (21).

Yet, as I noted in the first chapter, to see the indigene as "foreign" creates an impossible situation unless the text accepts an essential distance from the land that the white is attempting to inhabit. This appears to be the case in *The Desert Horizon* which states of an Aborigine: "All the alien quality of the land was concentrated in that figure" (23). The desire for the land, nature as country, is given its problematic by the natural man, so clearly different from the white observer. The agressively indigenizing Jindyworobak, Rex Ingamells, attempts to defeat any such distinction in *The Great South Land: An Epic Poem* (1951) by entwining nature/land/country with all Australian humans in his own version of an Aboriginal creation legend:

All Nature was, in this philosophy,
one vast extended family of Spirit,
immense and sacred Brotherhood of Being. (42)

This ontological embrace exceeds all limitations. It is a more flamboyant version of the natural power observed by the mixed-race boy at the end of Patricia Wrightson's *The Rocks of Honey* (1960): "He knew that this old country would fashion its people, all of them, to its own shape in its own good time; and this slow growth of the country was the best hope of them all" (184).

Many of the positive views of the indigene can be divided between the familiar ideologies of hard and soft primitivism. To a great extent, the animal references noted above define the split, between the hardy bears and buffalos, made strong by the hard primitive life, and the delicate birds, made pure by idyllic communion with the beauties of the soft. The latter sometimes goes even beyond fauna to flora, as in the example of the Aboriginal woman who provides the title of William Hatfield's *Black Waterlily* (1935). The extreme possibility of soft primitivism is represented by the various plays of Amy Redpath Roddick. In her *The Seekers: An Indian Mystery Play* (1920), a young Indian woman named Summer dances to the following:

My home's in the land of the yellow sand,
  Where washes the turquoise sea;
Where feathers the palm in the sunset calm,
  Then rustles and shakes with glee. (43)

This representation is admittedly the far end of the continuum, although representative of a number of poetic works of the period and slightly earlier. *Ranolf and Amohia* includes a bower for the Maori maiden which quite resembles that which Summer found in Canada:

Bright in the morning sunbeams lay,
With large-leaved roots and basking fruits
That lolled on beds weedfree and clean
As fairies had the gardeners been. (Domett, 1:160)

Yet even contemporary texts have similar tendencies. Idyllic berry-picking is presented as the essence of the natural Indian life in George Ryga's play *The Ecstasy of Rita Joe* (1967). *Poor Fellow My Country*, primarily an example of hard primitivism, often attempts to reject the sentimentalism suggested by Roddick and Domett, but the narration still refers to "those who come nearest to being Arcadians, the Australian Aborigines" (Herbert, 1325).

Hard primitivism similarly explores a variety of views. The young Indian man in *The Ecstasy of Rita Joe*, Jamie Paul, asserts his superiority to the whites by recalling his experience of surviving days on the trapline without food. Of course, hard primitivism is only in one sense the indigene *of* and *with* nature. In soft primitivism nature presents an opportunity. In hard primitivism nature presents an obstacle which is transformed into an opportunity. Thus when the title character in Howard O'Hagan's *Tay John* (1960) fights the bear, it is "An epic battle: man against the wilderness" (86). Whereas the most extreme version of soft primitivism tends towards the sentimental, the extremity of hard primitivism is shown in Theo Price's

God in the Sand: An Australian Mystical Romance (1934) to be reaching for mysticism:

> The Buddhist priest scarifying, sacrificing his body, caring nought for its needs in order that his soul may live, is only doing consciously what Nature, in harsh mood, has done for the Aboriginal tribesman. (40)

The elevating power of nature, whether through its caresses or its blows, is often associated with the hackneyed image assessed in Fairchild's *The Noble Savage*. The power of the phrase, "noble savage," has made it a constant epithet in criticism of the image of the indigene. But to see all positive representations of the indigene as noble savages defeats the useful specificity of the concept. There are many portraits in all three literatures which leave no doubts about aristocracy. The handsome Maori, Kowhatu, in Jean Devanny's *Lenore Divine* (1926), is a prime example:

> High purpose was stamped upon him; strength of mind and of body evulgated from him, and the softness of his race was there, the softness and poetry of his race, which doubtless found expression through the medium of his violin and vocalising. (127)

Lest this still be too restrained, the text then asserts that he is "possessed of a chivalry" (127). Kowhatu is part of a large tradition, from the Aborigines in W.H. Leigh's *The Emigrant: A Tale of Australia* (1847): "these very unfigleaved noblesse of the land" (175) to the Indians in the anonymous contribution to *The Literary Garland*, "The Indian's Dream" (1839): "the wild nobility of whose untutored souls shames the degeneracy of civilized man!" (61).

The *Literary Garland and British North American Magazine*, which the *Oxford Companion to Canadian Literature* refers to as "the leading literary journal in British North America" (454) of its day, provides a general reflection of the beliefs of bourgeois Canada in the mid-nineteenth century. Thus, it is important to note that it presents the noble savage as more than a simple product of the quality of the natural life or an inevitable characteristic of indigenous race. "The Indian's Dream" makes clear that there are variations on the theme when it expresses a fear that these nobles might become extinct before being documented:

> There will be nought to record the lofty independence of the natural lord of the prairie and the wild, or to distinguish him from the common herd of untamed barbarians, who have fallen before the all-grasping power of the European world. (61)

It would seem that the distinction here is between the elevated Indian and various similarly "untamed" but lesser races. It might also refer, however, to the difference between the elevated individual and the "common herd" of the Indians.

Although the Maori in general in Bracken's "Te Rauparaha" are only that "step beyond the brute," the title figure is

> Scion of heroic breed,
> Born to conquer and to lead!
> Strongest branch of noblest tree. (18)

Similarly, the title figures in various Canadian heroic tragedies, such as Robert Rogers' *Ponteach: A Tragedy* (1766) and Charles Mair's *Tecumseh: A Drama* (1886), are clearly superior to the common Indians whom they lead, even down to their language. While Ponteach speaks an elevated stage-Indian verse, his followers use an ungrammatical prose. One American officer says of Tecumseh,

> No need had he of schools or learned books –
> His soul his mentor, his keen lion-looks
> Pierced to the heart of things. (127)

The point is not that Tecumseh is noble because of the absence of civilization but that he had "no need" of civilization.

Te Rauparaha, Ponteach, and Tecumseh are noble savages but their nobility is linked to their state in life. The common indigenes have no elevated ideals. Rather than noble savages in the usual sense, Te Rauparaha and his peers are savages who are also noble, products of innate aristocratic qualities. In the two Canadian examples, they are perfect specimens for royalist, anti-American texts. They are no more results of their untouched primitive situation than an English king in Shakespeare is a direct result of civilization. The noble savage, as a specific category, tends to have this aristocratic distance from the general race. While seldom a direct product of nature, the point is often made that their natural context enables their aristocracy to flourish. As the romantic indigenizing Lefroy rhapsodizes in *Tecumseh*: "Free, and untainted by the greed of gain: /Great Nature's man content with Nature's food" (22).

Even when no specific claims to nobility are made, the central indigene characters of many texts from all three literatures are clearly differentiated from others of their race. Charles De Boos' *Fifty Years Ago* (1867) describes the Aborigines met by the white hero as men of mark in their tribe, for three finer specimens of the aboriginal race could scarce have been encountered, even in those early days. Straight as the saplings of their native forests, lithe and sinewy from constant exercise, they might well have been selected as models of combined power and activity. (3)

While their qualities are directly associated with the requirements of nature's hard primitivism, they are clearly superior to others of their race who share the same environment.

The search for the elevated indigene, perhaps as a quest for an idealized figure superior to the qualities perceived to be the norm of the existing indigenes, is found throughout the three literatures but it reaches its most interesting form in what might be termed the "lost tribe" novels. The majority of these are Australian, but there are Canadian and New Zealand versions. The whites leave civilization and enter the interior. In the Australian examples, they find gold, a freshwater lake, and an Aboriginal tribe far superior to any previously encountered. Psychological critics have often viewed such fictional adventuring expeditions as mythic representations of a quest for identity. In these examples, the adventure represents a search for a positive definition of country and an encounter with an element of the indigenous that will both supply such a definition and provide indigenization to the white explorer.

Many Australian novels follow this structure – from O'Reilly's *Moondyne* to Mrs Campbell Praed's *Fugitive Anne* (1903) to *God in the Sand*. There are many variations among them (see Healy, "The Lemurian Nineties" 1978 and Goldie, "The Necessity of Nobility" 1985), but the basic pattern is the same. The whites leave a reasonably hospitable land at the coast and move toward the centre through increasingly hostile country until they find a hidden paradise. The Aborigines there are far superior to those discovered elsewhere, whether because of their isolation or because they are remnants of some Asian, South American, or other immigration. In other words, behind the evil lie mineral riches, fertile nature, and an indigenous people suitable to various romantic ideals. Few Canadian novels follow this pattern although Harold Lowrey's *Indian Gold* (1929) does, exactly. *The Village of Souls* is a Canadian variant which, like *God in the Sand*, utilizes fragments of Jungian psychology in order to make extra-sensory connections in a mystical land.

For Mair, Rogers, and J.B. Mackenzie, author of a play entitled *Thayendanegea: An Historico-Military Drama* (1898) about Joseph Brant, the attraction of the heroic tragedy was linked to monarchist sympathies. One is tempted to say that long before the phrase was applied in Canada to left-leaning Progressive Conservatives, these dramatic versions of Indian heroes would have been perfect candidates for the label of "Red Tory." To go beyond the obvious pun, they might also suit the phrase in their joining of aristocratic bearing and attitudes and an overwhelming concern for their responsibility for the welfare of their people. In presenting an indigenous people who aided the British in understanding the land and repelling the Americans, these plays reflect nationalist and imperialist ideals of the period, and thus devotion to Canada as an idealized new version of the patria – the aristocrat of nature as source of nation.

This is quite different from the Australian "lost tribe" novels. The "Aboriginal royalty" represented by the guide King Jimmy in Carlton Dawe's *The Golden Lake* (1894) is no great leader but a comic assistant, quite at variance with the barbarian aristocrats his white masters discover. In these texts, the temptation for the Australian romantic was not to glorify the history of the land and subtly reshape it so the indigene became something akin to a friendly monarch. Rather, it was to reject history and contemporary reality and replace them with speculation. These texts reflect a general impression that Australia was a rather uncomfortable land at the coast which became even worse as you ventured towards the centre. It was *terra incognita* but also *terra hostilis*. It became tempting to speculate that beyond this dry, hot exterior which their alien consciousnesses had encountered might hide a pre-lapsarian heart.

The "lost tribe" novels imply an image of nature which must be changed. These texts create a specifically imaginary nature in an apparent attempt to avoid taking the side of white technology, of man as art, against nature. In Henry Lawson's "The Drover's Wife" (1894), development seems desirable but the land resists progress at every turn. The snake in the woodpile, the most overt symbol of the evil of Australian nature, an evil which might kill the beleagured figure of the title, seems but a more direct version of the Aborigine who, hired to build the woodpile, made it hollow. The indigene, quite appropriately unthinkingly and unintentionally, aids nature in the apparently inevitable defeat of technology.

The subtleties of this ideological assumption can be seen in two nineteenth-century texts. Howe's "Acadia" paints a rather romantic portrait of the landscape and then states:

So blooms our country – and in ages past,
Such the bright robe that Nature round her cast,

Ere the soft impress of Improvement's hand,
By science guided, had adorned the land;
Ere her wild beauties were by culture graced,
Or art had touched what Nature's pencil traced. (*Poems*, 10)

Domett's *Ranolf and Amohia* presents a slightly different version of the contribution of technology:

In days when Nature – ere discharmed –
Undeified by Science – swarmed
With bright Divinities akin
To the energies terrific
In her wilder phases working. (1:276)

For Howe, science was to fill out the basic form nature provided. For Domett, it was to erase the superstition which nature's power had suggested. For both, science was an aid greatly to be desired, as it was for Lawson, although his story is much less sanguine about its possibilities. In Lawson's text, the defeat of the woman's attempts to make her farm hospitable and productive represents the inherent evil of a landscape which thwarts Australia's possibilities at every turn.

Many earlier and later writers have taken a very different view. Jo Smith's play, "The Girl of the Never Never" (1912), depicts a very simple split between white and Aboriginal views. An American geologist states "I don't believe any race of people have a right to hang on to a country if they're not prepared to put it to a good use" (53). The Aboriginal servant Cinderella provides an emotive perception: "Wommera! My country – all belong my people –" (60). The agent of white technology considers nature to be no more than raw material. The Aborigine does not analyze but responds, extolling land as nation as communitas. Of course, the play still apportions this land to her sensitive white boss. The indigenizing white, Jeremy, central character of *Poor Fellow My Country*, is less convinced that there is a significant variation between different white invaders:

Will all this quiet loveliness be laid waste to satisfy the *kuttabah's* [white's] insatiable technology, which is really only a craze for artificiality, a hatred of what is natural because Nature makes him feel too small? (1302)

H.J.K.'s "Indian Address to the Mississippi" (*The Literary Garland* 1846) asserts,

The paleface will endeavour,
  Thy wild waves to restrain;
But may thy waters never
  Be sullied for his gain. (213)

Texts which represent the indigene as an emissary of untouched nature and fear the ecological dangers of white technology turn to the indigene as environmentalist. Rex Ingamells' "The Gangrened People" (1941) appeals to "the faith of vanished men" (*Selected*, 31) in order to make white Australia ecologically responsible: "Australia wants a race whose active bone/will mutter the white light of her limestone rocks" (32).

Texts which attack progressivist tendencies can be viewed as responses to either sociological or psychological forces. Kovel considers the divorce from nature as psychologically debilitating: "Abstraction and splitting gain power without awareness, and so serve the needs of repression. But they also diminish the self, and progressively cut it off externally from what is done to the world. The result is an inner void, which is filled synthetically, just as the machines fill in the gaps in the natural landscape torn up in the name of production" (158). The embrace of the indigene is thus presented in many texts as a return to a whole, before the "abstraction and splitting" of civilized life. To follow Dennis Lee's schema, the natural indigene is an explanation of the holistic indigene, the human who has not ceased to be part of an essential integrated planet, in which all is earth and there is no world to cause the fields to conflict.

Various aspects of indigenous life become part of this assertion of wholeness. Goody makes the following anthropological claim: "The contribution of the intellect in simple societies has been played down to such an extent that one is sometimes moved to ask "Do natives think?". Or do they just have constraining structures, special systems of classification, undomesticated thoughts?" (20). Goody's comment might be seen as a different version of Kovel's splitting. The "simple society" does not allow the intellect to lead and thus maintains the balance of mind and body and the integration of mind/body/nature, unlike the white technology which attempts to situate mind over both body and its larger self, nature. Most images of indigenous sexuality, orality, and mysticism can be viewed as in some way part of such an affirmation of "undomesticated" wholeness.

Recent overtly environmentalist texts reflect this absolutist opposition between indigene-nature and white-technology, often with one or two white characters who go through a process of indigenization which leads them to swear allegiance to the holistic cause of indigenous ecology. The basic pattern is exemplified by Grahame Webb's *Numunwari* (1980) from Australia, and Bodsworth's *The Strange One* from Canada. In both novels, a scientist is led by contact with indigenes to recognize that white technology is not only inadequate, it is part of a general assault on a delicate ecology. Still, neither text is as completely despairing of the effect of the pernicious white influence as the Canadian *Surfacing* (1972), by Margaret Atwood, or the Australian *The Jimberi Track* (1966), by Max Brown:

> The people had been taught to believe that their spirits came from the country and returned to the country. Just as the sinking of shafts, the felling of trees, the impounding of waters, the spread of cattle and sheep, were killing the old hunting life, so each tree felled, each rock split, each mine dug, each 'roo displaced, was a spirit source destroyed; and since these were the source of life, the people felt themselves impoverished and humiliated. (143–4)

The defeat of nature is thus a defeat of the indigene. In the same way that historicity makes the demise of the indigene inevitable, white technology *must* destroy the indigene because it must control nature and the natural essence of the indigene is destroyed by this control. The lament for this demise makes it no less assured in the various ecological texts. In *Surfacing* and Wayland Drew's *The Wabeno Feast* (1973) the indigene is already of the past. *Numunwari* and *The Strange One* both end with the death of an aged indigene who is a guardian of natural tradition. The extreme of this pessimistic ideology is seen in M.T. Kelly's *A Dream Like Mine* (1987), in which the degraded Métis, Arthur, kidnaps both the ecologically concerned narrator and a polluting capitalist, and in the tellingly titled *The Brown Land Crying* (1975) by Richard Beilby. In the latter, the violence of one Aborigine against a white, "this representative of the despoilers," is viewed to be "bestial and primitive, yet oddly natural, vengeance being wreaked in the name of a dispossessed race" (8).

Unlike earlier and even contemporary texts, *The Brown Land Crying* presents the bestial as "oddly," rather than inevitably natural. Partly, this results from an association of Aboriginal violence with a degenerate, detribalized society, but it also reflects a general assessment in the text that nature and the Aborigine have failed the test of the white onslaught and thus anything "natural" now is "odd," not belonging in the new context. The Aborigines had been "autochthonoi, sprung from the earth" (47), but they had been "deindigenized." The sense is often there, however, that the land under white technology is hardly worth retaining. Rose's *Country of the Dead* makes this view quite clear in its title. Unlike many early Australian texts, the barren land is not pre-white nature, the country of the Aborigine, but post-white de-nature, a technologized pseudo-patria which has alienated the Aborigine. A sensitive white stock-man cries, "We're killing the country" (50).

The philosophical assumptions of nature as pure which lie behind most of the environmentalist texts are a response both to observations of indigenous nature and to established theories of nature. A subtle but important inconsistency created by the distance between these two simuli appears in one short passage in Samuel Hearnes' *A Journey from Prince of Wales's Fort in Hudson's Bay to the Northern Ocean* (1975). At the moment when in closest contact with nature, he finds himself in fear of its emmisary, the Indian; Hearne turns to Young's *Night Thoughts* and its reference to "Nature's sweet restorer, balmy Sleep" (44). For him, the essence of nature as a philosophical construct was found not in Canada and the indigene but in Young and literature. To apply the observation more generally, the "natural" images recorded by the various explorers are at one level reflections of experience but also manifestations of an already existent semiotic field.

A belief in the inherent purity of nature creates a central conflict in one aspect of Maori technology, tattooing. Nicholas's *Narrative of a Voyage to New Zealand* is almost obsessed with the subject: "The mind revolts at the idea of seeing a fine manly race as any in the universe, thus shockingly disfigured; and producing associations similar to what may be imagined of so many fiends" (1:361). The text constantly displays the tension between assumptions that the Maori are "the children of genuine sensibility" (1:86) as described by Rousseau (referred to here as "the wayward philosopher of Geneva" [1:86]) and claims that the Maori are in need of "moral culture" (1:106). The result is a portrait of one leader who is perceived as somehow more Maori because untattooed: "nor were his regular features disfigured with the tattooing, but left undisguised to display the varied passions of nature" (1:230). Similarly, in William Satchell's *The Greenstone Door* (1914), the white hero is able to convince his Maori friend to avoid tattooing: "I shall hate to see you transfigured out of all likeness to yourself" (118). These assessments represent the natural indigene as defacing nature through an extravagantly semiotic art. Can man the signmaker be not man but nature?

The link of indigene and land which is used so often as a definition of belonging to a place is a particularly interesting process given that most of the indigenes considered here are to some degree nomadic. Even the indigenes with highly developed material cultures and strong village systems, the Indians of the British Columbia coast, for example, would periodically move their community. T.A.G. Hungerford's "The Only One Who Forgot" (1968) presents the travelling Aborigine as one more aspect of nature in the blood consciousness: "Through the years, his mind forgot, and his heart forgot, the thousand nomad lives that dreamed in his blood" (93). *Reading the Country: Introduction to Nomadology* (1984) attempts to combine the nomadic and the postmodern. Under the general direction of Stephen Muecke, a white Australian, the book incorporates edited transcriptions from tape recordings of Paddy Roe, an Aborigine, commentaries by Muecke, and paintings by a Morrocan immigrant, Krim Benterrak. Muecke depicts the traveller as an important political subversive of a rather Foucauldian type: "The citadels of the state distrust the nomads because they don't know where this other dynamism will *lead*" (Benterrak, 218). Then, the nomad is shown to represent the essential flux of anything, including the text: "These multiplicities occupy the space without counting it and one can only explore it in the act of travelling across it" (222). The Aborigine is thus the perfect example of belonging to the natural land without limiting it. The nomad "is always coming and going, but more or less in the same place" (224).

As in many other aspects of the natural indigene, the contradictions of nomadic belonging create inconsistencies which are at once resonant and troubling. Still, more important than the inconsistencies are the consistencies, the continued limitations of the semiosis. It is common in texts which assert the validity of indigenization and the importance of a natural way to reject the explicitly artful version of nature suggested in Hearne's quotation from Young. Child's *The Village of Souls* ridicules a "quadrille des sauvages américains" at the French court, complete with ostrich plumes and a unicorn (3). Yet the natural indigene of *The Village of Souls* is also a literary artifact, as are the other figures in the texts in this study. In most such texts, indigenizing whites are allowed to acquire nature through acquiring the indigene, whether sexually, ideologically, or in some other process. Even when no such agent of the text is clearly established, the text itself undergoes the process through its representation of the indigene.

In "Canada and Its Poetry" (1943), Northrop Frye declares, "Canadian poetry is at its best a poetry of incubus and *cauchemar*, the source of which is the unusually exposed contact of the poet with nature which Canada provides. Nature is seen by the poet, first as unconsciousness, then as a kind of existence which is cruel and meaningless, then as the source of the cruelty and subconscious stampedings within the human mind" (141–2). Even at the time of writing, this vision of nature as a consistently, and essentially, negative quality in Canadian literature is inaccurate, but it correctly identifies the internalization of nature in Canada, Australia, and New Zealand as "unconsciousness," as essence of the Other. Frye misses the important note that throughout literature the *cauchemar*, the nightmare, can be seen as divine guidance and those "subconscious stampedings" can be attractive answers to irrational questions. The nightmare of mysticism and the incubus of sexuality, both experienced through the indigene, are but two means of embracing nature.

The indigenes begin and, to date, end as "children of nature." Their role for the white culture is shown in Max Brown's *The Black Eureka* (1976), in which a white states that the Aborigines "expressed the country" (11). In the ardently pro-Aborigine television series, "Women of the Sun" (1983), by Hyllus Maris and Sonia Borg, one character says, "We are the land" (46). Yes. But does this semiotic field ever allow them to become more than the land, more than a suitable ground for the cultivation of indigenization?

CHAPTER THREE

Form

The title of this chapter reflects an impossibility. Tzvetan Todorov distinguishes between form and substance in many ways in "Poetics and Criticism" (1977) but he recognizes, "The literary work does not have a form and a content but a structure of significations whose relations must be apprehended" (*Poetics*, 41). In Chapter 1, I show that my analysis of the semiotic field of the indigene operates on a similar assumption. Yet there are questions of form which must be addressed which do not fit easily into the specific analyses of the commodities. Those which arise from dramatic texts have the major additional factor of theatrical presentation, and are thus dealt with in a separate chapter (although certain "closet dramas" are briefly considered here in association with epic poetry). If there is a general identifying term besides form it would be that equally vague formalist word, "literariness." The semiotic field of the indigene is similar throughout the cultures of Australia, Canada, and New Zealand, but it has aspects which are specifically shaped by the literariness of texts in which it appears. Most of this chapter is devoted to discussions of genre in poetry or prose but other elements of style or technique are also considered.

In general these various techniques are only slight variations from those employed in other literatures, in English and in other languages. This is true not only of the early, overtly colonial texts. For example, the various forms of "realism" that become important in the last decades of the nineteenth century and are a major factor in the transmission of the image of the indigene are a part of similar fluctuations in literary techniques throughout European-derived cultures at that time. Different forms enter the Canadian, Australian, and New Zealand contexts at different times and in different ways, but the earliest of note is the genre which at once accompanies and represents the entrance of European culture, the explorer's narrative. In some ways it establishes the form for all literature which follows it. Indeed, many critics have claimed that all narratives follow the structure of quests. A text begins with a goal, stated or unstated, and then describes the pursuit of the goal, a process epitomized by the explorer's narrative, in which a white figure pursues an overt quest, a goal of indigenization. Openly fictional texts such as novels or epic poems hide this pattern under various literary palimpsests but the arrivant text remains to be read.

The first reaction to the explorer's narrative might be an assertion of the absence of literariness. Northrop Frye maintains that such works are "as innocent of literary intention as a mating loon" ("Conclusion," 822). Frye suggests that rather than literary texts these discourses are "what the explorer saw." But like any other text each traveller's tale presents a series of manipulations as it attempts to convince its readers of the truth of its discourse. Mary Pratt writes, in "Scratches on the Face of the Country" (1985), of such narratives of Africa: "The explicit project of these explorer-writers, whether scientists or not, is to produce what they themselves referred to as 'information.' Their task, in other words, was to incorporate a particular reality into a series of interlocking information orders – aesthetic, geographic, mineralogical, botanical, agricultural, economic, ecological, ethnographic, and so on. To the extent that it strives to efface itself, the invisible eye/I strives to make those informational orders natural, to find them there uncommanded, rather than assert them as the products/producers of European knowledges or disciplines" (125).

Such texts in all the "new worlds" present an image of their authors' lives as overdetermined gatherers of knowledge. Peter Hulme, in "Polytropic Man: Tropes of Sexuality and Mobility in Early Colonial Discourse" (1985) claims, "For polytropic man every moment is unique, every touch on the rudder must be in response to an unrepeatable sequence of circumstances" (22). But this uniqueness is not the essence but rather the explorer's claims to be originary. He is the first, no matter when he arrives. Even such a late figure as Carl Lumholtz turns *Among Cannibals: An Account of Four Years Travels in Australia and of Camp Life with the Aborigines of Queensland* (1889) into a constant assertion of discovery, in which all the information is a beginning. The role of the white "discoverer" has become a vexing problem for historians in recent years, in deciding how a land with an existing population can be discovered. But the flavour of such encounters continues in fiction; even in a very recent text, M.T. Kelly's *A Dream Like Mine* (1987), an originary entry into

Indian dream produces information beyond that which the narrator-discoverer, laden with the facts of white history, can record.

Such self-conscious efforts are still quite different, however, from the task attempted in the narratives by the various explorers of all three countries, from the earliest, such as Stephen Parmenius's letter to Richard Hakluyt (1583), to Lumholtz. Todorov suggests that even a text such as Lumholtz's is of value, regardless of questions as to what he "in fact" experienced. To Todorov, *Among Cannibals* would represent a certain type of "verisimilitude. That is, an event may not have occured, despite the allegations of one of the chroniclers. But the fact that the latter could have stated such an event, that he could have counted on its acceptance by the contemporary public, is at least as revealing as the simple occurrence of an event which proceeds, after all, from chance" (*Conquest*, 55).

The section of Samuel Hearne's *Journey* known as the "Coppermine Massacre," his account of Inuit slain by Indians, presents his contemporary public with one such chance experience. The focus of the massacre becomes one Inuk girl. The description of her death is explicit and worth quoting at length:

> The shrieks and groans of the poor expiring wretches were truly dreadful; and my horror was much increased at seeing a young girl, seemingly about eighteen years of age, killed so near me, that when the first spear was stuck into her side she fell down at my feet, and twisted round my legs, so that it was with difficulty that I could disengage myself from her dying grasps. As two Indian men pursued this unfortunate victim, I solicited very hard for her life, but the murderers made no reply till they had stuck both their spears through her body, and transfixed her to the ground. They then looked me sternly in the face and began to ridicule me, by asking if I wanted an Esquimaux wife; and paid not the smallest regard to the shrieks and agony of the poor wretch, who was twining round their spears like an eel! Indeed, after receiving much abusive language from them on the occasion, I was at length obliged to desire that they would be more expeditious in dispatching their victim out of her misery, otherwise I should be obliged, out of pity, to assist in the friendly office of putting an end to the existence of a fellow-creature who was so cruelly wounded. On this request being made, one of the Indians hastily drew his spear from the place where it was first lodged and pierced it through her breast near the heart. The love of life, however, even in this most miserable state, was so predominant, that though this might justly be called the most merciful act that could be done for the poor creature, it seemed to be unwelcome, for though much exhausted by pain and loss of blood, she made several efforts to ward off the friendly blow. My

situation and the terror of my mind at beholding this butchery, cannot easily be conceived, much less described; though I summed up all the fortitude I was master of on the occasion, it was with difficulty that I could refrain from tears; and I am confident that my features must have feelingly expressed how sincerely I was affected at the barbarous scene I then witnessed; even at this hour I cannot reflect on the transactions of that horrid day without shedding tears. (153–5)

Much of the power in Hearne's piece is provided by the first person narration. In "The Eye of Power" (1977) Foucault discusses the control exerted by the "gaze" in a prison where the inmates' every act is observed. He refers to a comment by Jeremy Bentham which asserts that the gaze itself saps the inmate of power (*Power*, 154). Hearne's position seems to be that of the spectator-owner, as the Inuk woman is valorized within the standard commodity of sexuality. Still, to imply such power might seem quite inappropriate. Immediately before the above passage, Hearne emphasizes his own impotence: "I stood neuter in the rear" (153). Even when this "neuter-ality" is overwhelmed by the girl's grasp, he can be no more than a supplicant on her behalf. But in literary terms, his power is absolute, as his eyes, and then his pen, control the reader's perception.

The central commodities here are sex and violence. The Indian's question about Hearne's interest in the Inuk woman emphasizes both the power of the gaze and the value of the indigene maiden in imperialist discourse. Rather than "neuter" in the sexual sense, Hearne's perception demonstrates a sexuality which is hidden yet ardently there. Similarly, Hearne is far from neuter in terms of the Indian violence. The Indians had had territorial skirmishes with the Inuit long before Hearne's arrival but now their violence is as agents of the British invasion, as part of Hearne's admittedly commercial exploration. The full title of Hearne's text is *A Journey from Prince of Wales's Fort in Hudson's Bay to the Northern Ocean Undertaken by Order of the Hudson's Bay Company for the Discovery of Copper Mines, a North West Passage, &c. In the Years 1769, 1770, 1771, & 1772.* Hearne's "neuter-ality" is a guise in both contexts, a guise which Pratt sees as common: "In the body of the text, European enterprise is seldom mentioned, but the sight/site as textualized consistently presupposes a global transformation that, whether the I/eye likes it or not, is already understood to be underway" (125). The text is itself one element of the inevitability of imperialist progress.

The language of the passage from Hearne is shaped by the first person narration. Since the text avoids direct quotation, either of Hearne or of the Indians, the effect is a limited presentation of consciousness. Hearne eludes the layers of confusion suggested by the transliteration of Indian language, but he also misses the appearance of subjectivity which is a result of direct quotation in which, to recall Bishop Berkeley, the character exists because we perceive him perceiving. The Indians remain as objects in the piece, as, of course, does the girl. Hearne himself becomes subject as perceiver and object as actor. This effect becomes redoubled when the narrator is shown at the end of the piece to be well distant in time from the action. The emotive narrator of the conclusion is reacting to story rather than experience.

It is common in these explorer narratives to reserve these historicizing intrusions in the narrative for scenes of violence, for those moments in which the barbaric character of the new land has become clearly personified. Eyre provides an echo of Hearne when he recalls Aborigines killing an overseer:

> Though years have now passed away since the enactment of this tragedy, the dreadful horrors of that time and scene, are recalled before me with frightful vividness, and make me shudder even now, when I think of them. (2:7)

The focus on the first person in recollection makes the gaze itself an emotive sign within the apparent restraint of the "information" text.

The simile employed by Hearne, "like an eel," is a particularly striking figure of speech. It has all the more power because the rest of Hearne's description seems so bare and direct. This brief trope, like all such figurative associations between indigene and animal, reinforces the image of the indigene as nature. But its isolated appearance in Hearne's "factual" account gives it the power of a selected truth. The isolation gives an immediate veracity to the comparison which would not be the case in a florid prose full of Indianisms.

The simplicity of the syntax at the beginning of this passage might also be contrasted with the construction used at the centre: "I was at length obliged to desire that they would be more expeditious" and "otherwise I should be obliged, out of pity, to assist in the friendly office of putting an end to the existence." As the observer becomes participant, the stylistic emphasis turns to civilized circumlocution, in which action is cloaked by the passive voice. The intervention is that not of Hearne but of civilized society.

Two other elements are worthy of immediate note. The contrast in the final comment between the time of writing and the time of experience emphasizes the position of the indigene as an historical artifact. Those "transactions" are of a period before "reflect"-ion. This is an early example of what has been the norm in Canadian literature, the concentration on the indigene of history rather than the indigene of contemporary experience. The focus on the death of an indigene similarly reinforces the image of indigene as passing if not past.

My analysis here has not been concerned with historical context but with the Hearne passage "as it presents itself." However, this text might also be examined as an example of contemporary litera-ture, as it is a part of recent anthologies. The "Coppermine Massacre" in various forms appears in the very small selection of explorer's narratives in A.J.M. Smith's *The Book of Canadian Prose* (1965); in *Literature in Canada* (1978), edited by Douglas Daymond and Leslie Monkman; and in *An Anthology of Canadian Literature in English* (1982), edited by Russell Brown and Donna Bennett. Whether because of its undercurrent of Inuit sexuality, its overt presentation of "Indian barbarity," or its exemplification of the explorer's account, we, as contemporary Canadians, want to read this story.

Explicitly fictional quests similarly reveal the assumptions of the indigenizing cultures. The "lost tribe" novels noted in the chapter on nature are similar to novels exploring other strange lands, such as Rider Haggard's *She* (1886). That this pattern should arise in different tentacles of the British imperial octopus at very much the same time, with, in many cases, little likelihood of direct influence, gives some credence to the psychoanalysis of empire suggested by Conrad's *Heart of Darkness* (1899). Yet the popularity of the form in Australia and its limited use in Canada imply that different land-scapes or native people elicited different structures of representation. The genre of the "dark heart" which applied to Africa and Australia seemed less appropriate in a land which had been quite extensively explored well before the nineteenth century. But the few Canadian examples show that the structure could fit that context. The accurate distinction is perhaps less qualitative than quantitative. The Cana-dian text felt slightly less neuter, less in the rear.

In contemporary genres even this distinction is no longer valid. Paradoxically, greater geographical and anthropological knowledge has led to greater feelings of "neuter-ality," and recent texts from all three cultures provide more explicit psychological quests. One of the primary patterns in contemporary literature follows the indivi-duation of the central character. In Canada, Australia, and New Zealand, individuation is often joined by indigenization. The char-acter gains a new awareness of self and of nationality through an excursion into the wilderness. The transformation is often something akin to a sea change, in which the character plunges into the natural and in some association with indigenes partly removes the civilization which is seen to be inimical to his or her indigenization. Among examples of this in contemporary literature are Atwood's *Surfacing* and Kroetsch's *Gone Indian* in Canada and B. Wongar's *The Trackers* (1975) in Australia. Examples such as the Australian Kenneth Cook's *Eliza Fraser* (1976) and Bowering's *Burning Water* represent revisionist examinations of historical experiences. Drew's *The Wabeno Feast* explicitly parallels an eighteenth-century expedition and a contemporary journey. Among other variants are Hulme's *The Bone People* and Damien Broderick's *The Dreaming Dragons: A Time Opera* (1980), in which a Maori and an Aborigine, respectively, de-indigenized through various forms of assimilation, undergo a similar process in order to regain touch with their roots.

Some of these contemporary texts reveal an attempt to indigenize form which goes beyond simply following the thematic process of the central quest. The system of multiple beginnings and endings in *The Bone People* seems to replicate the traditional Maori designs that the central character has drawn on her floor:

> It was reckoned that the old people found inspiration for the double spirals they carved so skilfully in uncurling fern fronds: Perhaps. But it was an old symbol of rebirth, and the outward-inward nature of things. (46)

Surfacing similarly justifies deviant form by quoting a "scientific" article on Indian rock paintings:

> In treatment they are reminiscent, with their elongated limbs and extreme distortion, of the drawings of children. The static rigidity is in marked contrast to the rock paintings of other cultures, most notably the European cave paintings.
>
> From the above features we may deduce the creators of the paintings were interested exclusively in symbolic content, at the expense of expressiveness and form. (102)

Thus the novel's tendency to caricature and its severely limited action and emotion are part of an indigenization of the text, as, like *The Bone People*, it becomes indigenous by form.

Many white texts directly parody indigenous forms. Any text which in any way imitates an element of indigenous culture might be seen at some level as parodic, although in the terms defined by Linda Hutcheon in *A Theory of Parody* (1985) it might be better called an imitation since it usually lacks the irony Hutcheon looks for in parody, and denies rather than heightens the distance between itself

and the original. Where such texts seem particularly worthy of interest as parodies is in their use of what Hutcheon terms "transcon-
textualization" (32). The texts imply that each such replication of an
item of indigene culture transforms the white text and transposes
the context of the original to become one with the context of the
new. Such general transformations can be seen in many quite specific
examples. Various lyric laments written in the nineteenth century
are responses to references by explorers of all three countries to the
warrior boast proclaimed when near death. While many of the
poems include notes attesting to their authenticity, they clearly owe
just as much or more to heroic forms from the European literary
tradition, such as the various laments in Old English. A good example of this would be Henry Kendall's "The Last of His Tribe" (*Leaves*
[1869], 92–3), which, like most of the examples, has a *ubi sunt* theme,
in which great warriors and great events of the past are noted and
their passing lamented. This reinforces the impression of the indigene's stoic nobility and also reflects the standard commodity of the
prehistoric in its comment on the demise of indigenous peoples.
Mair's "The Last Bison" (*Dreamland*, 148–53) shows the degree to
which the genre was established. The poem represents a double
parody, as the inclusion of both bison and Indian within the semiotic
field of nature makes possible a chain in which the bison's lament
imitates a poetic imitation of a warrior's lament.

The sense in these works that some indigenous form exists which
suits a heroic topic presents only one side of the case. Kinahan
Cornwallis's *Yarra Yarra* (1858), one of the earliest of the Aboriginal
epics, consciously avoids too close an imitation of Aboriginal forms
"for, to speak candidly, aboriginal Australia is about as fruitless a
field for the employment of the pen as any region yet discovered"
(xii). G.W. Rusden's *Moyarra: An Australian Legend in Two Cantos*
(1851) and George Gordon McCrae's two epics, *The Story of Balla-
deadro* (1867) and *Mamba ("The Bright-Eyed"): An Aboriginal Romance*
(1867) emphasize veracity; but their forms, particularly the heroic
couplets, place them in an overtly alien tradition where, by virtue
of the same form, Bassett Dickson's Maori poem, *Honi Heki, in Two
Cantos* (1847), also belongs. Like various Canadian closet dramas,
heroic tragedies such as Mair's *Tecumseh* and Mackenzie's *Thayendanegea*, they overtly, if apparently unconsciously, manipulate indigenous subject to suit white form. The heroism of the central character
often seems an inevitable response to the vehicle, as is the strangely
inverted pseudo-Shakespearean speech found in many of these
works, including *Moyarra*: "Methinks the caitiff I could bless,/Who
drove thee thus to my caress" (10). This might be expected given

the assertions of poetic tradition in various prefaces such as the
following from Adam Kidd's *The Huron Chief and Other Poems* (1830):

> The little birch canoe, in which I have safely glided through the tranquil
> lakes of the Canadas, could not securely venture on the boiling surge,
> and foaming breakers, over which Childe Harold and Lalla Rookh trium-
> phantly rode in their magnificent Gondolas. (ix)

The attraction of nineteenth-century Canadian, Australian, and
New Zealand poets to the epic and the heroic tragedy might partly
be explained by various opportunities which the genres provided.
Eva Figes, in *Tragedy and Social Evolution* (1976), reflects one of these
when she looks to the studies of Australian Aborigines by Spencer
and Gillen to demonstrate how the basic elements of tragedy appear
quite clearly in "a primitive society" (12). In Figes's view, tragedy
has an unusual fit in "societies which are conceived of as inherently
static" (55). As shown as well in the historical romances, particularly
those of Rudy Wiebe and Patrick White, the indigenes, enmeshed
in the standard commodity of the prehistoric, and source of so much
frisson from the standard commodities of sex and violence, seemed
to offer a society much closer to the antique periods in which the
classics of the genres of high passion had been set, from Shakespeare's tragedies through Scott's novels.

Another appeal can be found in the historical context, a period of
nation defining. The epic in particular has often been defined as a
mythologized statement of beginning and of purpose for the nation.
Wole Soyinka, in *Myth, Literature and the African World* (1976), con-
tends the epic "concretises in the form of action the arduous birth
of the individual or communal entity, creates a new being through
utilising and stressing the language of self-glorification to which
human nature is healthily prone" (2). These poets combine their
individual need for indigenization with a collective statement on the
indigenizing of their community. Often, this process includes an
implied transformation of the Other nation, the indigenous, into an
extension of the self nation, and thus a suitable group for such self-
glorification. This provides an explanation for the apparent dichotomy in the image of the indigene in Howe's "Acadia". The poem
presents a vision of the founding of a nation and the Indian must
fit. Thus before the arrival of the whites the Indian is an extremely
noble figure, providing an extended history for the greatness of Nova
Scotia. After the whites take over, the Indian becomes the treacherous redskin, a justification to direct the readers' empathy to the
invaders rather than to those recently presented as an indigenous

aristocracy. The Australian pre-contact epic similarly establishes an ancient tradition for the land. The Canadian heroic tragedy demonstrates a nation-building coalition between the nobility of the indigene and the British-derived indigenizing.

Indigenized form as an overall shaping device for the "national literature" is only the macrocosmic manifestation of indigenization. Mair often used vaguely "Indian" words and phrases to make poems appear more rooted in the Canadian experience. Isabella Valancy Crawford flavoured her "Malcolm's Katie" (1884), a poem with no apparent interest in native peoples, with still more extensive Indianisms to represent nature:

> The South Wind laid his moccasins aside,
> Broke his gay calumet of flowers, and cast
> His useless wampum, beaded with cool dews,
> Far from him northward. (*Collected*, 198)

Alfred Bernie Bell's *The Diamond of Glen Rock* (1894) much less subtly justifies its simplistic sentimental story by vague Aboriginalities. George Cossins' *The Wings of Silence: An Australian Tale* (1899) represents a still more extreme, and still more common, version in popular literature, in which the exotic title is first represented to arise from a suitably violent bit of Aboriginal mysticism associated with a specific part of the Australian landscape and then left to hover over a story with no Aboriginal elements.

The most extreme examples of indigenizing metaphor are probably the poems of the Jindyworobaks, although to place them in such a limited context is unfair as their embrace of things Aboriginal was much more careful and much more general. In their battle to refute the European hegemony over Australian literary culture, they incorporated as many native elements as would be possible within the boundaries of contemporary poetry in English. The conflicting requirements of indigenization and genre led to severe formal limitations. The vast majority of Jindyworobak poems are brief lyrics in free verse, with an overt but limited subjectivity. The power of various disparate international movements such as imagism and social realism are apparent. Brian Elliott's introduction to *The Jindyworobaks*, claims: "It is, in fact, an unprofitable exercise to try to establish any connection between Aboriginal and Jindyworobak poetry, and even the striking forms and designs of Aboriginal visual art seem to have made only a picturesque impact" (xxix). Yet Elliott has much more trouble being dogmatic when he examines Roland Robinson's poems made out of stories taken directly from Aboriginal story-tellers: "I think in the end they must be accepted as poems and not merely as records and documentaries; and if they are poems, they are surely Robinson's as much as they belong to the Aboriginal speakers" (lix). The representation of indigenous form once more becomes an issue.

Claims to indigenous form play a still more important part in verisimilitude in prose fiction, particularly when narratives are presented as if told by an indigenous story-teller, as in Isabel Ecclestone MacKay's *Indian Nights* (1930). Fry's *Come A Long Journey* presents various stories, ranging from remnants of the distant past to the present. The different segments use different rhetorical techniques to signify the Indian narration. The first story uses a stilted yet simple and grammatical form of English:

> So perhaps when all this happened, life seemed no harder or easier for the people than now. They lived how they understood to live. (50)

The last story turns to a style which is highly ungrammatical:

> He wants all kinds fur, mostly he wants marten 'n he give little stuff, maybe little axe and knife 'n stuff like that, but he don't give gun, not much he don't give gun. (210)

The first uses a style which emphasizes a terse nobility, the Indian as past aristocrat. The second turns to the humbly colloquial, the Indian as downtrodden present.

W.P. Kinsella's stories (*Dance Me Outside* [1977], *Scars* [1978], *Born Indian* [1981] and *The Moccasin Telegraph* [1983]) are perhaps the best example of the verisimilitude problem in representations of the indigene. They are all "told" by Silas Ermineskin through cynical comments on white society, often in the form of an overtly "Indian" assessment of the stupidity of the white obsession with material progress. At times Silas and his friends are like the title character in Mordecai Richler's *The Incomparable Atuk* (1963), using white society against itself. But most of Silas's stories are more akin to Atuk's relatives, humour arising from misperceptions of the majority culture. In one story Silas interprets the white expression for pregnancy, "one in the oven," as a "kid in the stove" ("The Kid in the Stove," *Dance*, 81–4).

Kinsella's texts observe a number of important limitations. The usual standard commodities are there, the primary ones being sex and violence, but with a significant exception. Most of the stories avoid mysticism, the standard commodity which often is perceived to be the most romantic, the least "realistic," of the traditional Indian attributes. The other commodities are employed in ways which conform to the "realistic" tone, established by Silas's ungrammatical English which, like that in Fry, effects the aura of the storyteller, and gives him the veracity of orality.

There has been a simplistic acceptance of the verisimilitude of Kinsella's texts, even at the level which Todorov, in his list of definitions in "An Introduction to Verisimilitude" (1977), terms the "naive meaning, according to which a relation with reality is expressed" (Poetics, 82). Mikhail Bakhtin, in "Forms of Time and the Chronotope in the Novel" (1981), states that "we must never confuse – as has been done up to now and is still often done – the *represented* world with the world outside the text (naive realism)" (Dialogic, 253). A close analysis of Kinsella's texts shows that they should be recognized as what Todorov calls "verisimilitude as mask, as a system of rhetorical methods tending to present these [discursive] laws as so many submissions to the referent" (84).

Kinsella's texts shift the context of the semiotic field, as shown, for example, in the absence of natural metaphors. Kinsella changes the source: the field is shaped not by pantheism but by the stereotype of the Indian as manifestation of the welfare state. Instead of nature, a lethargic hedonism rules, with the primary mover the practical joke. Yet characters such as the priapically named Carson Longhorn and Frank Fencepost show that the altered source does not devalue the commodity, here sexual power. The ironic "voice" of Silas masks the portrait but does not change its valorization.

Kinsella's fiction remains circumscribed. The few Indians who deviate from the established semiotic field are given very limited roles. Any who are successful in the white world are immediately rejected as central subjects, unless they are perceivable as buffoons. The obvious problem for such characters in overtly "Indian" texts is that an Indian who does not fit within the semiotic field loses the shape identifiable as an Indian, an important element of the "exotic" in Kinsella's fiction. Some aspects of the field, such as mysticism, however, are too overtly "Indian" and deviate from the rhetorical methods of verisimilitude in contemporary fiction. The text is able to maintain an uneasy balance between a "stage Indian" and what would be considered by many white readers to be "not-Indian" partly because Silas is almost completely without introspection. The reader is thus not required to judge Silas's absent thoughts as "Indian" or "nonIndian" but is left with the paradox of an Indian narrator and no Indian consciousness. The moment at which mystical ritual and Silas's inner self are glimpsed in "Parts of the Eagle"

(*Moccasin*, 45–57) shows the severe limitations of the other stories and yet also shows the difficulties which arise when a text based on a restrained verisimilitude attempts to break the restraints.

Kinsella's texts might be placed in some perspective if compared to Norman W. McCallum's stories published under the pseudonym of the stereotypical Maori, Hori (*The Half-Gallon Jar* [1960], *Fill It Up Again* [1964], and *Flagon Fun* [1966]). The obvious exception is that while the Hori texts were printed by a small local publisher and are generally regarded in New Zealand as jokebooks of questionable taste, the Kinsella collections have been published internationally by major houses and given substantial acclaim. One could make various speculations on the reasons for these differing receptions. Other examples throughout this study show that it is an error to assume that the New Zealand image of the indigene is significantly different from that in Canada. Kinsella's texts have a more sophisticated display of literary techniques but, with the exception of more complex plot structures, it would be difficult to demonstrate an essential difference. The forms of publication are perhaps more important, in providing a very different impression to the reader. The imprimatur of the "serious" publisher is a factor too seldom recognized as a major part of the context of reading.

There are many genres in which verisimilitude is a primary concern. One, the sketch, might be associated with Kinsella's texts in the use of limitations: limited length allows a highly restrained description of an individual, usually contemporary, environment. It is particularly appropriate for brief ethnographies in which cultural definitions are a priority. Although some are rather more sentimentalized or more plot-centred than this suggests, a number of the Maori stories which Roderick Finlayson published between 1937 and 1972, collected in *Brown Man's Burden*, are representative. Finlayson's editor, Bill Pearson, claims: "The point of view is that of a compassionate helpless watcher, a God who sees his creatures destroy themselves but cannot interfere" (*Brown*, xviii). Similarly distant gods are found in various novels that, attempting a sparse impersonal realism, create the impression of a depersonalized portrait of the indigene as social problem in an object lesson. The titles of three such Australian texts are revealing: Joe Walker's *No Sunlight Shining* (1960), Nene Gare's *The Fringe Dwellers* (1961), and Sheppard's *Children of Blindness*. Although there are some points at which the texts represent certain psyches, in general they follow the form described by Todorov in "Language and Literature" as "the famous objective narration, a type used chiefly by American authors between the two world wars, in which the narrator knows nothing about his character, but merely sees his movements and gestures, hears his words; here story supplants discourse" (*Poetics*, 27).

The aspect of the text that "hears his words" suggests the inclusion of at least some subjectivity – denied in the passage from Hearne. The inclusion of indigene "speech" might seem to represent a prime example of the pattern noted by Bakhtin in "Discourse in the Novel": "These distinctive links and interrelationships between utterances and languages, this movement of the theme through different languages and speech types, its dispersion into the rivulets and droplets of social heteroglossia, its dialogization – this is the basic distinguishing feature of the stylistics of the novel" (*Dialogic*, 263). Bakhtin sees this dialogization as creating an important tension in fiction: "Every utterance participates in the 'unitary language' (in its centripetal forces and tendencies) and at the same time partakes of social and historical heteroglossia (the centrifugal, stratifying forces)" (272).

The "objective narration" attempts to avoid a ruling "unitary language" but, as both Todorov and Bakhtin note, the rhetoric of objectivity cannot deny that the form of the text is controlling the material presented, that story only *appears* to supplant discourse. Yet Bakhtin still maintains that there is a positive tension in what he calls a *"double-voiced discourse"* (324), in which the "self" of the text includes the "Other" within its vision while at the same time representing the social and historical vision of the Other. Bakhtin goes so far as to call it *"another's speech in another's language"* (324). This would seem to increase the subjectivity of the presentation. For the image of the indigene, the extreme example of objectivity, in this sense, reification, would be a novel in which the indigene is presented only as moving scenery, with no representation of an indigene consciousness, even to the extent of including dialogue. Further along the continuum would be a work in which some such speeches are recorded, then one in which an omniscient narrator penetrates the perceptions of one of the indigenes, and finally one in which the narrative is told through an indigene narration.

One might therefore see a significant shift in the form of the portrait of the indigene in Katharine Susannah Prichard's *Coonardoo* (1928). In earlier literature, the consciousness of the indigene is limited to the dialogue: the texts observe presence only from the outside. The few exceptions, such as the rarefied rhetorical introspection of some of the indigene heroes of epics, do not create a mask sufficient to achieve verisimilitude at any level. *Coonardoo*, usually considered of importance because of its representation of miscegenation, is perhaps of more interest because of the novelty of its rhetorical method. The omniscient narration concentrates on two parallel centres of intelligence, viewing the world sometimes through the white station owner, Hugh, and sometimes through the title character, his lover, a station black. This represents a significant difference not only from earlier texts but from many contemporary and later portraits of the indigene. In the Australian Vance Palmer's *Men Are Human* (1928) and Alan Fry's *How a People Die* (1970), for example, novels with similar concerns, the brief accounts told from indigenous points of view are so limited in depth as to offer almost no insights into the characters.

It should also be noted, however, that fewer examples of Coonardoo's point of view appear as the situation becomes more complicated and as her symbolic value becomes more pronounced. Prichard never reaches the strict balance of Hilliard's parallel *pakeha* and Maori centres of intelligence in *A Night at Green River*, a novel almost completely based on opposing defamiliarization as these two centres examine each other. A better example of the shift in perspective is perhaps Prichard's slightly later story, "Happiness" (*Kiss* [1932], 107–132). The narrative does not use an Aboriginal narrator but seldom deviates from one Aboriginal centre of intelligence. The skewed analysis is not primarily a comic device, as in Hori or Kinsella, but rather makes an overt attempt to create something close to Bakhtin's double-voice. "Story" is the tale of John, a white station-owner, and his marital problems; "discourse" is filtered through Nardadu, an aged station black woman who makes it clear that while John's life is her story, it is a minor factor in her worldview, particularly in comparison to her own duties and the success of her grandson.

Prichard's story is a significant change as a representation of both indigene consciousness and indigene ideology. For the former it presents the inner workings of the Aboriginal mind in an attempt at verisimilitude. The tropes and analyses avoid any elements which do not reflect Aboriginal experience. Similarly, if examined sociologically, the centre of intelligence reflects the ideology which governs Aboriginal practice. The kinship structures of the past and economic imperatives of the present combine to control the narrative of the alien white situation.

But the incorporation of Aborigine within white text remains limited. Once again, I would emphasize the masking procedures at play, in which the "unitary language" is denied and yet is the essential factor. An omniscient narration is hidden in various ethnographic references, a narration which re-establishes the position of the "centre of intelligence" as peripheral to the true centre of any discourse in white text. The indigenous centre of the discourse, so far from John's position as stranger to the land, remains an alien within the text. In opposition to Bakhtin's analysis I would suggest that this image of the indigene is an example of the negative confluence of the centripetal and centrifugal Other. It is centripetal because always subject to the system of white texts. Even here the Aboriginal "voice" "lives" only in Prichard's story. It is centrifugal because that Aborigine always reaches out to a clearly shaped semiotic field, here emphasizing the natural, which has defined the Image before its inclusion in the fluctuations of the individual text. The process continues even in contemporary texts which devote themselves entirely to an Aboriginal centre of intelligence. Todorov's *The Conquest of America* concludes with a consideration of the psychological process which would be involved in an "I" text which would be able to overcome the "I" sufficiently to eye the other truly: "And just as the discovery of the other knows several degrees, from the other-as-object, identified with the surrounding world, to the other-as-subject, equal to the I but different from it, with an infinity of intermediary nuances, we can indeed live our lives without ever achieving a full discovery of the other (supposing that such a discovery can be made)" (247). The image of the indigene suggests that this parenthetical half-reversal is where Todorov glimpses truly the impossible task of I reaching the plenitude of Other.

An important element of "Happiness" is ethnography. Prichard introduces a number of observations about kinship patterns and daily activities and uses a number of Aboriginal terms, which are glossed in footnotes. Ethnographic observations are a central part of many texts on the indigene, as one might expect of discourses which attempt to show the exotic revealing itself, from the "information" of the explorer's narratives to texts which strive for an indigenous point of view. David Ireland's novel *The Glass Canoe* (1976) parodies not indigenous form but the ethnographic obsession by depicting white urban pub culture through the anthropological frame of a participant observer narrative and a number of "Aboriginal" references: "While your tribe's waterhole flowed, you never went walkabout to another tribe's waterhole" (2).

Another possible gauge of textual attempts to make Bakhtin's second voice a part of the central discourse of the text is the number of indigenous words used and also the manner in which they are explained. For example, the reprint of "Happiness" in the *Penguin Book of Australian Short Stories* (1976) avoids almost all of the footnotes used in the original edition, in the apparent assumption that context is now sufficient to elucidate them. This seems to correlate with the general belief in our societies of a progressively greater knowledge of and more sophisticated response to indigenous peoples. A similar pattern appears in the ethnographic fiction of Donald Stuart, a novelist with an Aboriginal wife who lived in an Aboriginal environment for much of his life. His first novels represent various aspects of recent or contemporary experience with an emphasis on white-black interaction, particularly in miscegenation. There is little attempt to explore the subjectivity of the characters, white or black, in *Yandy* (1959) or *The Driven* (1961). *Yaralie* (1963) provides a somewhat more complicated portrait of a quarter-caste woman and her response to the social pressures of contemporary Australian society.

These texts describe the ethnography of a mixed society, with a strong emphasis on the experiences specific to that society but with few of the setpieces which overtly reify certain elements as particularly Aboriginal. Stuart's *Ilbarana* (1971) and *Malloonkai* (1976) demonstrate an emphatic shift in subject and in rhetorical method. Both use the title characters as centres of intelligence to describe the time of first contact. *Ilbarana* employs an extensive glossary, but *Malloonkai*, the story of Ilbarana's son, depends on context to explain Aboriginal words. Each text uses extensive estrangement to establish point of view when the Aboriginal centre creates its own ethnography of the white arrivants, and attempts its own form of assimilation:

> The proper men of the People of the country had placed the four pale men in the kinship system ... one Panaka, one Millanka, one Karimara, one Boorong, and had sent a young girl of the right face to each, though the Waibilla knew nothing of kinship. (*Malloonkai* 17)

At one level, this is not unlike the defamiliarization often used to denote an indigene perception, as in Donald Payne's *The Children* (1959), in which an Aboriginal boy observes two white children:

> Not only, he decided, were they freakish in appearance and clumsy in movement, they were also amazingly helpless: untaught; unskilled, utterly incapable of fending for themselves: perhaps the last survivors of some peculiarly backward tribe. (41)

The method in *Malloonkai* is much more sophisticated; the process of defamiliarization, is enhanced by the explanation by context and the use of a slightly stilted yet simple form of grammatical English to represent traditional indigenous discourse. But the whole is still representative of a number of texts from Australia, New Zealand, and Canada, and from different periods, with the exception that a complete novel is seldom devoted to such a perspective. The result is limited in that both of Stuart's texts demonstrate the same distance from the centre of discourse as that in Prichard and there is a similar lack of depth in their subjectivity. Both novels wear their ethnographies quite heavily. It is as though Stuart was too knowledgeable about the culture to commit the error of attempting psychic insight.

In prose fiction, verisimilitude in the representation of the indigene has been the primary concern of both writers and critics in all three countries, but there remain many other issues in the combination of generic forms and the standard commodities. For example, the central love relationship in the typical nineteenth-century romance usually conforms to certain structures. If A is the man and B is the woman, there is usually a C to complete the triangle. If C is a female, she is the sister of the male and sisterly to the female. In some nineteenth-century portraits of the indigene such structures prevent the text from considering the social effects of miscegenation. Catharine Parr Traill's *The Canadian Crusoes* (1852) presents a less than attractive portrait of Indians, but the final marriage of the strangely named Indiana to the young white Hector seems almost inevitable, given that they are the only three major characters and Hector's sister, Catherine, has already proclaimed her sisterhood with Indiana. Even sixty years later this structure holds significant power, as shown in Satchell's Maori novel, *The Greenstone Door*.

Still, as in the case of the epic, control by genre is most overt in poetry. The poetic traditions of nineteenth-century Australia have often been divided into the academic and the popular. Such a bifurcation is much too simplistic but its value can be shown by representative examples. Eliza Dunlop presents the following Aboriginal image in "The Eagle Chief" (1842):

> Bid joyous dancers fill the honied shells,
> Drink to the bold beneath his own blue sky,
>   Drink to the land where the Emu dwells,
> And the Ibis floats on high.

>   Light, light the pine! let cedar burn
>   To greet Maliyan's glad return! (*Aboriginal*, np)

An appropriate contrast is W.G. Wilks' ironic epic, *The Raid of the Aborigines* (1875):

> She stood with the air of a naiad of grace,
> And earnestly gazed on his jolly round face;

'Twas just such a gaze as I've seen an old glutton
Bestow on a saddle of five-year-old mutton. (37)

The ironic voice of Wilks' poem seems completely opposed to the heroic idyll by Dunlop, but this is more an opposition of genre than of philosophy. The general absence of this absurdly ignoble savage in prose fiction (and its presence in nineteenth-century drama) supports the assessment that it is a response to specific generic assumptions. This formal rather than essential separation of genres is reflected in Henry Kendall's poetry. Although "The Last of His Tribe" conforms to all of the heroic expectations of the warrior lament, his "Peter the Picaninny" (1880, *Works*, 184–7) maintains the generic requirements of the popular verse of the day in a rollicking portrait of the Aborigine as degenerate buffoon. Rather than revealing a considered position maintained by Kendall, the poems show the power of genres to create philosophical contradictions.

The bush ballad form, with its emphasis on ironic incongruities, also demonstrates the power of the individual word and its associations, a significant opposition to the incorporation of Aboriginal terms in the heroic poems. Wilks's reference to the "naiad" presents one such example. In "A Piccaninny," James Brunton Stephens, who achieved the most popular success with bush ballad depictions of the ignoble savage, refers to a female Aborigine as "A Helen in the nigger apprehension?" (*Works* [1902], 173). "Nigger" is a misnomer in its reference to a negroid race but significant in Australia in that it connects the Aborigine to an image of the American black as degenerate and servile, a connection which is particularly important in nineteenth-century drama. The overt colloquialism of "nigger" clashes with the elevation of the Greek reference and of the manifestly intellectual quality of "apprehension." Wilks uses a similar rhetorical figure in a reference to "sable hags" (34).

These examples play on other literary references, in which Greek comparisons and words such as sable have been used to elevate the indigene. The complicated irony which can result from this process is suggested by the words of John Mathew's "The Aboriginal Love-letter" (*Echoes*, 1902): "The nymph though dark is fair" (39). "Fair," a central signifier of the woman as literary object, and "dark," the essence of the alien Other, cross with the "nymph," part of both semiotic fields. The different words are part of a general system of indigene-linked terminology, which includes a variety of elements from the idyllic to the satanic, extending to the emotive indigenisms emblematic of the standard commodity of violence, such as "braves" and "war-paint," defined in North America and then transported.

The extent of this system of terminology is suggested by Crawford's Indianized nature and by Kenneth Mackay's description in *A Bush Idyll* (1888) of an Australian "fire-god":

> The drought-fiend lapped with thirsty sun–parched tongue
> Each spring and tank, and sucked with ghoul–like lips
> The very life–blood from the cracking soil;
> Fire came to blacken earth and mar the sky
> With charred and sable tokens of his wrath,–
> Undimmed by miles of smoke his savage eyes
> Gleamed like the outposts of the hosts of hell. (12–3)

There is no implication that Mackay intended an association with the Aboriginal image but almost every line contains a term from the Aboriginal canon, a rhetorical association of fear of the personified land.

Contemporary examples achieve a greater sophistication, but they show a clear continuation of the literary tradition. Les Murray's contemporary epic, *The Boys Who Stole the Funeral: A Novel Sequence* (1980), uses the heroic Aboriginal figure of pseudo-legend. Murray takes an apparently commonplace setting and characters and raises them to a national metaphor. As in the Jindyworobak tradition, white Australian maturation, both of the individual boys and of the nation, is linked to Aboriginal ritual, and parody once again appears when a white ex-warrior delivers a *ubi sunt* lament (18). The elevation of the narrative is enhanced and affirmed by the presence of a mystical Aboriginal figure who addresses one of the boys in an imitation of an Aboriginal dream vision and provides "the blood-history of the continent" (65).

Although its free prosaic verse is a clearly contemporary vehicle, Murray's overtly epic and thus depersonalized poem might seem more a derivation of an earlier white literary tradition, of the same lineage as Ingamells's *The Great South Land: An Epic Poem*. Much of contemporary poetry is more openly personal in tone than Murray's. This leads to a subjective and discursive portrait of the interaction between white and indigene. The loose form of contemporary poetry emphasizes expressions of empathy and at its most extensive presents an imitation of symbiotic transformation as the poet becomes the object which he/she has been examining, as in John Newlove's "The Pride" (1968):

> in our desires, our desires,
> mirages, mirrors, that are theirs, hard-

riding desires, and they
become our true forbears, moulded
by the same wind or rain,
and in this land we
are their people, come
back to life again. (*Fat Man*, 74)

Newlove's internalization is somewhat anomalous in the collective
claims made through the first person plural. Al Purdy's "Beothuck
Indian Skeleton in Glass Case" (*Wild Grape Wine* [1968], 109) is more
representative in its exploration of a first-person singular response.
But neither transforms the indigene to subject. The degree of white
subjectivity which the confessional form demands increases the
manipulation of the object and the reification of the indigene, a
process which Al Pittman's "Shanadithit" (*Drowning* 1978) both man-
ifests and describes:

I admit now
(putting this poem aside)
that my love for you has nothing
to do with you. Not as you were
or might have been in those few
of your own dead-end days. (45)

The many major and minor manipulations of form in poetry reflect
the pressures of literary convention on the indigene. In most ways
the image of the indigene was forced to conform to the literary
conventions. The heroic indigene of the epic is in this sense similar
to the indigene as stimulus to guilty introspection in the contemporary lyric. In both forms, the indigene is object to be manipulated
in the aid of the subject of the white text, whether it is the overtly
subjective first-person lyricist or the hidden subjectivity of the epic
text as poetic nation.

The sonnets of Duncan Campbell Scott provide perhaps the most
unusual convention in the poetry of the indigene. Various forms of
what might be termed "parlour poetry" have used indigene images,
usually fairy-like figures. The majority of these were published in
nineteenth-century periodicals, like the above example from Eliza
Dunlop. *The Literary Garland* presents a rather dismaying assortment
for the years 1848–52. Still, many twentieth-century examples are
to be found, as in the various works by Roddick. They might be
described as "Indigene as silly wood-nymph." Even Pauline Johnson, who identified herself as a Mohawk and who produced a num-

ber of texts in prose and verse which present a strong although ideologically undeveloped support of native people, is now best known for just such lyrics.

Scott presents an interesting exception. The agenda for his poems is suggested by the comments of his friend and sometimes mentor, Archibald Lampman, who liked to torment the establishment through his occasional column "At the Mermaid Inn," in the *Globe* newspaper (1892). Lampman's "improper" and even "malevolent" persona he called "my friend the sonneteer" defended his "atrocious and impudent" versions of sonnets with "a defiant glare. 'The best way to impress your subject on the reader is to cast it in a totally unsuitable form. It's the contrast that does it, you know'" (*Selected*, 63). In terms of the present study, Scott's "Indian sonnets" must be seen as limited achievements as they seldom show even slight deviations from the standard semiotic field. "Watkwenies" (1898) and "The Onondaga Madonna" (1898, *Selected Poems*, 133–4), for example, concentrate on the standard commodities of violence and the prehistoric.

Yet they demonstrate the value of not the appropriate but the inappropriate form through the sonnet, which most would assume a prime example of a genre inimical to a new land. Perhaps the answer was not to attempt forms in which the indigene could find a "natural" place, such as the epic, nor even the various prose versions of verisimilitude, to show the indigenes "as they are," but rather to turn to an ardently oppositional convention, to present the semiotic field in a form which highlights the problematic, the ideological moment, rather than masking it in the appearance of double voice as in Kinsella. The impossible goal of seeking a form which will liberate the indigene, which will go beyond the indigene as signifier to the referent, would be replaced by a presentation which shows the manipulation of the signifier and thus represents the manipulation of the referent.

CHAPTER FOUR

Sexuality

Sexuality is a major, if not the major, element of human life. Since Freud, psychoanalysis and other theories of the human mind have done much to turn it into a focal point for our view of the individual psyche. We regard sexual attitudes, desires, energies, as central to the definition of each person. From this perspective it requires but a small adjustment of the lens to regard western society as a collectivity of these individual sexual psyches.

Foucault's *The History of Sexuality* (1976) attempts to understand the changes in attitudes towards sexuality which took place in the nineteenth century, which is more or less the starting point of the present study. Foucault asserts: "People often say that modern society has attempted to reduce sexuality to the couple – the heterosexual and, insofar as possible, legitimate couple. There are equal grounds for saying that it has, if not created, at least outfitted and made to proliferate, groups with multiple elements and a circulating sexuality: a distribution of points of power, hierarchized and placed opposite to one another; 'pursued' pleasures, that is, both sought after and searched out; compartmental sexualities that are tolerated or encouraged; proximities that serve as surveillance procedures, and function as mechanisms of intensification; contacts that operate as inductors" (45–6).

Foucault here tries to reconcile the difference between the severely circumscribed forms of sexuality that our society appears to consider normal and the complicated array of sexualities existing within that same society. To the suggestion that society represses those forms of sexuality regarded as deviant, or that at best are not sanctioned, Foucault replies: "Because this repression is affirmed, one can discreetly bring into coexistence concepts which the fear of ridicule or the bitterness of history prevents most of us from putting side by side: revolution and happiness; or revolution and a different body, one that is newer and more beautiful; or indeed, revolution and pleasure" (7). To Foucault the very force of repression creates a space in which repressed elements can be voiced. In a society without the confidence of repression such elements might be too frightening, too dangerous in their opposition to the status quo. Within a repressed society they can be instead a source of energy.

The combination of these views, Freud's of humanity as sexually driven and Foucault's of the gap provided by sexual repression, suggests the importance of the standard commodity of sexuality in the semiotic field of the indigene. It is the selection of participants rather than the actual form of sexual activity which is deemed illegitimate, but the suppression of sexual relations between whites and indigenes has been just as strong as in the case of most other "perversions." And yet, because the form of sexuality itself seems to be "normal," there is an admissible erotic attraction for the reader. The few accounts of homosexuality with indigenes, such as those in Keneally's *The Chant of Jimmie Blacksmith* and Bowering's *Burning Water*, admit no positive component but show the acts as the depraved perversity of violent white rapists.

A claim could certainly be made, however, that many accounts of indigenous females do not emphasize their attractive powers. The Australian explorer, Charles Sturt, in *Two Expeditions* (1833) claims that "the loathsome condition and hideous countenances of the women would, I should imagine, have a complete antidote to the sexual passion" (2:126). Hearne asserts the same in *A Journey*: "perfect antidotes to love and gallantry" (89). But the very testimonial to the medicinally anti-erotic properties of these potential objects of miscegenation implies a fear of their attractions. The possibilities of that "repression gap" are thus brought into play.

Mannoni looks at the role of sexuality in a specifically racial context: "In his urge to identify the anthropoid apes, Caliban, the Negroes, even the Jews with the mythological figures of the satyrs, man reveals that there are sensitive spots in the human soul at a level where thought becomes confused and where sexual excitement is strangely linked with violence and aggressiveness" (111). The masculinist assumptions of Mannoni's comments are perhaps the central issue of the commodity of indigene sexuality. The confusion of thought in the sensitive human soul, which Mannoni observes is of "man" is a male confusion. This is not to claim that a similar confusion does not exist in texts by female authors. While the expression of indigene sexuality in Mazo de la Roche's *Possession* (1923) seems very similar to that in texts by male authors, the repression of sexuality in Praed's *Fugitive Anne* might have some specifically feminine, although not feminist, attributes. But the basic *view* of the indigene as sexual figure is an extension of the masculinist reification of the Other. Mannoni provides a simple explanation for the basic attraction of the indigene: "romantic literature has made use of the sexual appeal of racial differences as if they reinforced the purely sexual differences. The more remote people are, the more they seem to attract our projections – the easier it is for a 'crystallization', as Stendahl called it, to take place" (111).

Mannoni's use of the word "projections" has an additional power because of its implication of a filmic image. The static Other reflects the gaze of the observer and returns the image which the male gaze requires. Berger suggests that the nude in a painting tends to look out rather than at some other figure who shares her canvas because she looks "towards the one who considers himself her true lover – the spectator-owner" (56). Berger examines at some length the difference between the images of men and the images of women in western art. He comes to the following conclusion: "One might simplify this by saying: *men act* and *women appear*. Men look at women. Women watch themselves being looked at" (47). This gives some suggestion of the role of the indigene in these literatures. The primary role for the male indigene is found in the standard commodity of violence. This male is reified but he is, if possible, an active object. The female, in the standard commodity of sexuality, is simply an object. As noted below, she often has a very limited interaction even with the central white male of her narrative. It is as though he, in this context, acts as persona for the "spectator-owner," the author, the reader, the culture, and is guided by the repression of that masculinist, antimiscegenist culture.

Thus the commodity of indigene sexuality can be seen as an extension of the patriarchy. Although both indigene and woman are object of the white male subject, the "patria-archal" assumptions of imperialist violence and of imperialist views of indigenous violence place the male indigene in a slightly different perspective from the traditional reified female figure identified by so many feminist critics. The female indigene is instead the female refemaled in a variety of contexts. She represents the attractions of the land but in a form which seems to request domination, unlike her violent male counterpart who resists it. The image of the female as receiver of the male power provides an explicit opportunity for the white patriarchy to enter the land. If, as in the majority of the early works and many of the later, the sexual relationship is repressed or even denied she becomes still more explicitly object, as the domination is not through sexual "inter-action" but through the spectator-owner. And at all times she represents a passionate heterosexuality with the limited perversion of miscegenation – with all the tensions that, as Foucault shows, are so productive of discourse.

Foucault considers those tensions in the following comment: "What is peculiar to modern societies, in fact, is not that they consigned sex to a shadow existence, but that they dedicated themselves to speaking of it *ad infinitum*, while exploiting it as the secret" (*Sexuality*, 35). This is seen throughout the images of the indigene, particularly in the nineteenth century. The term "black velvet" has long been used in Australia to represent sexual relations between white males and Aboriginal females. It has the aura of Foucault's secret in that it represents something "unmentionable" which is often "mentioned," similar to the description of indigene sexuality in Alexander Mackenzie's *Voyages* (1802). *Voyages* begins with an introductory history of the fur trade which first notes the evil effects on the Indians of their encounters with whites but then adds: "At the same time they were not, in a state of nature, without their vices, and some of them of a kind which is the most abhorrent to cultivated and reflecting man. I shall only observe that incest and bestiality are among them" (xcvii).

The Chant of Jimmie Blacksmith presents black velvet as a ubiquitous passion among the outback males: "For they nearly all knew what it was to slaver after dark women" (109). In the nineteenth century, however, the Australian unmentionable was more like Mackenzie's. The secret is maintained by phrases such as that of the explorer, Edward Eyre, writing in 1842. He describes the ugliness of the older Aboriginal women in phrases not unlike those of Sturt above but then asserts: "When young, however, they are not uninteresting" (2: 208). A later but less sophisticated observer, W.H. Willshire, is more explicit in his awareness of the attractions of Aboriginal women in *The Land of the Dawning* (1896). He first rejects an article which he has just read which comments on "harmless flirtations with dusky princesses" (29), but then a page later gives the following artful account of just that:

Under the gentle influence of chaste Luna, several haughty, dusky beauties, the perfection of womanly grace, used to commence dancing a vigorous and unrefined sort of can-can for the edification of the tribe. Now and again I said, "hear, hear," and put more wood on the fire, so I would not lose the better part for want of light. In their barbaric sensuality they began skipping around me. I always had a keen sense for natural beauty, and an admiration for the weird and wild mysteries of unknown regions.

When a woman makes what he deems to be a direct overture to him, Willshire states that he "declined with thanks, and bowed most courteously; she with equal politeness returned the courtesy" (30).

Willshire's text begins in parody, the reference to "chaste Luna" being placed in juxtaposition with these women who are presented as far from chaste. The second point of irony, as he adds wood to his voyeur's fire, seems far less assured. The "barbaric sensuality" of the women has no such irony. The "natural beauty" and "weird and wild mysteries" could be viewed as ironic, but there is nothing in the immediate context to make such an interpretation necessary. The ambivalence of the rest of Willshire's text is similarly unhelpful in achieving a unitary meaning. It seems that regardless of Willshire's attempt to describe "without garnish" (4) he falls into Foucault's trap of mentioning the unmentionable. Then, however, he resorts once more to a confident irony in his account of the proposition, and is thus able to thwart the assumptions of his autobiographical portrait of the appeal of black velvet. Willshire adds fuel to his fire but does not penetrate the land, remaining as spectator-owner of the female indigene and holding his active powers for his violent attacks on the males elsewhere in the text. Eyre uses a still more creative form of deflection to camouflage some of his "interest" by employing a nineteenth-century "scientific" practice and presenting his most lengthy and most explicit descriptions of Aboriginal sexuality in Latin. What better example could there be of the secret *ad infinitum*?

Sexuality is perhaps the most complicated of the standard commodities of the indigene, seldom employed without ambivalence. Other commodities are often valorized in more straightforward ways. For example, the reaction to the violent indigene is usually negative. The sexual indigene is only very seldom an object of absolute aversion but even when she seems an image of unalloyed attraction, as in Domett's *Ranolf and Amohia*, there are usually elements to modify that image. Amohia's death is one more example of the demise which liberates the white hero from miscegenation.

The indigenes of Australia, Canada, and New Zealand are never so remote in Australian, Canadian, and New Zealand texts as Mannoni's figure from romantic literature. The latter might be compared to that noted by Sander Gilman in "Black Bodies, White Bodies" (1985): "one of the black servant's central functions in the visual arts of the eighteenth and nineteenth centuries was to sexualize the society in which he or she is found" (209). But in these examples, the servant is seldom the sexual object. The white female performs this role and the servant acts as association with a remote realm, quite undefined, which signifies lascivious sexuality. The role of the sexual indigene, in particular the indigene female, is quite different. The indigene maiden is not an emblem of boudoir sexuality nor an emissary of an undefined distant place. Both of these values in the economy of the painting in Gilman's example clearly remove the black servant from the context in which the painting was produced. The indigene maiden is instead a manifestation of the land in which the text is produced and is a major factor in the attempt to make that text of that land.

The primary valorization of the indigene maiden is as an ethereal romantic figure. She appears throughout all three literatures, and the early acknowledgment of her prominence is suggested by some of Willshire's phrases above. She can best be understood as a series of absolutes: absolute purity, absolute beauty, and absolute devotion. Ranolf says of his Maori love:

> But Amohia! What a glorious creature
> In every gesture, every feature!
> Such melting brilliant eyes!

He follows these exclamations by assessing her hair:

> black abundant floods
> Of tresses (1:34)

before he concludes:

> But these are graces to be left unspoken
> Beside the soul – the spirit's charm
> That from some well of witchery infernal
> Comes dancing up. (1:135)

The essence of the indigene maiden is a sexual interest but also a sexual restraint. In many instances there is no overt reference to any sexual interaction. It is an example of the repression of miscegenation, but this not in the form of a fear of interaction with a lesser creature. Rather it cloaks the issue in an ethereal aura which suggests the impossibility of sexual congress with a spiritual entity. It is a pure temptation with the titillation but none of the confusion caused by a fulfilment of the temptation. The text's associated comments on the land are usually positive, with many references to the attractions of the topography. Yet there is often a sense of some distance, both from the indigene and from the land, as is appropriate in the usual distinction between temptation and the realization of that temptation.

The many versions of the maiden owe their basic shape to a long-established female vision, as suggested by the various references to Diana, in texts from the Canadian *An Algonquin Maiden* (Adam and Wetherald 1887) to the New Zealand *Half-Caste* (Baume 1933), to the Australian "The Lost Tribe of Boonjie" (Meredith 1940). The relatively recent Australian *No Sunlight Singing* (Walker 1960) shows the limits of historical change in the image of the indigene: "One, lovely as a vision of eternal youth, ran fleetly as the Goddess of the Chase, the first Diana, who no doubt was olive-complexioned" (95). Like Diana, she and the others combine sexual attraction, chastity, and nature. This goddess maiden is presented as the essence of the race and yet superior to it. In Bodsworth's *The Strange One*, Kanina Beaverskin has "an exotic, nonconforming beauty": "She was an Indian like the others, yet strikingly different; she seemed more Indian-like in some respects – the very brown skin and the coal-black hair – yet she was extremely attractive" (96). For some of the maidens, such as the title figure in *Half-Caste* and Hatfield's *Black Waterlily*, a mixed-race ancestry is presented as an explanation of the variation between her attractions and those of other indigenes. Both texts first emphasize the white attributes: "Now she was a young Diana; her brown eyes shining from her sweet face as they shine over the sun-tan of perfect blondes; not a native trace anywhere, unless one who knew" (Baume, 103); "She's utterly irresistible. Marvelous white skin, night black hair, lips like poinsettia blooms, and large hazel green eyes" (Hatfield, 69). Yet their indigene status is always clear and a major part of their sexual attractions. Hatfield's Lily asserts her own passionate sexuality: "I'm a breathing, palpitating little savage who'd *kill* if anything came between me and my man" (172).

The limited importance of racial mixture for the indigene maiden might seem a strange element. The results of miscegenation had long been an issue throughout the "new world." C.D. Rowley's *Outcasts in White Australia* (1970) notes that the Victoria Aboriginal act of 1869 made specific reference to "half-castes" (5). In *We Are Métis* (1980), Duke Redbird states of the equivalent group in the Canadian context: "the Métis were being identified as a group as early as 1670" (3). In Canada, the valorizing term has usually been not Métis but "half-breed," a product of debased sexuality. The Australian "half-caste" seems more a statement of the rank of that product. Still, the images associated with these fractionated hyphens are very similar. Xavier Herbert's *Capricornia* (1973) lays extensive claims for their virtues as what his *Poor Fellow My Country* refers to as "a created people" (53). John Liddell Kelly's poem, "In Maoriland" (1896), calls for much the same: "May conquering and conquered

blood be blent/And breed new beauty and virility!" (*Heather*, 148).
As a white in Stuart's *Yaralie* observes to a pregnant part-Aboriginal
woman, those of mixed race achieve indigenization through simple
biological fact: "It will be a child of the country, Scot, and your
mother's people, and Chinese and Filipino, it will belong, as all
your people have belonged" (206). Don Gutteridge's *Riel: A Poem for
Voices* (1972) records an old priest's view of the Métis, for whom
Riel resonates as the leader of their rebellion against the Canadian
government:

> The Métis were like the Red River (the priest had said)
> Where it was joined by the Assiniboine, two great
> Currents fused in one strong flowing to the lake
> Of the sky that waited for, and cared for them all. (3)

A character in Thomas Ronan's *Vision Splendid* (1954) simply states,
"The Australian half-caste is the best-bred physical specimen in the
world" (137).

Within the standard commodity of violence, mixed race is represented as intensifying the evil, but the female is no more and no
less sexual than her full-blood sisters. Her varied background might
be used to justify her unusual attractions but the result is very little
different from the pure examples represented by Kanina Beaverskin
or by Amohia in Domett's poem. The only significant variation is
when the racial blend leads to psychological confusion within the
woman, as in Baume and in Leonard Mann's *Venus Half-Caste* (1963).
Duncan Campbell Scott's "The Half-Breed Girl" (1926) has racial
memories of her Scottish ancestry, "The heritage of an age-long life/
In a legendary land," and is unable to reconcile these memories:
"She fears for something or nothing/With the heart of a frightened
child" (*Selected Poems*, 63). Yet regardless of suggestions of internal
quandaries, it is her external role which earns her a place as object
of the white male subject. And as object she remains the indigene
maiden.

The usual emphasis in all such figures is on romantic devotion,
as in Tecumseh's daughter in Mair's *Tecumseh* and the Maori girl in
Angus McLean's *Lindigo* (1866). In both works, the unacceptability
of interracial love is raised, but the problem is erased by the death
of the indigene woman in the service of her love. In Richardson's
Wacousta, the sexual issue is avoided: while Oucanasta's attentions
to Captain de Haldimar are the subject of ribald commentary by
other soldiers, the narration provides no suggestion that the devotion is sexually based, regardless of the clearly romantic pattern of

the relationship. Oucanasta is not unlike the many other indigenes in voluntary servitude. In E.L. Cushing's "The Indian Maid," (1846), through *Ranolf and Amohia*, to *Poor Fellow My Country*, in which Jeremy's Aboriginal wife, Nanago, calls herself "servant" and him "master" (1282), indigene women become devoted "slaves" for a white man, attending him with "dog-like" fidelity.

The forms of repressed sexuality in many texts provide interesting reflections on Foucault's observations. The many romances found in *The Literary Garland* employ Indian love objects, such as the afore-mentioned "Indian Maid," even less corporeal than might be expected. But a text in the same genre, *An Algonquin Maiden*, combines this pure romantic devotion with a nude scene of its "Diana," in her "barbaric splendour." As Berger describes the nude in paint-ing, "This nakedness is not, however, an expression of her own feelings; it is a sign of submission to the owner's feelings or demands" (*Ways*, 52). As such, she represents the power of the spectator and thus of the imperialist patriarchy, but in this text the potential fear of her racially-based sexuality becomes more evident. The reaction of the observer figure in *An Algonquin Maiden*, "Hence-forth be blind for thine eyes have seen too much!" (61), suggests Foucault's comment on the attitude of nineteenth-century society: "As if it suspected sex of harboring a fundamental secret" (69). This is clearly the case in Brian Moore's *Black Robe: A Novel* (1985), in which the Jesuit Laforgue, an inadequate indigenizer at best, observes a young Indian woman performing fellatio on his young assistant and "as though possessed" (55) is driven to masturbate. "He stood sobbing in that wild place, bereft of all hope, beyond all forgiveness" (56). Even a masochistic scourging provides little relief from this confrontation with the fundamental secret.

It would be possible to view the fairyland figure of the indigene maiden as one of a pair of opposites with the unattractive squaw at the other end. An Aboriginal version of the latter might be seen in Vance Palmer's *The Man Hamilton* (1928):

> In the dark, broad-featured face there was no expression save that of empty amiability, and the brown eyes had the wild look seen in animals that have been tamed and domesticated a long time. An olive-skinned, placid-looking woman, whose blood moved as sluggishly as her thoughts! This was Hamilton's wife. (40)

She might be linked to a variety of other figures, such as the mis-sionary's Indian wife in A.M.D. Fairbairn's play, "A Pacific Coast Tragedy" (*Plays*, 1935), whose bland exterior covers a malevolent interior. Yet these two "wives" are in one sense very like the maiden. Both maiden and squaw are manifestations of the white culture's felt temptation by the indigene and by what the indigene represents in the land. But if one looks at them as emotional signs, as something like Eliot's objective correlative, the variation between the two becomes apparent. The maiden represents the positive anticipation, and thus temptation; the squaw is the fruition, the aftermath, of that temptation, and becomes fear. The maiden represents the optimism that the land holds, the potential of a positive indigenization; the squaw represents the pessimism, the potential that this alien realm will be a negative indigenization, a destructive takeover of the soul.

These two "squaws" are identified within the texts as "wives" and thus the focus is on the evil ties that they have on their husband, both to themselves and through them to the land. All "squaws" are by no means wives, and there are a number of wives, such as the Indian Helen in Augustus Bridle's *Hansen: A Novel of Canadianization* (1924), "some great northern flower" (271), and the Maori Ngaire in *Half-Caste*, who are much nearer the perfect beauty of the maiden. Still, even the elevated Ngaire proves a problematic spouse, as might be suggested by her squaw-like mother: "Thick lipped, chin tattooed, Rewa was as dark as coffee and shapeless as a sack" (10). The conclusion of the novel is ambivalent about the future of Ngaire's marriage. The very idea of marriage, a state-controlled relationship, seems a significant deviation from the vision provided by Amohia. The legal commitment which marriage entails might thus be seen as the "reality" in opposition to the "aesthetic theory" of the attraction of the maiden, a "reality" which is not the joyous indigenization expected from accepting the temptation of the indigene maiden.

In many texts the only variation between the maiden and the squaw is the overt sexuality. The squaw is thus not an essentially different commodity from the maiden but rather receives a different valorization: the white man who gives in to the physical attractions of the maiden is doomed. Vance Palmer represents the tenor of many works of all three countries in the title of *Men Are Human* (1928). The Indian Onawata in Ralph Connor's *The Gaspards of Pine Croft* (1923) suits the Indian maiden stereotype, "beautiful, proud" (28), "with the fleet and silent movements of the wild things of the forest" (25). Her husband, Gaspard, recognizes "her lofty sense of right, her Puritan holiness of spirit" (28). But once again the reality of miscegenation destroys this ethereal power and Gaspard asserts, "I'm a perfect savage, Mrs. Pelham. I have been living among savages, I have become dehumanised" (90).

The only escape from this situation is the usual one, the death of the indigene. In this as in many other texts, whether she remains the distant image or becomes the reality of miscegenation, she must die, must become of the past, in order for the white to progress towards the future and move beyond the limitations of his sexual – or at least romantic – temptation and achieve possession of the land. A suggestion of this imperative is provided by one of the few narratives in which the indigene as object of desire does not die, *Possession*. For Derek at first Fawnie is the spectator's object:

> She seemed to rise, a dark water-lily on its stem, a flower of unearthly beauty, springing from the water, fed by the flames, filling the night air with the perfume of her desire. (52)

Like Hatfield's Lily, Bridle's Helen, and many other maidens, Fawnie is the floral beauty of the land while in her position as object of the gaze. Later her sensual drive is revealed: "It's awful to feel the way I do. Like as if my blood was dancin' in my body" (71). The combination of this "unthinking" (229) power and Derek's weakness leads to his indigenization which he recognizes as a reversal of the domination suggested by his earlier position as farmer of the land and spectator of the indigene: "What a strange thing possession was! You thought you were the possessor when, in truth you were the thing possessed" (288).

The female indigene as emanation of the land is a source of indigenization but in various ways. In many works, particularly nineteenth-century examples such as *Wacousta* and *Tecumseh*, her careful protection of a white male suggests the possibility that the white might find within the apparently inimical land an element which will save him. In both texts she is presented in explicit opposition to the violence of the male indigene which would thwart the white domination. In Eleanor Dark's *The Timeless Land* (1941), the "white blackfellow" Johnny, through his Aboriginal wife, "rediscovered the earth" (323). The title character in Prichard's *Coonardoo*, perhaps the most famous indigene maiden in the Australian canon, provides a native counterpart to the male hero's white devotion to the land he owns. When he has sex with her, Hugh "gave himself to the Spirit which drew him, from a great distance it seemed, to the common source which was his life and Coonardoo's" (64). As for Derek in *Possession*, sexual ownership of the indigene seems to fill in the spiritual – and sensual – gap left by the legalistic fact of white ownership. The extent of the powers which Coonardoo as indigene offers to fill that space are made still more clear at the end of the novel:

She had loved Wytaliba and been bound up with the source of its life. Was she not the well in the shadow? Had she not some mysterious affinity with that ancestral female spirit which was responsible for fertility, generation, the growth of everything? (199–200)

This is not to say that this relationship between the white male and the female spirit of the land is entirely positive, particularly in the examples of overt sexual contact. Hugh is obsessed with Coonardoo and yet cannot face this obsession and so, in a pattern very similar to that in *Possession*, sends her away, which destroys himself, her, and the land:

Coonardoo's spirit had withered and died when she went away from Wytaliba, was something of what Chitali said. And that withering and dying of Coonardoo's spirit had caused a blight on the place. (199)

As the traditional image of the succubus would suggest, the acquisition of hidden knowledge through a sexual encounter with a female source has its dangers.

In Robert Kroetsch's *Badlands* (1975), a group of archaeologists are initiated into the land by a young Indian woman, Anna Yellowbird. The expedition leader, Dawe, is overwhelmed by sex with her:

It was the moment of descent that came to obsess him. The hot, cascading instant when, in which, she eased her body down onto his. The secret opening, the perfect mass of her cunthair yielding its secret gate, forcing his entrance; at that split second of penetration he must, he would, raise up with him into that underworld of his rampaging need the knowledge of all his life. (194–5)

Even in such an explicit description, sex remains Foucault's secret, but the phrase reveals it to be doubly enfolded because opening of miscegenation and gate to indigenization. The experience breaks time – an instant – a split second. Dawe should be the power (assuming that an unstated "he" is the subject of "forcing his entrance"), but he enters a consciousness which is unconscious; he descends into the dangerous underworld which will incorporate, possess whatever alien knowledge he may bring, as Fawnie does of Derek in *Possession*. *Badlands* asserts: "at each moment of entry into the dark, wet heat of her body the outside world was lost" (195).

It is tempting to employ the orientation known as gynocriticism and assess *Possession* as a woman-authored text. Nancy K. Miller's "Writing (from) the Feminine: George Sand and the Novel of Female

Pastoral" (1983) looks at the "female plot": "By female plot I mean quite simply that organization of narrative event which delimits a heroine's psychological, moral, and social development within a sexual fate" (125). Women writers provide an alternative: "But female-authored fiction generally questions the costs and overdetermination of this particular narrative economy with an insistence such that the stories produced provide internal commentary on the status of female plot itself. They thereby solicit a reading of narrativity that takes into account the ideology at work in this genderization of experience. Whether such a reading can in turn reveal the unmistakeable traces of a specifically female (re)writing remains of course an open question – or an article of faith" (125–6). Female authorship does not absolutely prove the faith as the death of Coonardoo at the end of Prichard's novel fits the typical white patriarchal pattern. The fact that Hugh has been destroyed psychologically simply fulfills the usual male fear of the succubus. But Fawnie reverses the dead indigene maiden, surpassed by the indigenized male, and instead subverts the patriarchy through possessing the man and repossessing, in both senses, the land. Then Kroetsch's narrative, which ends with Dawe dead and a surviving Anna Yellowbird indigenizing Dawe's appropriately named daughter, Anna, could be a male acquisition of the gynocentric vision.

But such an interpretation makes teleological inversion paramount and dismisses the continuing limitations of the standard commodity. Both Fawnie and Anna remain tightly circumscribed as unconscious expressions of natural sexuality. The semiotic field is the same as overtly negative white encounters with that sexuality, such as those in the Australian narrative, "The Blood of Marlee" (1939–40), by Charles Broome. There Marlee, "the Wild Spirit of the Bush" (September 1939, 48), destroys the men she attracts. This sexual spirit might be almost a revolutionary sign, as the Union Jack dress worn by a woman in Conrad Sayce's *Comboman* (1934) is "The flag of a conquering race worn by a black woman because she had vanquished a member of that race" (26).

The latter two texts might be seen as the literary equivalent of a flashing billboard: "Beware of indigene maiden." Yet the female figures on that sign are little different in function from those in the more sophisticated and more sensitive texts: *Men Are Human, The Man Hamilton, Coonardoo, Possession*, and even from Anna Yellowbird. In the earlier texts, unlike *Badlands*, the white hero's penetration of a sexual unconsciousness is not presented as justification for abandoning the values of the outside world but in all, including *Badlands*, the attraction of the land leads to miscegenation and indigenization, while the transformation, Dawe's loss of knowledge, figuratively or physically destroys the white male. Possession of the subject of desire reveals the terror hidden within that object.

The image of the indigene as sexual essence depends on the distinction between self and the Other. The pure beauty of the indigene maiden is usually completely object, existing only for the spectator-owner. Although not the equal of the violence of the male indigene, the squaw or the succubus has a much more active power than the maiden which can overwhelm the self and turn the female indigene from temptation into fear. In both instances, however, the statement being made is on the sexuality of the Other rather than of the self, as in Palmer's title, *Men are Human*. The normative sexuality of the white male is confronted by the aberrant sexual powers of the female Other.

Of course, the normative sexual relationship of the white male with the indigene female is rape, violent penetration of the indigenous, although this is not the primary image of sexual interaction. Rather, most texts imply sex is, as Olaf Ruhen suggests in *Naked Under Capricorn* (1958), the "ultimate communication" (72). Still, particularly in recent texts concerned with white guilt, rape is a common motif. In Eleanor Dark's historical romance, *No Barrier* (1953), one of the white characters recognizes the applicability of rape as trope: "They had barely begun to know this land; had they ever tried to learn it, or had they merely attacked it savagely with axe and plough? A rape, he thought – all taking, and no love" (339). In Roger McDonald's *1915* (1982) a young man's rape of an Aboriginal woman seems almost a rite of passage, an inevitable part of the violent side of Australian culture. Grace Bartram's historical novel, *Darker Grows the Valley* (1981), has a scenario in which the valley in fact becomes progressively whiter although darker in moral terms. The mixed-race character, Haddon Torquane, the product of an English aristocrat's rape of an Aboriginal girl, becomes obsessed with the evil way he is treated to the point that he rapes his girlfriend, daughter of the liberal owner of the local property:

In Phillip's mind there was an explosion of fast-spinning memories, memories that spun away into the past where a black child was being raped by a huge white man, and somehow Lizbeth became that black child and at the same time she was his white child being raped by a black man, and yet subject to the same humiliation and outrage as the black child Banijuljul so long ago. (132)

Yet the guilt expressed by the text cannot deny the limited valorization of the indigene as a commodity of sexuality. In *1915* the woman is the only Aboriginal character, unnamed, alone, when the teenage male is at a dangerous stage of his sexual and national maturation. The natural Aboriginal female is an object for the white attack, as available as the "unoccupied" land. The natural Aboriginal male expresses his sexuality *against* the white female, the weak arm of the patria-archal penetration. His act is a passionate explosion of frustration but in no sense suggests the domination figured in the earlier white rape.

Some texts, perhaps in an inverted expression of guilt, emphasize the limitations of white sexuality rather than its domineering power. These works, all but a very few published in the second half of the twentieth century, divide their narratives between a white anti-sexuality or perversion of sexuality and an indigenous, natural sexuality. In Mitchell's *The Vanishing Point*, Carlyle Sinclair at first expects a virginal purity from his Indian student, with the telling name of Victoria. He is not conscious of how his attitudes have been shaped by his virulently anti-sexual Aunt Pearl, an emblem of white repression. His triumph over her proscriptions seems akin to the anality in Kovel's stridently Freudian view of the sexual attractions of the American black: "Here was the magical excremental body itself, the body-as-a-whole: black, warm, odorous, undifferentiated – the very incarnation of that fecal substance with which the whole world had been smeared by the repressed coprophilia of the bourgeois order" (193). As might be suggested by Kovel's analysis, Carlyle is overwhelmingly awakened when he comes to terms with Victoria's sexuality. He is drawn into her world through the incessant drumming of the Prairie Chicken Dance. The next morning: "He could feel her touching warmth beside him. The drumming cut loose again outside – but inside himself as well – urgent at his throat – clubbing him with his own heart" (387).

Keith Sinclair's "Memorial to a Missionary" (1952) presents a similar pattern in the suggestion that the New Zealand missionary Thomas Kendall was redeemed from alienating religious beliefs by Maori sexuality. Various accounts of the Tasmanian Aborigines, particularly *Queen Trucanini* (1976), by Nancy Cato and Vivienne Rae Ellis, and Drewe's *The Savage Crows* show Robinson, the missionary-like Protector of the Aborigines, tormented by the sexuality or even nymphomania of "the last Tasmanian," Truganini. Betty Roland portrays the Aborigines in *Beyond Capricorn* (1976) as "schooled in the mysteries of sex" (47). For Leonard Cohen in *Beautiful Losers* (1966),

Catherine Tekakwitha is both an object of lust and a symbol of white perversion; she is the "first Iroquois Virgin," an offensive Christian imposition on the open Indian sexuality (254).

In *Poor Fellow My Country*, Herbert praises Aboriginal sexuality as he rejects white limitations. He claims that sin is "another name for Nature" (1330). Like many other commodities of the semiotic field of the indigene, indigenous sexuality is a signifier which extends beyond the specific "nature" of the land as "the nation" to the more general "nature" as "before artifice." Indigenous sexuality becomes another aspect of the indigene's valorization as freedom in the semiotic field of nature. The "natural" result of sex, procreation, is thus linked to indigenous sex. In Alan Fry's *The Revenge of Annie Charlie* (1973), the title character's open sexuality is part of her desire not to limit her fertility, something which her white boyfriend finds difficult to understand, a situation very similar to that of the Maori Netta in Noel Hilliard's *Maori Woman* (1960–74) trilogy. In Margaret Laurence's *The Diviners* (1974), Musgrave's *The Charcoal Burners*, and Kinsella's *Dance Me Outside*, white infertility, whether innate or technologically contrived, is contrasted with the fertile powers of the Indian. Beilby's *The Brown Land Crying* extends this image to the following portrait of an Aboriginal woman: "For all the youthfulness of her body, there was mother-earth readiness about it, a fertility waiting to open and receive" (270). *The Chant of Jimmie Blacksmith* and *Poor Fellow My Country* similarly emphasize a maternal sexuality.

There are many ways in which indigenous sexuality is linked to other standard commodities. One of the most obvious is mysticism, as in Patrick's *Inapatua*. Illuta accepts her violent initiation in association with the indigene concern for fertility: "The spirit children were waiting to enter her body and a passage must be made for them" (66). Male subincision enjoins mysticism and the image of the Aborigine as prehistoric remnant: "Manala said the heroes of the dreamtime probably began Arilta because they wanted to enjoy coition more fully" (118). In a number of works the commodity orality is connected to sexual attraction, from the "bird"-like songs of a variety of indigene maidens to the direct power of Doolie "singing" her lover in Thomas Keneally's play, *Bullie's House* (1980), to the association of sexual energy and the corroboree in Henrietta Drake-Brockman's *Men Without Wives* (1938).

Most of these texts present these associated commodities in opposition to the limits of white sexuality. In *Bullie's House* the white characters are sexually powerless in response to the singing of both Doolie and Bullie, although the whites retain complete power over their general destinies through rational administrative systems which are so alien to the Aborigines in the play. Foucault discusses at length the concern in Western society for a *"scientia sexualis"* based on "the physiology of reproduction and the medical theories of sexuality" (*Sexuality*, 58, 55). He also notes the careful split usually made between these two aspects of the *scientia*. Many novels and plays about indigenes, particularly the most recent ones, reject the scientia in favour of what is perceived as the indigene's holistic, to some degree unconscious, view of the world. In many of the above texts, the scientia of reproduction is only an aid of repression. In *Poor Fellow My Country*, an injury Jeremy receives leads a doctor to suggest castration; instead Jeremy uses Aboriginal medicine to save his manhood. In Musgrave's *The Charcoal Burners*, Matty's tubal ligation is viewed by Dan, her Indian lover, as a symbolic castration.

In early works, the castration might not have seemed such an evil. There, even the slightest suggestion of the male indigene's sexuality is an emblem of fear rather than temptation, as shown in the many captivity narratives in various forms. John Mathew's parallel poems "The White Captive" and "Song of the Black Captor" (*Echoes* [1902], 17–9) show the Aborigine as capable of romantic devotion but the object of that attention can have no response other than terror. In Gilbert Parker's "She of the Triple Chevron" (1894), the hint of sexual intentions by an Indian chief is a glimpse of horrendous evil. Even a contemporary example, Cook's *Eliza Fraser* (1976), shows Aboriginal women as nubile attractions while the sexual energies of the Aboriginal male are manifested in an aged figure who shows a frightening desire for the title character. The sexual element in Kombo, the faithful protector of *Fugitive Anne*, is never more than a slight implication, although his name reflects the term "combo," Australian slang for a man who has sex with Aboriginal women.

The situation in most of the literature of recent years is very different. Jack Hibberd's "Captain Midnight V.C." (1972) and Keneally's *The Chant of Jimmie Blacksmith* transfer the American tradition of the priapic black male to the Australian Aborigine. Mannoni's image of the Other as satyr is used in opposition to the absent or perverse sexuality of the whites. In "Captain Midnight" the defective genital apparatus of the white capitalist is compared to the title character's prowess. *Jimmie Blacksmith* refers to "the white phallus, powerful demolisher of tribes" (20), but the phallus destroys not by virility but by disease. This is but one of several examples of evil white male sexuality in this text. The white boss, Mr. Newby, shows his recognition of Jimmie's sexual power when he confronts Jimmie's white wife and "expose[s] his patriarchal blunt genitals, slug-white and sitting in his hand for her information" (69). The symbol may be patriarchal but it is far from a signifier of sexual vitality, the representation of many male and female Aborigines in the text. The appropriately named Frank Fence Post and Carson Longhorn in Kinsella's "Indian Struck" are the equal of either Jimmie or the Captain. The male indigene's sexual exploits at times even have an implicitly revolutionary effect, as suggested by the degrading way Frank refers to the white girls who are attracted to him: "We got a truck full of chicken dinner here, a little white meat be soft and tender and warm and taste good" (*Born*, 19–20). The inadequately genitalled capitalist of "Captain Midnight" fears:

> Soon we'll be a nation of brown bludgers like India, whose citizens, as is well known, are sapped of all energy and drive during the day by the conjugal excesses of the night before. (58)

In a number of contemporary novels with a female author and protagonist, the pattern of a search for individuation and, to varying degrees, indigenization, is associated with sexual contact with a male indigene: in *The Diviners*, a Métis, in *The Charcoal Burners*, an Indian, in Townend's *Travels With Myself* and Sheppard's *Children of Blindness*, Aborigines, and in Sue McCauley's *Other Halves* (1982), a Maori. The transference is an interesting one. It could be seen as simply an overcoming of the racist exclusion of the male indigene from the potential of miscegenation. Rather it seems that some works with a structure based on an overt or implied feminist awakening find an appropriate signifier in a character who has most of the same semiotic tags as the indigene maiden had in the past. In *Other Halves* and Hilliard's *Maori Woman* the attraction that a white woman feels for a Maori man is explicitly defined as "difference": I don't know how to put it. But it's the difference that *makes* the difference" (122). The reification of Other is thus maintained.

McCauley's novel ends with a suggestion of an ambivalent hope for the Maori-white relationship. Even this tenuous future, however, is quite at variance with the experience of many of these white female figures. In Laurence, Musgrave, Townsend, and Sheppard, the male indigene is, like so many of the maidens, a transitional figure who is left behind when the white protagonist has achieved certain development. It is as though the element of "difference" provides a necessary catalyst for the process of individuation but, like other catalysts, it forms no part of the final product.

This process might be compared to the analysis of Lacanian desire by Coward and Ellis: "It is not a question of the assumption by the subject of the traits of the Other, but rather that the subject has to find the constituting structure of his desire in the same gap opened up by the signifiers in those who come (through transference) to represent the Other for him, in so far as his demand is subjected to them" (117). When the focus becomes *her* desire, the same gap is at issue as in Foucault's comments about repression. The semiotic field of the indigene, as constituted in the commodity of sexuality, provides the signifiers and controls the "structure" even more than the analysis by Coward and Ellis would suggest. The "demand," whether her or his, is very much subject to these signifiers. Still the various elements of the overall sign of sexuality must be recalled. As Berger suggests, traditionally, male sexuality is a signifier of power while female sexuality is a signifier of receptivity. It would be difficult to find this pattern emphasized in the valorization of the indigene in these feminist novels. The new indigenous incubus, like the old succubus, has the power to confer indigenization. But the incubus is no better able then the succubus to use this power as "demolisher" – or even controller – of the white tribe.

The element of fear is probably more general in the image of male sexuality, but it is usually only tangentially related to the commodity of sexuality and represents rather the fear of the violent male indigene. With the exception of *The Diviners*, all of these texts of feminist individuation, and others which could be mentioned, show that the danger lies in the necessity which the sexual relationship creates for intense proximity with the violent indigene. In *Fugitive Anne* the sexuality of Anne's relationship with Kombo is almost completely suppressed, but the form of the relationship remains that of the typical inversion of the male maiden, with the usual danger of Kombo's tendency to "a burst of barbarianism" (19). The common fear found in the text with male subject, the sexual possession of de la Roche and Palmer, seems absent.

The female white invader may become an invadee in terms of the sexual metaphor, but the balance of power remains a racial one. These male indigenes are more indigene than male in the economies of the texts. In fact, far from threatening males they tend to be agents of liberation *from* threatening males, such as the restrictive, confining husbands whom the heroines of *The Diviners* and *Other Halves* must escape in their processes of individuation.

The situation is quite different in narratives, such as Hibberd's play and *Inapatua*, with both a male author and a male subject. In the latter, Charles Carson, an Aborigine brought up in a white environment, returns to his homeland. As he becomes reindigenized he takes an Aboriginal wife, Illuta: "She possessed a blending harmony with her country that transcended beauty and can belong only to the functionally perfect" (4). In his ambivalent situation, however, he once more tries civilization, to live with a white woman, Helen, sexually inadequate, physically deformed, and psychologically damaged, the dysfunctionally imperfect blend of civilization. Their relationship fulfils fantasies of the potent Aboriginal male and the masochistic white female. Then Helen disappears and Charles, now "Irritcha," returns to the land. As Illuta gives birth, Irritcha completes his exemplification of virility by going hunting: "Dust still hung in the still air, the fierce song of the family was loud in the land as I hacked a huge slab of meat from the quivering flesh" (201). The threat of the male indigene's sexual power for the white female is reasserted, supported, and then shown transformed into a vital fertility through the sexual power of the female indigene.

One of the most interesting views of the indigene in contemporary fiction is Frank Moorhouse's "Imogene Continued" (1980), a text which explicitly valorizes the commodity of sexuality and then examines that valorization, through the narrator, the former lover of the female centre of the action, a white anthropologist named Cindy. When three Aboriginal delegates to a conference violently rape Cindy, their conformity to white stereotypes leads to anguished self-examination, as in the following conversation between the "victim" and the narrator:

> "Shit no, I couldn't bring in the police, not after what we did to the aboriginals for two centuries."
> "Other times, other mores. We didn't do it to them."
> "O shut up, you're not entitled to an opinion." (97)

The narrator, as a white male, is expected to be completely voiceless in a liberal world. But Cindy realizes that just being white is bad enough. She recalls, "I was even warned by another woman, an anthropologist, and I thought, and I thought she was full of racist rape fantasies" (97). No consideration of the event is safe: "In the cab back to the conference she commented sourly that she had probably got vd from last night. 'And that's a racist thing to say too'" (103). Later, Cindy calls for more time at the conference for "colonial victims": "She talked of 'compensatory time' for historical wrongs" (110). The black African male who is chairing the session reacts: "May I suggest that time be set aside for the white Australians to consider their confusion, their wounds" (113).

Moorhouse's Aborigines conform to the indigene semiotic field as established from the beginnings of Australian, Canadian, and New Zealand cultures. The basic scene, in which the whites fail to maintain their guard against the indigenes, presents the same pattern as

many of the Australian "squatter novels." As in many of those nineteenth-century texts, the white female's sentimental view of the
indigene contributes to the disaster which befalls her, and the white
male who should be protecting her is beset by oppressive feelings
of impotence. Thus "Imogene Continued" becomes something like
an ironic captivity narrative.

But the specifics of the drunken rape might seem to involve different factors. The terrifying power of the earlier indigene was an
expression of an innate, natural sexuality, unbounded by the necessary restraints of civilization. The actions of the rapists in "Imogene" seem a symptom of decadence in the Aboriginal culture, a
product of the debilitating encounter with civilization. In many of
the texts which present the indigene as "social problem," sexuality
is primarily a reflection of that social problem, as in *Venus Half-Caste*,
No Sunlight Singing, and Fry's *How a People Die*. John McGarrity's
Once a Jolly Blackman (1973) makes this explicit: "Often they copulated
with complete abandon in front of the gawking, giggling children.
The drunker they were, the more unnatural their fornications" (44).

Yet there is a sense in many texts, as in Kinsella, that this is not
in essence "unnatural" but rather a deformed continuation of the
open sexuality of indigenous tradition, the natural sexuality, perverted when indigenous tradition becomes defeated society. In
Venus Half-Caste Beatrice survives as a mistress for a white man
whose sexual abilities are shown to be limited, but when she encounters an Aboriginal lover, "he was seized by her, by her hands and
by her mouth with fierce and hungry devouring passion" (230). Just
as a general attempt to separate a "realistic" picture of the indigene
in contemporary literature from the "stereotypes" of the past will
lead to a constant rediscovery of the fences of the semiotic field, so
does a specific effort to assert the line between traditional and
degraded indigenous sexuality. In both, sexuality is a pervasive force
beyond the control of the civilized restrictions of white society. And
often, as in Sheppard's Aborigines, Fry's Indians, and Hilliard's
Maori, contemporary indigene society, which is presented as
depressed and degraded in its sexual expression, offers the same
potentials for indigenization and its many associated facets as the
overtly romantic figures of the past. Rex Ingamells's poem, "Lilliri"
(1940), observes an Aboriginal domestic repressed by civilization:

They called you some colourless name
in their puritan lack of shame,
little dressed-up gin
who sat in the lighted tram. (65)

But no form of repression can overcome her powers:

> You have the unexpected beauty,
> the dim suppleness, the animal grace,
> the wild questioning, the smouldering fire
> and the inevitable pain
> of a man's first-dreams.
>
> Business men in the tram stared over their newspapers,
> stared from their dull accustomed lives,
> and for you in their hearts, I am sure,
> forsook their white wives. (*Selected*, 65)

There have been a series of transformations in the various aspects of the commodity of sexuality. The maiden has ranged from ethereal goddess to voracious succubus. In her capacity as the agent of indigenization she has been perfect temptress and perfect terror. The male has been a captor, the phallic rage of the wilderness, and an incubus as agent of feminist liberation, an indigenizer to equal his sisters. Yet throughout the indigene remains the same commodity, the same object of white desire and white fear.

Susan Gubar's "'The Blank Page' and the Issues of Female Creativity" (1985) notes how common it has been to view the female as art form or even more as the material from which the art will be created. Woman has no need – and no right – to create the poem because she is the page from which the poem will be created. Gubar looks to the act by the woman writer through whom "the blank page is transformed into living wood that sighs and sings like a tree in the wind" (309). It is easy to see the attraction of Gubar's organicist metaphor but, if one looks at the actual role of the tree in book production, the process might better be reversed as an assessment of the female indigene as sexual object. She is beyond the semi-tamed beginning point of artifice which is the blank page and instead represents a sexual analogy to the natural orality of the singing tree. As object for the white male creator she is the rawest of raw material, a perfect Galatea – or even recently a Galateus – for the indigenizing Pygmalion of the new worlds. Long live the Maori maiden. And long may his temptations thrive.

CHAPTER FIVE

Violence

Neither the dialectic, as logic of contradictions, nor semiotics, as the structure of communication, can account for the intrinsic intelligibility of conflicts. 'Dialectic' is a way of evading the always open and hazardous reality of conflict by reducing it to a Hegelian skeleton, and 'semiology' is a way of avoiding its violent, bloody and lethal character by reducing it to the calm Platonic form of language and dialogue. (Foucault, *Power*, 114)

Foucault's rejection of semiotics as a method of analyzing conflict is both understandable and surprisingly ingenuous. It is understandable because "reducing" the ultimate experiential reality of violence, blood, and death to a system of signs seems quite unsatisfactory. It is surprising, however, because Foucault is usually so aware of the limitations involved in his own position, the ideological centre from which he assembles his genealogies. Yet here, Foucault's discourse, which can be no more than a semiotic construct, is depicted as somehow superior to semiotics.

My analysis of violence and the indigene is based on semiology partly because of a recognition of just such limitations but also because the subject treated here is only discourse. To use a distinction which admittedly Derrida has made questionable, this study is of texts rather than experience. The violence under consideration here is dripping with blood only to the extent that a text can portray red flowing from the page. Yet such essentialist violence can be seen in texts, as in the response of the central character in A.C. Grant's *Bush-Life in Queensland or John West's Colonial Experiences* (1881), as he enters the Australian wilds:

In imagination he peopled those green hills with a savage, bloodthirsty race, whose ancestors had gone on the warpath, and followed the chase over those silent valleys and rugged mountains for hundreds, ay, perhaps thousands, of years. (1:18)

Violence is yet one more of the standard commodities through which the indigene as imaginative textual creation is valorized.

Before considering these images of violence and the various permutations and transformations they represent, a simple observation must be made about the histories of these three countries. The etymology of violence connects it to "violate" and the white invasion of Australia, New Zealand, and Canada was nothing if not a violation. Todorov sees violence in Christian proselytizing: "Yet is there not already a violence in the conviction that one possesses the truth oneself, whereas this is not the case for others, and that one must furthermore impose that truth on those others?" (*Conquest*, 168). But there is no need to extend the meaning of the word beyond the physical. The history of white "settlement" is clearly a history of physical violence because a violation of physical space, as are the journeys of Todorov's missionaries. In this sense, every element of this study, and every consideration of the relation between white and indigene, can be seen to be a consideration of physical violence.

Frantz Fanon's *The Wretched of the Earth* (1961) suggests that violent exploitation itself diverts the indigene's attention from mystical tradition towards reality: "During the struggle for freedom, a marked alienation from these practices is observed. The native's back is to the wall, the knife is at his throat (or, more precisely, the electrode at his genitals): he will have no more call for his fancies. After centuries of unreality, after having wallowed in the most outlandish phantoms, at long last the native, gun in hand, stands face to face with the only forces which contend for his life – the forces of colonialism" (58). Fanon's image of emasculation suggests the close connection between the standard commodities of sexuality and violence. When the white text represents the sexuality of the indigene as fear rather than temptation, sex and violence often become one. One example was discussed earlier: the two rapes in Bartram's *Darker Grows the Valley*. A debased aristocrat rapes an Aboriginal girl and then the child of that act rapes a young white woman. The first is shown to be the result when civilization attempts to loosen its usual restraints and embrace what appear to be the tempting resources of the land. The second is the effect of civilization reimposing those restraints, making it impossible for white and indigene to rejoin except in violence.

Dan, the Indian lover of Matty, the central character in Musgrave's *The Charcoal Burners*, is always violent and potentially dangerous, a

strong element of his appeal for Matty. When he returns from cattle
rustling:

> His body was glowing and he was breathing heavily, the way he breathed
> after making love. He always wanted her before they went hunting,
> wanted to roll her on the ground and make love like the animals. (26)

In McCauley's *Other Halves*, the central character's sexual relationship with a Maori contributes greatly to her individuation but it also
has a very violent moment. These texts link the emotional signs of
temptation and fear, of Indian maiden and treacherous redskin,
much more clearly than do novels such as Palmer's *Men are Human*,
in which the miscegenating white man's only fear is of degradation.
A sexual relationship with a male indigene foregrounds both primary
values of the Other, combining the sexual allure of the various indigenous nymphs and the terror of Egerton R. Young's *Children of the
Forest: A Story of Indian Love* (1904): "Few sounds are more dreadful
than the blood-curdling war-whoops of a party of wild Indians"
(121).

This short line from Young demonstrates how the signifiers of
indigenous violence are more limiting and repetitive than even those
of the sexual indigene. The Indian maiden's "bird-like voice" and
"flowery bower" cannot compare to "blood-curdling." The very common adjective, "wild," has come to have an inevitable association
with the term Indian. As I have indicated in Chapter One, the many
specific Indianisms of formal violence, such as "war-whoop," were
also applied to Aborigines and Maori.

Many of the words associated with indigene violence suggest the
gothic romance in their direct association with satanic powers.
Words such as "devil," "fiend," and "demon" are ubiquitous in nineteenth-century images of the indigene in all three countries. The
Indian attack in Richardson's *Wacousta* provides a typical example
with "devilish war-cry," "image of hell," and "clangor of a thousand
demons" (175–7). Bracken's "The March of Te Rauparaha" describes
the attacking Maori as "like fiends unloosed from hell" (30). T.L.
Mitchell's documentation of experience in *Three Expeditions* (1839)
provides an extended account of the "demoniac looks" he receives
from a group of Aborigines:

> In short, their hideous crouching postures, measured gestures, and low
> jumps, all to the tune of a wild song, with the fiendish glare of their
> countenances, at times all black, but now all eyes and teeth, seemed a
> fitter spectacle for Pandemonium, than the light of the bounteous sun.
> (1:247–8).

Such a literally flamboyant image might be examined as a stimulant for the reader. Association with the Christian hell should create as intense a vision of evil as would be possible for a Christian reader. Fanon claims, "The colonial world is a Manichean world... As if to show the totalitarian character of colonial exploitation the settler paints the native as a sort of quintessence of evil" (*Wretched*, 41). An interesting variant on this image of biblical evil is found in the depiction of the Aborigine in A.J. Boyd's *Old Colonials* (1882): "nothing but a sneaking, filthy, thievish, murdering vagabond – a very Cain, whose hand is against every man, and every man's hand against him" (219). It would be difficult to think of a better metaphor for the Other as evil than the paradigm of fratricide.

But, as noted in my introduction, in reference to the more carefully defined Manichean theory of Abdul R. JanMohammed, the indigene as "absolute evil" (Fanon, *Wretched*, 41) in an essentialist sense suggested by such demonic terms, is contradicted not only by the many positive images of indigenes but also by positive images of indigenous violence in which Cain's action is opposed to Abel's repression. It seems more appropriate to consider demonic violence as an extreme version not of the moral principle of good vs. evil but of the emotive energy stimulated by self vs. Other.

Renate Zahar's *Frantz Fanon: Colonialism and Alienation* (1969) includes an analysis of violence as liberation which seems as close to Herbert Marcuse as to Fanon: "Through the act of violence the colonized is capable of freeing himself from his reified status and becoming once more a human being" (77). Yet when the violence is, as in these texts, a standard commodity, a value of Other, a reflection through which to explore the self, the reification is not overcome but reinforced. A liberating violence would enable the indigene to somehow subvert the text and deny the violent native as object through an even stronger subjectivity.

Once again it is tempting to consider the psychological reasons for the attraction of this violence. Marcuse, in *Eros and Civilization* (1955), claims, "The adjustment of pleasure to the reality principle implies the subjugation and diversion of the destructive force of instinctual gratification, of its incompatibility with the established societal norms and relations, and, by that token, implies the transubstantiation of pleasure itself" (13). Marcuse's interpretation of Freud could explain how society uses a civilized form, the text, to divert the instinctual gratification of sexual pleasure by representing it in association with the indigene who still lives with unadjusted pleasure. Marcuse goes on to observe, "In the Freudian conception, civilization does not once and for all terminate a 'state of nature.'

What civilization masters and represses – the chain of the pleasure principle – continues to exist in civilization itself" (15). Thus, the sexual pleasure is both without, in the Indian maiden, and repressed within, as the white text represents its almost mastered sexual energies through the reflection of the maiden.

In the frisson provided by the violent indigene, the treacherous redskin can be a figure of temptation. The pleasure of violence is kept without, in the bloodthirsty Aborigine, but flickering within, as the white text represents the blood to appease the almost-mastered thirst of the white reader. The situation is not unlike that noted by Foucault in *Power/Knowledge*: "And here is what is directly of concern for the confessor: how is one to lend one's ear to the recital of abominable scenes without sinning oneself, that is, taking pleasure oneself" (214). Whether the violence is by the indigene or to the indigene, the text's depiction of evil creates the pleasure of the text.

This pleasure might be part of the reason for the many explicitly detailed portraits of indigenous violence, particularly in nineteenth-century texts. Explicit portrayals of the sexuality of indigenous temptation were limited by the moral values of Canadian, Australian, and New Zealand societies. However, barriers to depicting the violence of indigenous fear were much less absolute, as shown in the vision of the Maori warrior in Domett's *Ranolf and Amohia*:

> From his broad axe-blade dripped and drained
> The blood; and all with hostile blood
> His hoary hair and beard were stained. (2:199)

Still more extreme images are provided by Charles Harpur's "The Creek of the Four Graves" (*Bushrangers*, 1853):

> his own
> Warm brains were blinding him!
> . . . .
> And four stark corses, plundered to the skin
> And brutally mutilated, seemed to stare,
> With frozen eyeballs up into the pale
> Round countenance of the moon. (67–9)

Louisa Meredith's *A Tasmanian Memory of 1834* (1869) adds another:

> "Is it *her* head – her pretty hair,
> "Clotted with mire and blood down there?
> . . . .

"The Baby's underneath,
"Mangled to bits – each small bone broke." (16–17)

Canada has a finely tuned child murder in Howe's "Acadia":

The wretched Mother from her babe is torn,
Which on a red right hand aloft is borne,
Then dashed to earth before its Parent's eyes,
And, as its form, deform'd and quivering lies,
Life from its fragile tenement is trod,
And the bruised, senseless, and unsightly clod,
Is flung into the soft but bleeding breast
To which so late in smiling peace 'twas press'd. (*Poems*, 24–5)

It requires little imagination to think of the thrill of horror experienced by a nineteenth-century reader or the horror of a very different kind which would have been the response to a similarly explicit sexuality.

Most literary images of the indigene present violence as an essential characteristic. W.D. Kearney's *The Open Hand* (1864) reports that "torture is the chief delight/Of all the Indian race" (28). In Wilfred Campbell's "Daulac" (*Tragedies*, 1908) the Indians are only an offstage threat until they enter for the final martyr-like tableau. In nineteenth-century and early twentieth-century fiction the treacherous indigene is often asserted through the casual inclusion of words such as "blood-lust," at times in narratives which have little overt interest in violence. This is particularly true in the many texts from all three countries that are in some sense apologias for the white conquest – best represented by the Australian squatter novels, exemplified by the fiction of Praed and Boldrewood. No similar term has been used in Canada but fiction by Ralph Connor and others fits the same mold. A number of more recent works with apparent pro-indigene intentions, however, such as O'Hagan's *Tay John*, Hilliard's *A Night at Green River*, and Roland's *Beyond Capricorn*, similarly show indigenous violence as omnipresent.

The contradictions of many aspects of the standard commodities, such as the silent savage and the orator, two aspects of orality, are noted throughout this study. The violent indigene, in many ways a reflection of hard primitivism, contradicts the indigene maiden and her less prominent friend, the indigene poet, both reflections of soft primitivism. Charles Mair's narrative poem, "The Legend of Chileeli" (1901), which he labelled "A Transposition from 'Schoolcraft,'" attempts to reconcile these commodities. The Indians are

All fond of gawds, all fond of spoil and blood,
They flew from chase to chase, from feud to feud. (134)

But the chief's daughter is

a loving creature who was all men's praise
. . . .
A maid so infinitely kind. (133)

Her lover, Chileeli, is rejected by the chief for like qualities:

So this young swain, who was a poet, not
A vengeful man by nature, in despair
Fled to the wilds to nurse his passion there. (133)

He turns warrior and amazes the chief:

Why, this is strange! The youth has brought
Outlandish spoils, unheard of, out of thought!
Not scalps alone, but breasts of maidens fair,
And infants' arms wound in their mothers' hair. (140)

Chileeli thus wins the daughter, but she turns into a bird, after first admonishing him because he

Bewrayed thy poet-function, thrust apart
Thy finer nature, and abused thy heart,
Therefore the Father of pure thoughts hath ta'en
Me from thy path, and from the bitter pain
Of thy unhallowed love. (*Dreamlands*, 142)

In Mair's text, the Indian is generically violent but other commodities such as orality, ethereal sexuality, and even a monotheistic mysticism can supersede that violence. At the end of the poem, when the tribe remains violent, Chileeli "fled away, and ne'er was heard of more" (143). Through the hero and heroine, the romantic narrative makes idealized commodities the primary structural functions but the treacherous redskin retains general cultural supremacy.

David Thompson's *Narrative* (1840s) presents customs of retaliation among the Indians as a "pretext" to allow violence: "Such is the state of society where there are no positive laws to direct mankind" (260). (What Thompson saw in European law as "positive", presumably something which produces good behaviour rather than simply limiting bad, he does not record.) Most recent historical narratives, and some which describe contemporary indigenous society, accept certain violent acts as part of indigenous systems of law, often suggested to be at least no more negative than the white. Archie Nicotine's education of the indigenizing white, Carlyle Sinclair, in Mitchell's *The Vanishing Point*, includes a course in violent retribution when Archie slashes the face of an Indian pimp. When he imposes a less bloody sentence Archie instructs: "It was personal, Sinclair – kickin' him in his blueberries was the right way to do it" (176). There seems little doubt in the text that Archie's independent legal process is "the right way."

In contemporary Australian literature, the word "law," at times capitalized, frequently combines aspects of the standard commodity of orality, the power of the unwritten, and of historicity, the power of the tradition beyond time. "The Miringu" (1978), by B. Wongar, uses an Aboriginal term to define an epistemological distance between Aboriginal law and the white perception of it: "They call it *miringu*; all the local tribes do, but the white man has a different word for it – revenge" (*Bralgu*, 34). In the same collection, "The Tracker" reverses the distinction through the Aboriginal narrator: "The white men have made strange rules called 'law' and it's pretty hard to live by it" (*Bralgu*, 43). Social control by violence in the Canadian context is seldom called by more than that "different word," "revenge," and seldom represents the same overt epistemological distance, but there is no essential difference between "miringu" and the "ancient justice" in R.D. Cumming's *Paul Pero* (1928), when the Indian hero kills the white man who raped his wife: "Could we class the ancient justice/As a crime against society?" (3). There seems almost an absolute separation between texts such as Thompson's that treat violent retribution as a demonstration of the absence of law and those such as Cumming's that show it as a superior form of government. But in both, violence rules.

Stoicism is presented as the logical complement of ritual violence in Mair's poem, "The Iroquois at the Stake" (1901 *Dreamland*, 160–3), and in his play, *Tecumseh*, in which the Indian hero asserts that both torture and the stoic endurance of torture are statements of character:

> Look upon our warriors
> Roped round with scars and cicatrized wounds,
> Inflicted in deep trial of their spirit.
> Their skewered sides are proofs of manly souls,
> Which, had one groan escaped from agony,

Would all have sunk beneath our women's heels,
Unfit for earth or heaven. (29)

Douglas S. Huyghue's *Argimou: A Legend of the Micmac* (1847) represents this power as surviving even the final torture:

Passing the bodies of the Indians, they found that they were all quite dead, but an expression of stern ferocity, which even death could not eradicate or tame, still lived upon their bronzed visages, the latest they would ever wear. 'Twas the last seal of the unconquerable spirit ere it left its perishable tenement forever. (125)

Stuart's *Ilbarana* portrays a similar stoicism in Aboriginal initiation:

The blood that had spattered them, as they had lain each of them held on the bodies of three men, that too had been most meaningful. How could a man cry out, or in any way show himself less than a man, when the blood of a proper man was mingling with the blood of his own ordeal? (58)

This stoicism is a blending of hard primitivism and tradition but also a mystical communion of mingled blood. As in many other texts, the blood itself is central to the image, whether in this stoic *jouissance*, in terms such as "blood-thirsty," in Domett's vision of the Maori warrior above, or even in the unnamed blood in Duncan Campbell Scott's sonnet, "Watkwenies" (1898). The title figure, whose name means "The Woman Who Conquers," kills the sentry: "Her long knife flashed, and hissed, and drank its fill," leaving behind its thirst only "her dripping wrist" (*Selected Poems*, 133). In each case, the texts utilize the image of blood to represent an essential violence, whether positive or negative. That the white texts should so often find indigenous violence to be "blood-curdling" seems appropriate, as essence breaks through to essence.

In most texts, the white response to indigene torture is just such "curdling," and to stoicism, is amazement, but "Brébeuf and His Brethren" (1940), E.J. Pratt's epic poem about seventeenth-century missionaries, uses both aspects of the violence commodity to claim a superhuman religious power for the Jesuits. When Brébeuf is tortured, the Iroquois marvel at his stoicism:

Where was the source
Of his strength, the home of his courage that topped the best
Of their braves and even out-fabled the lore of their legends? (*Selected*, 148)

The source is Christianity but the standards by which Brébeuf is valorized are provided by Indian torture and stoicism, as established literary values. Here indigene violence is a demonic quality which defines Brébeuf's virtues through opposition, which is usually the process in similar texts which praise indigene stoicism. The title character in "The Iroquois at the Stake" extols violence but it is his stoicism in the face of his enemies' violence which ennobles him. *Honi Heki*, Dickson's poem for the Maori leader, is unusual in its praise for anti-white violence by a contemporary aristocrat, but violence ennobles a great warrior of the past in a number of texts, as in Alexander McLachlan's "To an Indian Skull" (1860s):

Tradition links thy name with fear,
And strong men hold their breath to hear
What mighty feats by thee were done –
The battles by thy strong arm won!
The glory of thy tribe wert thou –
But where is all thy glory now? (*Works*, 69)

This violence is the battle legend of an aristocratic artifact. Some historical narratives, notably *Tecumseh* and William Lighthall's *The Master of Life* (1908), show the essential violence of the indigene manifested in both the noble savage, Tecumseh or Hiawatha, and the demonic, the Prophet or Black Wolverine. The Indian heroes constantly reject what Tecumseh terms "bloody sacrifice" (Mair, 14), but both remain, as Hiawatha is called, "the man of battle" (Lighthall, 135).

In some contemporary works a similar portrait of noble historic violence is opposed to contemporary experience. The title figure in Bruce Mason's *The Pohutukawa Tree* (1960) commemorates a great Maori victory, "a sign of blood between Maori and pakeha for ever" (24), but now it is an ironic comment on Maori failure to hold the land. In David Ireland's *Image in the Clay* (1964) Gunner's name represents his prowess in the Australian army but old Gooroh refuses to use it: "Gunner is not a name I like to hear. Your fathers fought with weapons of a man, not crouched in trees a mile away, with telescopes to set the crosshairs over a man's heart" (44). Gooroh seems to be establishing a distinction between technology and what might be called natural violence. Jean-Paul Sartre's preface to Fanon's *The Wretched of the Earth* states, "Violence in the colonies does not only have for its aim the keeping of these enslaved men at arm's length; it seeks to dehumanize them" (15). Fanon's text makes the process still more explicit when it states that the colonial

"Manicheism" "turns him [the native] into an animal" (42). Most literary representations of the violence of the indigene do the same, whether this violence is attacked or praised by the text. This violence is shown to be of the indigene essence in that it is an expression of nature; it is not a human response by the indigenes to oppression.

The attack on natural violence can be represented by Traill's *The Canadian Crusoes* and Satchell's *The Greenstone Door* which present Christianity as a literally God-given opportunity for the indigene to overcome the debilitating effects of a violent society. The young Indian woman in *Crusoes* tries to reject Christianity.

> Yet when she contrasted the gentle, kind, and dove-like characters of her Christian friends with the fierce, bloody people of her tribe and of her Ojebwa [sic] enemies, she could not but own they were more worthy of love and admiration. (222)

In opposition, Herbert's *Poor Fellow My Country* and Randolph Stow's *To the Islands* (1982) in Australia and Bodsworth's *The Sparrow's Fall* (1967) and Fry's *Come a Long Journey* in Canada all depict the anti-violence tenets of Christian religion as white interference in the indigenous system of nature red in tooth and claw. *Poor Fellow My Country* reflects the traditional paradox of the split between man and nature by presenting the violence of Aboriginal justice as more human than white society because closer to natural man. The authoritative hero, Jeremy Delacey, asserts "that some degree of diabolism is essential in human behaviour" (40).

Indigenous violence is partly a reflection of nature as hardship: to survive in this land requires violence. The Chippewa woman in Duncan Campbell Scott's "The Forsaken" (1905) finds herself with a starving baby and no bait with which to fish:

> Valiant, unshaken,
> She took of her own flesh,
> Baited the fish-hook. (*Selected Poems*, 43)

Many years later, when she is "old and useless,/Like a paddle broken and warped," (44) she is abandoned by her family to die, but once again she is "Valiant, unshaken" (44).

The simplicity of diction in the poem reflects her stoic acceptance of life, but images of indigenous violence can be much more ornate, particularly in examples of indigenous tradition. The many representations in all three literatures of indigenous dance as a frenzied prelude to violence suggest the power of the image of indigenous culture as a dark ritual of fear. Alfred Grace's *Tales of a Dying Race* (1901) observes "this awful devil-dance" of the Maori: "The dense mass of savages lash themselves into even greater fury" (239). In many Australian texts, traditional dance ceremonies provide mystical reverberations of indigenous violence, as in Helen Hudson's *Flames in the Wind* (1918):

> Against the dreadful background danced the warriors in weird figures of the Bora ceremony. Across the rushing of the flames, like wind beating a mighty sea against a rock-bound coast, came the terrible sound of the bull-roarer. It tore the silence far out in the forests, and played on the strings of the white man's heart, so that of its sound there would nevermore be any forgetting for him.
>
>   It was a terrible accompaniment to the flames burning the lives of his comrades away. (2)

The standard commodities of orality and mysticism, encompassed in a simile of natural power, transmit the essential violence of the Aborigine through to the "heart," the essence of the white. The title character in Bridle's *Hansen* is equally struck, drawn by the Cree dance into a "state of corporate consciousness" (280):

> This rite was the remnant of the great drama dance in which every summer before the tribal battles the red men made braves by torture while the others danced and the tomtoms and the tune went incessantly on from one sunset until the sixth beyond. (279)

A similar Indian dance in B.A. McKelvie's *The Black Canyon: A Story of '58* (1927) draws from one white character the comment, "Don't it look like hell?" (28). McCrae's *The Story of Balla-deadro*, however, suggests a more organized militaristic response as the Aborigines leave the dance "In martial rank, by music fired" (23).

At times reflecting and at times contradicting historical documentation (see Goldie, "Contemporary" 1984), cannibalism is a significant part of the violence commodity in the portraits of Maori, Indians, Inuit, and Aborigines. Its literary power is suggested by the title of Lumholtz's *Among Cannibals*, a work which only slightly treats the subject. For most early texts cannibalism is primarily another kind of violence, but for later ones it provides an opportunity for much metaphysical play. Robertson Davies's shaman, in *Question Time* (1975), is a Jungian eater par excellence. Bowering extends his narrative introspections in *Burning Water* with George Vancouver's speculations on tasting Captain Cook. Cannibalism is a prime subject for black humour, in both senses, in nineteenth-century material, particularly for bush ballads such as Wilks's *The Raid of the Aborigines*, with its Aboriginal coquette:

And she pinch'd his fat cheeks as she sat on his knee,
Crying, "Budgery goori belonging to me."
Like thunder the horrid conviction did greet him –
The cannibal jade only wanted to eat him! (39)

This continues in the twentieth century in McCallum's pseudony-mous Maori Hori who threatens to turn obnoxious *pakehas* into gastronomic experiences, in *The Half-Gallon Jar* (42) and *Fill It Up Again* (33).

The meanings derived from cannibalism seem limited only by the number of interpreters. Eric Maple's *The Domain of Devils* (1966) considers various cannibals as story and practice: "It is possible that deep within the subconscious minds of all of us there lies a secret desire for cannibalism. Sporadic cases of this lust for human flesh have cropped up time and time again throughout history evoking a fascinated interest which is possibly second only to that of sex. Even the intense horror felt by the great majority at the very sug-gestion of cannibalism is a clear indication of the potency of this dynamic fetish among so called normal human beings" (101). Kovel treats cannibalism as a discourse which reveals both politics and psychoanalysis: "Now, we know that cannibalism is both a universal infantile wish arising in the oral sadistic phase of development (by virtue of which it becomes an element of the mass unconscious), and a well-defined cultural custom in some aboriginal groups. Both of these truths are being represented here, but are combined with a third one: that the culture of the West is representing by projection what it has done to the culture and peoples of Africa, namely eaten them up" (66). Such metaphoric interpretations are particularly relevant in various texts by Rudy Wiebe and Patrick White.

W.P. Kinsella's stories might be compared to the Hori sketches in their use of comic violence. The threats of contemporary scalping by Kinsella's Indians are like Hori's cannibalism, extensions of vio-lent rituals of the past into contemporary society. The contrast between noble, albeit terrifying, violence and modern degradation produces the incongruous comedy. Hilliard's *A Night at Green River* provides a much more subtle look at traditional and contemporary violence. The central white character learns from his Maori neigh-bours the joy of a much less restrictive lifestyle and when he returns to his own home, he participates in a bit of the random violence he had seen in the Maori. As in Kinsella's Indian stories, violence becomes not fear but temptation, an emblem of the indigene as freedom.

Yet at many points in Kinsella, as in other portraits of the contemporary indigene, violence may be freedom but it is also decadence. As in similar representations of sex, violence becomes a signifier of the loss of the traditional values which supported the indigenous society. This violence is often directed against whites but it is just as likely to be inflicted on other indigenes. Sartre suggests that the cause is not simply decadence but a failure to discover the productive violence of revolution: "If this suppressed fury fails to find an outlet, it turns in a vacuum and devastates the oppressed creatures themselves. In order to free themselves they even massacre each other" (*Wretched*, 18). This internalized violence is a constant among the male characters in Hilliard's *Maori Woman* trilogy and in Gare's *The Fringe Dwellers*. An interesting reflection of this pattern is found in Ireland's *The Glass Canoe*. Ireland presents white alcoholics as a tribal group, suitable for anthropological study because, like Aborigines, they engage in forms of tribally sanctioned behaviour such as sex and violence that deviate from the "norm." The narrator gives the following description of pub fighters: "As in the aboriginal tribes we'd pushed out, there was no chief in our tribe. Just a fairly loose system of elders, who laid down laws and dispensed wisdom from the shoulder" (25–6). Yet such explicit connections are not the primary validation of this comparison with Aboriginal society. There is an unstated assumption that such a decayed and degraded society will immediately suggest Aboriginal analogies.

Alcohol has the same value. Alcohol is a significant aspect of the semiotic field of the indigene but its valorization is much simpler than the variations of the standard commodities. It is used primarily as a cause for sex and violence, when these are presented as manifestations of the degraded indigene. In the nineteenth and early twentieth centuries the drunken ignoble savage was often a vehicle for humour, with the emphasis either on the still greater stupidity of the indigene when drunk or on the foolish insights which such a figure might inadvertently produce. These do not vary significantly from the many non-racial jokes about "a drunk who..." Such characters are seldom found in recent literature, although as the "Hori" titles *The Half-Gallon Jar*, *Fill It Up Again*, and *Flagon Fun* suggest, the undercurrent is still there. Similar reinforcement is provided by a recent American comic strip that depicted an overweight Indian deciding to change to "lite firewater," thus combining a signifier of the contemporary urban social drinker with a typical Indianism for alcohol.

In most texts, early and recent, alcohol is used only to demonstrate the decadence which civilization has created for the indigene. In Meredith's "The Lost Tribe of Boonjie: A Romance of the Australian Wilds", a group of Aborigines come to a miners' camp: "There they were supplied with tobacco and rum with the inevitable result: they became the degraded slaves of the white miners" (Aug. 1940, 48). This degradation is usually explained in connection with the semiotic field of nature or the commodity of the prehistoric. Either the indigene society is too pure and natural to handle such an evil as alcohol or else the indigene society is at too early a point of evolution and, like any child, lacks the sophistication to handle such a delicate tool of social maturation as alcohol. A white character in *Goonoo Goonoo* (1956), by Frank O'Grady, uses a variant of the latter to explain how a white man caused Aboriginal violence: "He filled the natives with rum, the poor innocent blacks who knew no better, and set them against us" (141). In some contemporary texts, this innocent response leads to an almost complete destruction of indigene life, as in Fry's *How a People Die* or McGarrity's *Once a Jolly Blackman*.

Each negative comment on the position of alcohol in indigene society has at least a subtextual attack on the results of the white conquest. Most texts fail to extend this to a consideration of white violence as a general and essential part of that conquest, but there are a number of notable exceptions, most particularly in contemporary depictions. The opening scene of Bill Reed's *Truganinni* (1977) makes a statement about the indigenes as passive object of both white sexuality and white violence, as an actor in a black mask is chased by an actor in a white mask:

> He catches her, beats her into submission, and rapes her. Then gets up, looks down at her, bends down as if in tenderness or sympathy, and then simply stabs her in the back. (1)

Yet there are many earlier texts with similar images. In Kidd's *The Huron Chief*, the whites are said to be "like demons of the raging storm" (128). In John Mathew's "Myal Creek" (*Ballads*, 1914), the white attackers are described as "dark and devilish," "savage," "fiendish," and "hellish" (18–21). A.J. Vogan's *The Black Police: A Story of Modern Australia* (1890), which might be called an "anti-squatter novel," employs the same type of gruesome tableau seen in the works of Meredith and Howe, with the major exception that the murdered mother is Aboriginal. The power of established signifiers for indigenous violence is used in the opposite cause, to establish the barbarity of some of the civilized, but the text makes a clear distinction between the blatantly evil violent whites and the equally imperial yet benevolent hero.

Such texts seem to maintain that the white invasion was evil only in methodology. They imply the superiority of the liberal white text over the history of white society and suggest that the invasion could have been other than violent, that present Canada, Australia, and New Zealand could have been created by some other means. They refuse to accept the white society as violent in its essence. This distinction from the intrinsically violent indigenes is related to Todorov's distinction between sacrifice and massacre: "The sacrifice is performed in public and testifies to the power of the social fabric, to its mastery over the individual. Massacre, on the other hand, reveals the weakness of the same social fabric, the desuetude of the moral principles that once assured the group's coherence" (*Conquest*, 144). Some texts present indigene violence as sacrifice, as maintenance of defined indigene values, while others emphasize massacre, an anarchy of blood and gore. Almost never, however, is white violence against the indigene perceived as sacrifice, fulfilling the essence of white principle. It is always massacre, usually reflecting a certain aspect of white society which has broken the coherence which the text still reveres.

But a strong argument could be made that the white violence is, if not an essential, at least a systemic, part of the imperial principle. Any opposition to the system of order imposed by imperial invasion, an opposition which was also inevitable given the different epistemes of the indigenous peoples, required the violent reaction of the white powers. In *Five Lectures* (1970), Marcuse asserts: "Here is the conflict of rights before which every opposition that is more than private is placed. For the establishment has a legal monopoly of violence and the positive right, even the duty, to use this violence in its self-defense" (89–90). Almost none of the texts under examination here, whether early or contemporary, recognize that this violence is, regardless of how analyzed, a direct and unavoidable product of imperial invasion. They seldom consider the economy which creates the violence. It perhaps overstates the case to see a simplistic reversal of the Manichean allegory in these texts, but there is a sense in which the text is presented as moral observer, at a distance from the apparently indiscriminate violence of the whites and from the pathetic passivity of the indigenes.

In a number of texts, the instigator of white violence is what might loosely be called, in reflection of the Australian situation, the convict element. In some, such as *The Black Police* and *Burning Water*, lack of civilization seems to be an aid in the development of the natural indigene, but it leads to a vicious violence in the convict, the shepherd, the sailor, etc. Mitchell's *Three Expeditions* (1839) instead creates an association through conflict between the Aboriginal "wild beasts" (1:274) and the convicts, both clearly at variance with the expedition's carefully civilized procedures:

> I was, indeed, liable to pay dear for geographical discovery, when my honour and character were delivered over to convicts, on whom, although I might confide as to courage, I could not always rely for humanity. (1:275)

Aboriginal violence is a product of their bestial nature; convict violence is a product of their failure to be of civilized humanity.

Some texts link the evil of the convicts to civilization's oppression of the lower classes. In this sense, even the violence by the convicts against the indigenes can be seen, in the context of convictism, as part of the search for liberation from European oppression. Ingamells's *The Great South Land* presents the convicts as an evil invasion of a land of mystical purity, but it remains ambivalent as to whether the convicts are evil in themselves or a product of the more general evil of Europe:

> The face of life is vile at Sydney Cove –
> a haven of Alcheringa invaded
> by sordidness and vice from oversea. (271)

The future, however, is much more assured: "The fathers and mothers of many of them are lags,/but their children's children will fight in the cause of Freedom" (278).

Comparisons with convicts might suggest a class-based analysis of violence that would suit Henry Reynolds' consideration in "Race and Class in Colonial Australia" (1984) of the position of the Aborigine in the context of the British class system: "The introduction of sheep, the dismantling of a traditional society with, above all, its relationship to the land, and the associated endeavours to turn those who no longer had access to the means of production and subsistence, into landless labourers while simultaneously inculcating in them those values which would make them punctual, regular, and reliable, all can be observed, contemporaneously, in Australia and the remote parts of Britain, especially in the Scottish Highlands" (15). The situations of Canadian Indian and New Zealand Maori are slightly different, and the convict and sailor classes cannot be associated directly with the landless labourers of the Highland clearances, but there are many ways in which all these groups can be related on the basis of class, on their manipulation by those in control of the means of production, and by their value as the basic tools of imperialist expansion. Their violence against the controllers, however, is seldom presented as class-based and potentially revolutionary but, once again, as a rather purposeless, "uncivilized" response to a difficult life. Ireland's *The Glass Canoe* provides a useful analogy. One character "had his lips permanently pushed forward to cushion a sudden attack of king-hit, the main tribal and inter-tribal disease" (73). The lips might suggest Aboriginal physiology, the innate, the "natural," but the reference to disease makes the degeneracy of the permanent violence clear. The violence is a response to the malaise of their depressed society, divorced from the values of the majority culture, but there is little sense of the economic base of that divorce.

Texts which highlight white violence often represent it as an aspect of the technological culture opposed to the natural life of the indigene. *The Great South Land* recognizes that violence is a standard commodity of the Aborigine but suggests that white violence is more telling:

So diabolical becomes the slaughter
of native folk by outlaw and by settler;
that they are harried to a swift extinction
by power of steel and lead and minds more brutal,
far more barbaric, than the stone age camp
could counterpose in its extreme of vengeance. (287)

The "native folk," a diminution which suggests the inadequacy of indigenous violence, are no match for white technology. In a more symbolic yet also more graphic version of white violence against the natural indigene, the perverseness of shooting the wallaby up the anus in *Once a Jolly Blackman* is continued in the whipping which results in the black youth being nicknamed Jody Scarback. Not unlike the way in which sex with indigene females is often used to show the immorality of the white in power, this form of violence demonstrates the white mistreatment of a pitiable and passive group.

One might expect a more positive image of the potential of indigenous violence in pro-indigene texts. Fanon claims, "Violence alone, violence committed by the people, violence organized and educated by its leaders, makes it possible for the masses to understand social truths and gives the key to them. Without that struggle, without that knowledge of the practice of action, there's nothing but a fancy-dress parade and the blare of the trumpets" (*Wretched*, 147). Fanon's text itself seems to recognize the symbolic potential of this view in a brief description of the guerrilla: "Each fighter carries his warring country between his bare toes" (135).

Bartram's *Darker Grows the Valley* makes Aboriginal violence positive by allowing it to be intrinsic yet ineffective. The Aborigines were "like children in paradise. The only fights they had with each other were as the fights of children, soon over" (162). Even when there is a suggestion of revolutionary violence on the part of the indigenes, a directed "violence against the system," it is often tragic, particularly in historical texts, and often not so clearly oppositional, as in Mair's *Tecumseh* where the title figure battles the Americans in support of the British. Dickson's *Honi Heki* is unusual in that Honi Heki's fight is allied with no white cause:

> He was a patriot such as ancient Greece
>   Had viewed well pleased, had he been then existent;
> His only wish his country to release
>   From hated bondage to a nation distant. (10)

The text often emphasizes that Heki's violence was restricted to absolute necessity by his Christian beliefs, but even with this modification he is anomalous, particularly in light of the concluding description.

> Hoping his heroic deeds may yet inspire
> Tasmanian patriots with an equal fire.
> Where'er their injured country stands in need
> Of patriot swords, then patriot hearts shall bleed
> In its defence, till stern oppression rue
> The foiled attempts to fetter hearts so true.
> Here ends our tale – we part from it with grief;
> Yet HEKI lives, an independent Chief. (32)

Heki is perhaps unique, both as inspirer of general indigenous opposition to imperial rule and as survivor of revolution.

Most revolutionary indigenes, such as the Aborigines in John Hooker's *The Bush Soldiers* (1984), are rather pathetic. In Craig Harrison's *Broken October: New Zealand 1985* (1976) a contemporary Maori uprising dissolves into despair. The title character of Keneally's *The Chant of Jimmie Blacksmith* attempts to justify his attacks on white farmers with the words, "Tell the p'lice I said I declared war" (86), but his actions are shown to be the indiscriminate thrashings of one soul in pain. Arthur, in Kelly's *A Dream Like Mine*, has a clear political agenda but his behaviour, and particularly his suicide, suggests not revolution but psychosis. Violence is ubiquitous in Kinsella's stories but even more purposeless. Their narrator, Silas Ermineskin, explains his lack of interest in white parties: "They don't dance or yell up a good time, and except for a writer once in a while, they hardly ever fist fight" ("I Remember Houses," *Born*, 124). Some Kinsella characters claim revolutionary intentions but they are similarly comic devices: "AIM usually stand for American Indian Movement but most people around here call them Assholes in Moccasins" ("The Moccasin Telegraph," *Moccasin*, 22).

Perhaps the most pathetic images are those of indigenes participating in violence sanctioned by white society, in war or, particularly in Australian literature, in boxing. The figure begins in Australia with "black troopers," Aborigines used by police to track other Aborigines. Whether represented as manifestations of Aboriginal or white evil, they are uniformly negative. In *Southern Saga* (1940) by Roy Connolly, one trooper, a Murra, is manipulated by his white master, Hampton, until uncontrollable:

> From then onward, Debil-Debil became an object of terror to the station women of this new country, a shadowy figure, but an imminent menace; a Murra filled with hatred against the whites, consumed with desire to square accounts by his molestation of white women. Hedley Hampton was not only of twisted nature himself. He had most successfully accomplished the twisting of another nature. (324)

No Indians are so formally part of the white system of violence, but the ubiquitous faithful Indian guide is often placed in this position. When Charcoal, in Duncan Campbell Scott's story by the same name, kills another Indian for seducing his wife, he is followed by trackers:

> The Mounted Police, the Indian agent, and the Bloods, the people of his own clan and totem, who had learned well the white man's treachery, were banded together to hunt him down. (*Selected Stories*, 45)

From white manipulation of indigenous violence within the country, it is but a small step to a similar manipulation in external conflicts. In Laurence's *The Diviners*, the Métis Jules has many stories of his ancestor's battles against the Canadian government but, of his own experience in the Canadian army at Dieppe, the text records only "?" (149). Reflecting the historicity involved in the semiotic field of the indigene, contemporary violence, both against white society and as agent of white society, is only a slight glimmer of the operative violent traditions of the past.

In McGarrity's *Once a Jolly Blackman*, the sanctioned violence of one generation is linked to that of another. Jamie Gumboots receives the Victoria cross but sells it to the pub owner for liquor. At the end of the novel, his son Jody has died in his last prize fight, and his cup as commonwealth champion is on display in the same pub. The indigene's violent abilities can lead to success in white-sanctioned violence, but the end result is invariably an even more pitiable state than that of his fellow indigenes, and usually a greater degree of de-indigenization. The Aboriginal boxers in Gavin Casey's *Snowball* (1958) and Raymond Aitchison's *The Illegitimate* (1964) both fight barnstorming American blacks, the effect of which is to de-emphasize their indigenous heritage and present them instead as downtrodden by colour and thus seeking to "rise" through sport in the American fashion. The Indian prizefighter is not a similarly common figure, but Kinsella includes Merton Wolfchild who uses his boxing fame to become a used car dealer and then makes his money cheating other Indians ("Manitou Motors," *Scars*, 86). Even Merton, one literary indigene for whom boxing does not mean absolute degradation, uses violence approved by the white system to violate his people – the treachery of the black tracker in one more guise.

At the centre of the blending of white and indigenous violence is the male character of mixed race, a very different factor from the sexual female enshrined in Mann's title *Venus Half-Caste*. A more likely phrase for the male is provided by Willshire's *The Land of the Dawning*: "the bastard gift of shameless Nature" (4). According to this, the part-Aborigine is "a spurious compound of white and black parasites of a poisonous nature," reflecting on both the Aboriginal mother and the belief that the debased white progenitor would have been, if not convict, of the convict class, "the offscouring of Australia" (4). The result is a character of "merciless treachery" (4). In W.A. Fraser's *The Blood Lilies* (1903), a white character suggests the applicability of Willshire's text to the Canadian experience: "A breed's part Injun, part white man, an' altogether devil" (243).

Regardless of claims, often in association with a mixed-race version of the indigene maiden, for the potential of mixing races, her male counterpart is usually violent. In Herbert's *Poor Fellow My Country*, the violence is presented as the result of society's failure to recognize this potential and instead to treat anyone of mixed race as "a Bloody Nothin'" (587). Sayce's *Comboman*, entirely devoted to the degradation of the white by miscegenation, shows the hope of the title character to remove his mixed-race son from any contact with Aborigines, but the boy's perusal of an anthropological study of the corroboree leads to his participation in one: "He danced in triumph round his father and cursed him with obscene barbaric curses. It was the victory of his black blood" (286). The assumptions of miscegenation can be seen in the anonymous *The Story of Louis Riel the Rebel Chief* (1885), which carefully defines Riel as "one-eighth Indian": "He is not, as so many suppose, a half-breed, moved by the vengeful, irresponsible, savage blood in his veins" (5).

The role of miscegenation in the standard commodity of violence is perhaps best seen in *The Chant of Jimmie Blacksmith*. Brought up by missionaries to believe that he should adopt white values as much as possible, Jimmie finds himself constantly mistreated by white society and turns to violence. He himself is confused by the source of this violence, however, and questions newspaper accounts of himself as "black": "The white seed might have been the bad seed" (127). Jimmie's comparisons between himself and the bushranger Ned Kelly (119, 135) suggest that he sees himself as part of a white Australian tradition of representative anarchic opposition to authority. Yet the imagery of Jimmie's violence defines it as Aboriginal: "He felt large with a royal fever, with rebirth. He was in the lizard's gut once more" (78).

Jimmie's error is in seeing his violence to be seminal rather than sanguine. The guiding adjective, "bloody," for the violence of the tableau in the nineteenth-century novel, is also the definition of the violence produced by miscegenation. As shown again and again, the savage blood prevails, even in so small a portion as that one-eighth attributed to Riel. The history of white invasion in these three countries provides a clear source of blood, but in the image of the indigene the blood of the Other is passion and the blood of the white is a product of that passion. When the blood is of the indigene as victim, it becomes such as parody of white blood as product. In such texts, the evil white is presented in terms defined by the tradition of the treacherous redskin; the fear created by the pathos of the dying indigene reinforces the tradition of the opposite. Battle blood, definition of the indigene as warrior, is similarly renovated in the blood of the street fighter, definition of the indigene as suicidal culture. The violence of the indigene lives as the indigene dies.

CHAPTER SIX

Orality

The orality of the Indian, the Maori, and the Aborigine seems an intrinsic part of their image, as it is of most representations of indigenous peoples. Films about Africa or South America are full of oratorical natives and of vignettes in which those same natives are literally enthralled by the power of writing. The split between literate and non-literate is often used as the defining point for an absolute division between white self and indigene Other.

Much of the material in this chapter is examined in the light of Walter Ong's comments in *Orality and Literacy* (1982). This is not because I share Ong's phenomenological philosophy; I rather see his claims for existential presence as in need of deconstruction. My own belief in the value of a semiotic approach to the analysis of culture is directly antithetical to many parts of Ong's text, perhaps most obviously to his simplistic assertion that "Words are not signs" (75). I employ Ong, however, because his phenomenological assumptions are the same as the assumptions underlying those poems, novels, stories, and plays which valorize the standard commodity of orality, what might be termed "oralist" texts. Such texts share Ong's belief that there is an essence contained within oral culture which written culture at best transmutes and at worst destroys.

It must be noted, however, that orality need not be seen only as what Ong presents it to be, even in the context of the indigene. Franz Fanon considers the white view of black "orality" to have a psychoanalytical impetus. In his opinion it is, like anality, an infantile stage with pejorative implications: "The Negro loves to jabber, and from this theory it is not a long road that leads to a new proposition: the Negro is just a child. The psychoanalysts have a fine start here, and the term *orality* is soon heard" (*Black*, 20). While the image of indigene as child is an important one as a primary manifestation of the standard commodity of the prehistoric, orality is not of major significance in that context. The term "jabber" is almost never applied to Maori, Inuit, or Indian. The "jabbering blackfellow" is a figure in nineteenth-century Australian literature, in James Brunton Stephens's bush ballads or the squatter novels of Rolf Boldrewood, but seldom after, except in a limited, "popular," context, such as Mary Grant Bruce's children's books about Norah of Billabong. If infantile orality as a psychoanalytical concept is central to any commodity of the semiotic field of the indigene, it is not as the spoken oral but as the oral as ingestion in cannibalism. Rather than an example of inadequacy, orality as a factor of language and communication is usually portrayed as an unusual attribute.

It is important to differentiate between orality, an essential quality, and illiteracy, the negative value of the same state which is not a quality but a lack. Orality is the Ongian ideology that Jacques Derrida confronts; it is the belief that speaking has more subjective presence than writing. This belief can be observed in many contemporary discussions: "Words assume a different relationship to action and to object when they are on paper than when they are spoken. They are no longer bound up directly with 'reality'; the written word becomes a separate 'thing', abstracted to some extent from the flow of speech, shedding its close entailment with action, with power over matter" (Goody, 46). In *Orality and Literacy*, Ong similarly asserts that "among 'primitive' (oral) peoples generally language is a mode of action and not simply a countersign of thought" (32). Yet earlier in this study Ong implies what might seem the opposite: "Not only communication, but thought itself relates in an altogether special way to sound" (7). The answer to this discrepancy is suggested in the first phrase's "not simply" and encapsulated in the following: "all sound, and especially oral utterance, which comes from inside living organisms, is 'dynamic'" (32). This is the basic appeal of orality in the context of my study. In turning to the Maori, Aborigines, Inuit, and Indians, what Ong would term "primary oral cultures," cultures untainted by print, various New Zealand, Australian, and Canadian texts try to make contact with this essential dynamism, a phenomenological presence of life.

The oralist nature of these texts is a reaction to the profound gulf which is usually seen between the two forms of communication, the oral and the written, and the connected assumptions about the major differences between those cultures which are literate and those which are not. Yet there is another philosophical distinction to be made between such works and those, primarily nineteenth-century, which emphasize illiteracy. Illiteracy represents a lack but it might also be seen as an absence in opposition to orality's presence. Commentators such as Goody and Ong emphasize the presence, the human that is speech and the inhuman that is writing. Some nineteenth-century writers emphasize the absence, the lack, of science shown in the inability to write.

As absence, therefore, orality is illiteracy – or better "non-writingness". This distinction can be glimpsed in another passage from *Orality and Literacy*: "Oral cultures indeed produce powerful and beautiful verbal performances of high artistic and human worth, which are no longer even possible once writing has taken possession of the psyche. Nevertheless, without writing, human consciousness cannot achieve its fuller potentials, cannot produce other beautiful and powerful creations ... There is hardly an oral culture or a predominantly oral culture left in the world today that is not somehow aware of the vast complex of powers forever inaccessible without literacy. This awareness is agony for persons rooted in primary orality, who want literacy passionately but who also know very well that moving into the exciting world of literacy means leaving behind much that is exciting and deeply loved in the earlier oral world. We have to die to continue living" (14–15). Elsewhere Ong adds, "The fact that oral peoples commonly and in all likelihood universally consider words to have magical potency is clearly tied in, at least unconsciously, with their sense of the word as necessarily spoken, sounded, and hence power-driven" (32).

As a rational writer engaged in analysis, Ong is torn between his attraction to orality and his recognition of the literary scientific process of his text. As a result, his commentary slides between both points of view. Orality finds its power in the spoken magic of human presence. Literacy finds its power in the addition of analytical tools. Even when wearing his analytical hat, Ong would not privilege the lack of those tools with a word such as illiteracy. Of a similar term, Ong states, "'Preliterate' presents orality – the 'primary modeling system' – as an anachronistic deviant from the 'secondary modeling system' that followed it" (13). And yet he clearly shows an acceptance of the limitations of non-writingness and of illiteracy as an historical stage which will be followed by literacy. Ong seems to have no problem with the implications of such historicity, although he would perhaps rather reverse his "anachronistic deviant" and refer to the "secondary" as post-orality. This historicist sensibility seems quite representative of the view which I would label illiteracy. It assesses non-writing as transitional, not essential.

This view can be opposed with the underlying implications of Ong's phenomenological view of orality: "In a primary oral culture, where the word has its existence only in sound, with no reference whatsoever to any visually perceptible text, and no awareness of even the possibility of such a text, the phenomenology of sound enters deeply into human beings' feel for existence, as processed by the spoken word. For the way in which the word is experienced is always momentous in psychic life. The centering action of sound (the field of sound is not spread out before me but is all around me) affects man's sense of the cosmos. For oral cultures, the cosmos is an ongoing event with man at its center" (73). Orality is thus human presence but primary orality, in being only human presence, is much more. Thus, the division between writing white and oral indigene is on the level of a different episteme. Orality represents a different order of consciousness, one which makes the indigene so clearly Other, something far more alien than simply an older, a more primitive, a more sexual, a more violent society. Orality provides the white observer with both a manifestation of and a definition of Otherness. It reaches its height in Cohen's *Beautiful Losers* as the narrator extolls the interjection with which the members of one Indian tribe conclude their speech:

> Thus they essayed to pierce the mysterious curtain which hangs between all talking men: at the end of every utterance a man stepped back, so to speak, and attempted to interpret his words to the listener, attempted to subvert the beguiling intellect with the noise of true emotion. (9)

The most obvious portrait of orality as a quality profoundly different from illiteracy is found in the inflated diction with which the nineteenth- and even twentieth-century indigene is often represented. Standish O'Grady states in *The Emigrant* (1841) that in Indian society "Right reason rules, no orator excites" (67). Even for 1841 this seems a surprising idea in light of the many previous suggestions to the contrary, although David Thompson claims, in reflecting on his journeys in the late eighteenth and early nineteenth centuries, "I have never heard a speech in the florid, bombastic style I have often seen published" (384). Connor's *The Patrol of the Sundance Trail* gives a view of the Indian orator much more typical than those in O'Grady or Thompson. Corporal Cameron of the Mounted Police observes Copperhead speaking to his people:

> A spell held them fixed. The whole circle swayed in unison with his swaying form as he chanted the departed glories of those happy days

when the red man roamed free those plains and woods, lord of his destiny and subject only to his own will. The mystic magic power of that rich resonant voice, its rhythmic cadence emphasized by the soft throbbing of the drum, the uplifted face glowing as with prophetic fire, the tall swaying form instinct with exalted emotion, swept the souls of his hearers with surging tides of passion. Cameron, though he caught but little of its meaning, felt himself irresistibly borne along upon the torrent of the flowing words. (190–1).

In this brief passage, Connor incorporates many of the elements of the standard commodity of orality, the presence, the prehistoric, the communal, and the mystical.

Throughout nineteenth-century literature, the typical "transla-tion" of indigenous speech uses inverted syntax and various archaisms such as second person singular. The archaisms might be part of the general tendency to emphasize the indigene as a people from the past, as in Connor, but they more likely represent the general assumptions entailed in the term, "poetic diction." The seventeenth-century explorer Henry Kelsey used the unusual but not unique term of "poets" instead of "tribe," as in "the Naywatame poets" (*Papers* [1690], 5). In what might seem like an inversion, the indigene is presented as more of a "writer" because unable to write, closer to the bardic ideal of an Ossian.

There are a number of eighteenth- and nineteenth-century texts which "document" such poetic flourishes in indigenous oration. Ong views similar elements in early written texts as emanating from a specifically oral world: "The fulsome praise in the old, residually oral, rhetoric tradition strikes persons from a high-literacy culture as insincere, flatulent, and comically pretentious. But praise goes with the highly polarized, agonistic, oral world of good and evil, virtue and vice, villains and heroes" (45). In Ong's highly subjective view, the "oral world" is shaped by the purity of opposed essences. This suits his analysis of oral narrative: "Oral memory works effec-tively with 'heavy' characters, persons whose deeds are monumen-tal, memorable and commonly public. Thus the noetic economy of its nature generates outsize figures, that is, heroic figures, not for romantic reasons or reflectively didactic reasons but for much more basic reasons: to organize experience in some sort of permanently memorable form" (70). Ong presents a realm in which heroism and rhetoric have an essential symbiotic relationship making the great number of oratorical Indians, Aborigines, and Maori, from Rogers' *Ponteach* (1766) to Herbert's *Poor Fellow My Country* (1975), seem almost inevitable.

Such works often emphasize the poetic traditions which the indigenes maintain, as in the comments in Satchell's *The Greenstone Door* on the elevated "oral learning" of the Maori (114). Many writers depict a quest for this learning as the most appropriate method for the white author to seek indigenization. Thus Roland Robinson refers to Aboriginal legends as a "once epic whole" (*Legend* [1952], 12), and both his own poems and those of the others associated with the *Jindyworobak Review* attempt to make that epic a part of their literature, to transform Aboriginal orality into Australian writing. The many collections of legends in all three countries represent similar efforts along a continuum. At one end are those which assert an absolute fidelity to the original legends. Many, such as MacKay's *Indian Nights*, in order to assert orality and veracity, imply that the entire text is the product of an indigenous storyteller. At the other end are those that make no absolutist claims of truth but pretend an imitation of indigenous style. Examples include many of the narratives employed by James Houston or the movement from traditional legend to personal story in Laurence's *The Diviners* and Fry's *Come a Long Journey*. In both novels the Indian character is shown using the historical forms of his orality to transmit new personal experience narratives.

All these inclusions of indigenous culture within white texts might seem no more than attempts to incorporate indigenous history and philosophy but indigenous orality is also central to the process. In each of the texts mentioned here, the orality of the tradition is emphasized through its source in the indigene storyteller. When, as in Houston and Laurence, no claim is made that the narratives are other than fiction, even more effort is placed on creating a context of orality. The atmosphere is again similar to one defined by Ong: "Primary orality fosters personality structures that in certain ways are more communal and externalized, and less introspective than those common among literates. Oral communication unites people in groups. Writing and reading are solitary activities that throw the psyche back on itself" (69). The solitary author creates both indigenous tradition and indigenous community through indigenous orality.

Even in those texts which emphasize the illiteracy of the indigene rather than the orality, there is often a felt need to incorporate indigenous narratives. In Mrs Campbell Praed's squatter novel, *The Head Station* (1886), the poet, Mr Durnford, aspires to write "an Australian Hiawatha," but his friend points out that his only Australian source could be "the blacks' vulgar superstitions and dirty ways" (2: 65).

Durnford is still able to create his great work but rather than turning to an Aboriginal form he goes directly to a place sacred to the Aborigines and "suddenly his imagination conceived a wild legend" (2: 97). Praed's text suggests that Durnford's inspiration came from "natural phenomena" (2: 97) rather than an Aboriginal source, but in many works there is little separation between the two. Speech is deemed to be more natural than writing and therefore the oral culture is much closer to nature than one that writes. Ong refers to "the world of sound, the natural habitat of language" (8). A character in Rose's *Country of the Dead* says of the Aborigines: "Their songs are full of the small detail that only people who live close to the earth can give" (115). The perceived experience gives a particular validity to the natural similes and metaphors which are a constant part of the image of the indigene. The fluidity of possible metaphorical connections between the indigene, the oral, and the natural can be seen in Wongar's description of Aborigines in *The Trackers*: "The day was a continuous song and not a burden; they seemed as free as the wind" (57).

In each of these oralist works, the untamed natural life of the oral attempts to subvert the enclosed alienated text, as might be expected in the light of the following observation by Ong: "By contrast with natural, oral speech, writing is completely artificial. There is no way to write 'naturally'" (82). As seen throughout this study, texts with a positive bias towards indigenes tend to seek some version of a "natural" path. If Ong's point of view is representative of such pursuits of the natural, as I think it is, both an attraction to orality and an aversion to the written text itself seem almost inevitable. In its praise of orality the white text most clearly shows how its attraction to Other is linked to a desire for an alienation from self, an alienation which is impossible to fulfil.

In *Reading the Country*, Stephen Muecke's commentaries demonstrate his extreme sensitivity to the tension between white and Aboriginal views, but Muecke's guard slips in his assertions about the validity of his representation of Roe's contribution. At first he simply suggests that Roe is "to tell the story of his country once again" (11) but then Roe's voice and the voice of nature become melded to "break through silence into form" (11): "The *voice* is then the material of this text. The voice, which we so often take for granted, is a concrete force: it murmurs, it shouts, it cajoles, it squeals and protests, it bounces along and leaps into song, it groans in our sleep or it makes the little cries of ecstasy which mark our greatest pleasures. In all this, the materiality of the voice cannot be denied, its substance is a vibration which penetrates the bodies of those listening or present" (20–1). Regardless of Muecke's care, when the text pretends to be oral it falls into the metaphysics of orality, into the tendency for the white text to claim the "natural" presence of voice and the subversion of what the oralist text would itself deem the artificial absence that is writing.

As suggested by Ong's "world of sound" above, the power of nature is found not only within the indigene's voice but within all the indigene's sounds. In the theatre, drums and didgeridoos are often used to create a metaphysical indigenous aura. Throughout Duncan Campbell Scott's poems, and particularly in "The Height of Land" (1916, *Selected Poems*, 55–9) and "Powassan's Drum" (1926, *Selected Poems*, 66–70), Indian sound, the song and the drum, becomes the "throbbing" of nature, not unlike the atmosphere Connor creates in the passage above. Muecke comments on this omnipresence of sound within indigenous orality: "Each Aboriginal story has its moment in which an animal noise is imitated, or the sound of a windmill, or the song belonging to one of the characters. These mimetic moments are the central point of access for the listener, the surprising moments when language is put aside and the illusion of being there is complete" (54). Once again, the orality provides both "being" and "there."

Indigenous communication is then natural presence and presence of nature, a connection that creates a corollary of a greater validity for the emanations of that communication. Thus many indigene names demonstrate an unusually accurate assessment of character, with villains such as "Tigerface" in Hampden Burnham's *Jack Ralston* (1902) and Duncan Campbell Scott's "Bad-Young-Man" ("Charcoal" [1947?], *Selected Stories*, 41–9) and beautiful maidens such as the title character in Hatfield's *Black Waterlily* and "Plume of the Huia" in *The Greenstone Door*. A.M. Klein's poem "Indian Reservation" (1948) states that such titles from nature put "fur on their names to make all live things kin" (*Collected*, 295). *Beautiful Losers* provides perhaps the most extreme example: a vanishing tribe is said to have been labelled by their neighbours with a name which signified "corpse" (5).

The power of indigene naming continues in the awarding of indigenous names to whites, as in the use of "mullaka" as an almost mystical honorific in Mrs Aeneas Gunn's *We of the Never-Never* (1908) and in *Poor Fellow My Country*. The latter emphasizes the importance of this title given Jeremy Delacey in that it is applied both by the Jewish refugee, Rifkah (1309), represented as having many of the attributes of the Aboriginal earth mother, Koonapippi, and by Bob-

wirridirridi (1425), an even more otherworldy wise man of the Aborigines. A similar situation arises in O'Reilly's *Moondyne* where the
title given the hero by the Aborigines "had some meaning more than
either manhood or kingship" (14). Long before O'Reilly the absurdity
of such titles was noted in W.T. Thomas's *Van Diemen's Land: An
Operatic Drama* (183?), in which an Irishman is called "Fire-destroy-
ing-white-man" or "Derry-bo-rang-bo-roo" (42), a witty transformation of the name of the Irish hero Brian Boru.

This incorporation of indigene naming in the white text and of
the white character in the indigene-naming system allows for several
layers of meaning. At one level it represents a simple inclusion of
one more aspect of the indigene; at another it represents an acquisition of the communal presence of orality in opposition to the indi-
vidualizing writing. Thus the named white is included but even more
is included within an inclusionary system. He becomes a presence
within presences, as in Ong's spoken word: "The word in its natural,
oral habitat is a part of a real, existential present. Spoken utterance
is addressed by a real, living person to another real, living person
or real living persons, at a specific time in a real setting which
includes always much more than mere words. Spoken words are
always modifications of a total situation which is more than verbal.
They never occur alone, in a context simply of words. Yet words
are alone in a text" (101). The named white becomes, even more
than other words, "real," "present," "communal," "total."

More than that, he becomes the land, as all indigene words,
including his name, are the land. Stephen Muecke makes perhaps
the most overt statement about the process of transformation which
the white text hopes to achieve: "This book is a record of Paddy
Roe's dreaming at its most important nexus: the country itself. Of
course, as the spoken voice is transformed into writing and the
country then becomes the book, the traveller in turn becomes a
reader" (14). The power of Aboriginal orality which Muecke hopes
for is effusively expansive: "The book can only be a white man's
artifact in the end, but Paddy Roe's texts can be read independently
(and must be read) as paradoxically *included* in the book, and thus
incorporated in the broader culture, but extending before and
beyond the covers (already crossing the country before the book was
thought of), one word after the other like footsteps: lively spoken
words" (23).

This vision might seem a great distance from "Derry-bo-rang-
bo-roo," but the latter is simply an extreme parody of the white
attraction to orality which permeates Muecke's text. The absurdity
cannot deny the similarity of the impetus to thus overcome the line

between indigenous and white semiosis. The situation can be related to the general problem of the representation of the indigenous consciousness, as in the above "translations" of indigenous speech. There are many examples in the nineteenth century of indigenous "songs" which when "translated" by a white author become more reminiscent of an English drinking song or of one of the more ethereal lyrics found in minor anthologies of the period. All were searching for a means of acquiring the power of the semiosis and the power of the orality, felt both in texts for which temptation is the operative sign and in those, such as Sayce's *Comboman*, overwhelmed by fear:

> He looked back at the group of niggers and had a sudden and almost irresistible desire to join them in their filthy occupation. At the same time he felt an influence working within him which made him want to shout. He knew that if he gave up control of his tongue for a moment it would utter wild barbaric words, unintelligible to him but in perfect accord with the fragment of chant he had just heard. (252)

In other texts where the indigenes are attraction rather than repulsion, the power of the oral, and of the naming, seems part of an indigenous process superior to the white. When Robinson, the Protector of Aborigines, gives new names to those in his care, such as Princess Lallah Rook for Truganinni, in Drewe's *The Savage Crows*, he explains that the new names "sounded so much more euphonious and dignified than either their native or vulgar 'whiteman's' names" (220). Yet the text allows no inference that this is to be deemed the equivalent of "mullaka," nor is it only a simple suggestion that the indigenes should be named within their own culture since it also reflects an assessment of the indigene naming as intrinsically better. Jack Goody examines languages in terms of the local (oral), world (oral/written), and classical (written). This conforms to his assertion that the written is easily decontextualized while context is inevitable for the oral. He claims that the written word is not "attached to a person; on paper, it becomes more abstract, more depersonalized" (44). The indigenous naming system resonates of the spoken, of the context. Robinson's names are alienated from context to the point that they could be seen in Goody's terms as almost classical. They are writing names, White-ing names. "Oral peoples commonly think of names (one kind of words) as conveying power over things ... Written or printed representations of words can be labels; real, spoken words cannot be" (Ong, 33). Here, the written name is deficient, lacking in power, a mere superficial wrapper – the inadequacy of writing from which the oralist white text turns. Elsewhere in Ong a more sinister side of the chirographic tendency is examined: "Writing, moreover, as will be seen later in detail, is a particularly preemptive and imperialist activity that tends to assimilate other things to itself without the aid of etymologies" (12). There can be little question why Muecke and so many others attempt to liberate orality from their written texts.

Indigenous naming systems are natural in a more direct way than simply as part of the speaking indigene. As in some of the above examples, they often refer to various animals and plants, and thus are less an element of the human reshaping of the world than white names are. As participators in the natural context they correlate rather than constrict. Thus Lefroy, in Mair's *Tecumseh*, can refer to the flowers as "unnamed" (21) before the arrival of the whites. Kumkleseem, who becomes Tay John in O'Hagan's novel of that name, is dissatisfied with his Indian name, which means "coming soon." But it proves prophetically accurate when he destroys himself by attempting to fulfill the role prescribed for him through his white name. The Indian name captures his essence while the white label is an illusion which dooms him. As Jackie, the white storyteller, affirms, "The unnamed – it is the darkness unveiled" (80). Within the white semiosis, the indigenous name is in a sense no name but paradoxically it unveils elements of the darkness which the white name only redrapes. The failure of that "redraping" in Australia is suggested by Eleanor Dark in *Storm of Time* (1948):

> One could fasten an English or an Irish name upon a place, and that was warming to the nostalgic heart; or one could leave a native name, and that was quaint, and still acceptable. But when the land took one's language it was taking one's people, and made strange, faint distortions and adjustments so that a word was still an English word, but not quite, there was a hint of forces not to be controlled. Forest – woods – woodland – coppice ... She shook her head. They were words which had struggled here for life where alone words can live – on the tongues of the people – and they were dying." (344)

The death of orality left only Ong's labels, words, for maps, for charts, writing, White-ing words. These textual words could not achieve a new orality, "on the tongues of the people." They had not lived but were dying.

The indigenous languages are usually represented as appealing. In texts with an apparent pro-indigene intent this would not seem surprising, but it is also the case in many early works which show little sense that the indigenous culture in general is attractive. Perhaps this is because the languages are assessed as sound rather than as vehicles of communication, as suggested in the constant use of the adjective "musical" in representations of indigenous speech. At least part of this musicality seems to reflect a desire to see orality as a metaphysical, unknowable power. This is reflected in one of Lévi-Strauss's explanations for his famous assertion, "the savage mind totalizes" (*Savage*, 245). Lévi-Strauss calls language a "totalizing entity but one outside (or beneath) consciousness and will. Language, an unreflecting totalization, is human reason which has its reasons and of which man knows nothing" (252). A description not unlike many Romantic definitions of music, it is an appropriate depiction of the apparently unanalyzed musical language of primary orality. Lévi-Strauss's comments in a slightly later work seem to support this interpretation: "But since music is a language with some meaning at least for the immense majority of mankind, although only a tiny minority of people are capable of formulating a meaning in it, and since it is the only language with the contradictory attributes of being at once intelligible and untranslatable, the musical creator is a being comparable to the gods, and music itself the supreme mystery of the science of man, a mystery that all the various disciplines come up against and which holds the key to their progress" (*Raw*, 18). In an analysis worthy of Pater, this music language becomes metaphysical by virtue of its untranslatability, not unlike the music language of the indigene. In "The Height of Land" Duncan Campbell Scott perceived this orality beyond interpretation in a "long Ojibwa cadence" (*Selected Poems*, 55) rising from the land, as indigene sound becomes the pervasive musical presence of nature. Musicality is another element of orality which provides an opening into the mystical.

In a number of works the attributes of indigenous language go well beyond sound. Cheney's "Singing Bird," the devoted consort in "Jacques Cartier and the Little Indian Girl," rejects white words as lies: "our race are renowned for truth, and such words are never spoken to us" (December 1848, 565). A more general suggestion of a similar assessment is found in examples such as Drew's *The Wabeno Feast*, in which white equivocation in support of destructive technology is countered by "this saying of the Ojibwa" (202). The key problem of Bodsworth's *The Sparrow's Fall* is that the central character, Jacob, fails to see the Christian hymn from which the title is taken as metaphor rather than the direct truth of orality. He is thus unable to hunt:

The *Manito*'s hymn says he sees even the little sparrow fall, and he loves them all, and if he's sad when just a sparrow dies, he must be sadder when one of his big ones like the *atihk* [caribou] or the moose dies. (12)

A possible compromise between indigene orality and the Christian "Word" is provided in Mitchell's *The Vanishing Point* by the innovative scriptural renderings of the lay preacher, Ezra Powderface, who describes Jesus riding up on the "Jerusalem Wendigos" (158).

Truth as a quality of indigenous language is presented as a general principle. It is closely connected to the oral character of the "spoken," of the "saying." The truth is supported by the communal experience of the tradition, on which Goody comments in the following account of the process of transmitting culinary skills: "But in any oral culture new recipes have to be learnt by one individual from another in a face-to-face situation. The concrete context would stress the relation of teacher to pupil, e.g. of mother to daughter. For oral learning tends to reduplicate the 'initial situation,' the process of socialisation" (142). More than just presence, orality establishes the timelessness of the culture and its veracity by virtue of being passed from speaking person to speaking person within the context described by Connor in the excerpt above from *The Patrol of the Sundance Trail*. This is emphasized in the various apprenticeship relationships so common in images of indigenous peoples. Goody and Ong are concerned with apprenticeship only within the primary oral culture but various Australian, Canadian, and New Zealand works expand the context to provide a more general opportunity for the acquisition of orality with all that it entails. In *Poor Fellow My Country*, the partly Aboriginal Prindy is reindigenized through learning from an aged tribal sage. In Houston's *Spirit Wrestler*, the white northern officer is drawn into his Inuk apprenticeship against his will by a power greater than his own.

The naturalness of indigene language is sometimes presented through reference to sex and scatology. In Moore's *Black Robe*, these elements of the Indian language appear to be consciously prurient, in what seems like one more reaction to the anal-retentive white attitude attacked in Kovel. The novel is responding to the attack on the Indian as the "natural man" in the seventeenth-century *Jesuit Relations*, which Moore gives as documentary justification for his use of what might be termed obscene language when an Indian hunter happens upon the lost priest they call "Nicanis." "'Shit!' the Savage cried. 'I thought I had a moose but all I have is this silly prick, Nicanis'" (75). *Black Robe*, which describes well-balanced Indians and neurotically, perhaps even psychotically, repressed Jesuit intellectuals, rejects the *Relations* and rather states "Mind = bad, body = good." Scatological and sexual language simply represents one more way in which orality transmits natural truth.

Elsewhere, however, indigene naturalness is usually seen in opposition to obscenity. In Bowering's *Burning Water* the Indian woman acquires lascivious words for sex from the white. And in most other works the impression is conveyed that while the indigenes are "natural," they are too natural to encapsulate the natural elements of life and present them as expletives. Sociolinguistics states that we use scatology and sex as obscenities *because* they are taboo subjects, a strange comment on the freely sexual yet foul-mouthed Indians of *Black Robe*. The Maori Netta in Noel Hilliard's *The Glory and the Dream* (1978) attacks whites for words such as "sparrowfart":

> We don't have rude words. We have names for things and that's all. You say *te* in Maori, that's exactly what it means. But you say it in pakeha, it means a lot of other things as well. Rude things. Lot of pakeha words like that. Not names but rude. (5)

Netta later finds the *pakeha* problem carried to another level in a comic book, where "that word," presumably "fuck," is written down: "'It's one thing to know about it,' she said. 'It's another thing to write it down.'" But she doesn't reject the action behind the word: "'I can understand people getting excited about that. Because it's real. Sure. But not by seeing the word in a book'" (121).

"Real" words opposed to "book." A very different situation from that in many earlier texts in which "book" represents "Book," the Bible. David Thompson asserts that it was the lack of writing which gave the Indians an inadequate religion: "The sacred Scriptures to the Christian; the Koran to the Mahometan give a steady belief to the mind, which is not the case with the Indian, his idea on what passes in this world is tolerably correct so far as his senses and reason can inform him; but after death all is wandering conjecture taken up on tradition, dreams and hopes" (362). In Gilbert Parker's story, "A Prairie Vagabond" (1894), the taciturn Indian is able to assert his existence only after his suicide in his jail cell, when he leaves the written exclamation, "How" (73). Previously a meaningless expletive, signifier of the silent savage, "How" becomes the climax of the story when scratched on the door. There is a complete reversal from this view in *Burning Water* in which an American's attempt to enter orality is rendered absurd:

> "What is this 'How'?" asked the first Indian of his companion.

"Search me," said the second Indian. "But we may as well go along with him." (199)

Bowering's presentation hinges on a sense of an orality which the writing man cannot touch, a view typical of the nineteen-eighties. Parker's written "How" is a scientific achievement, a sign of the rise from illiteracy which many nineteenth-century texts sought. It bears with it a residue of Thompson's sacred book, as in Homi Bhabha's "Signs Taken for Wonders" (1985), an analysis of a nineteenth-century account of a Bible's impact in India: "The discovery of the book is, at once, a moment of originality and authority, as well as a process of displacement that, paradoxically, makes the presence of the book wondrous to the extent to which it is repeated, translated, misread, displaced. It is with the emblem of the English book – 'signs taken for wonders' – as an insignia of colonial authority and a signifier of colonial desire and discipline, that I want to begin this essay" (144). Here Bhabha commences his discourse with a writing which is both imperialist, in the Ongian sense, and Imperialist.

If this "displacement" is a vexing issue within Hindu culture how much more so in the primary oralities of Canada, Australia, and New Zealand. Domett's *Ranolf and Amohia* makes much of Ranolf teaching his Maori love, Amohia, how to write. Ranolf asks, "On this unlettered Soul so white/ What characters am I to write?" (2: 130). It might seem incongruous to view a Maori soul as white, and perhaps even more so in the present context to link "white" and "unlettered." But Amohia's response is direct. She seeks a charmed form of writing, "the mystery deep/ Of letters" (2: 148–9), which she believes will be an extension of orality, "seeing talk," "unspoken speech unheard" (2: 148). This is not simply the traditional assumption that writing is only speech recorded. It seems an attempt by Amohia to achieve the power of orality transformed in writing. One might note here any of the passages quoted above from Stephen Muecke. Or the following comment from Ong, a hortatory hope which seems to contradict some of his other fears of imperialist writing: "But, in all the wonderful worlds that writing opens, the spoken word still resides and lives" (8). This sense of an extension of presence, of the spoken, the living, can be linked to Domett's elevation of the Maori storyteller as "a *living* book" (2: 300). Ong similarly asserts the humanness of oral knowledge: "When an often-told oral story is not actually being told, all that exists of it is the potential in certain human beings to tell it" (11). For Ong such knowledge is part of apprenticeship, but an apprenticeship through osmosis: "Human beings in primary oral cultures, those untouched by writing in any form, learn a great deal and possess and practice great wisdom, but they do not 'study'" (9).

Much fiction and much poetry, however, seem to reject even the limited technology implied by these "non-studying" apprentices. T.F. Young's "The Indian" (1887) "had read from nature's hand/ A book unwrit, yet wise its page" (*Canada*, 58). There is a sense in both Domett and Young that the indigenous orality is an emanation of nature which might be touched by the written, might even be partially expressed in the metaphor of writing, but in the end has a power which cannot be contained by it. As the American soldier in Mair's play says of Tecumseh, "To be free/Required no teacher, no historic page" (127).

These texts consider orality in an attempt to somehow embrace its power and to overcome the effect of writing. In what would seem an impossible paradox for works which write about orality, most white texts describe writing as failing when it tries to encapsulate orality, apparently because of the inadequacy of its Ongian imperialism in the face of a vast epistemological chasm. A white character in Stuart's *Yaralie* is said to have learned "something, despite all his reading, of their way of speech" (69). And yet that great gap at times seems less Indigene/White than Oral/Written. There are moments when a white orality holds such potential as in Ian Mudie (*Dream*, 1943), who is drawn to both Aboriginal song and "the immortal singing swagman" (3). Such's *Riverrun*, a highly oralist novel about the Beothuk Indians, takes its title from that contorted epitome of white orality and textuality, James Joyce's *Finnegans Wake*. Herbert's Rifkah in *Poor Fellow My Country* is a storyteller comparable to the Aboriginal examples, although the text suggests that as Jew she is other than, presumably Other than, white. In Murray's *The Boys Who Stole the Funeral* the possible fluidity of written renderings of the oral allows the Aboriginal presence to engage in an ethnographic float from Birrigan through Berrigan to conclude as Birroogun (62). As in other Irish figures elsewhere, and as in the character of Rifkah, assumptions of a white ethnic orality allow a transition between indigenous orality and text. For *The Savage Crows*, however, such written inconsistencies are not emulations of the oral but their own ironic commentary on the death of the last male Tasmanian Aborigine, called William Lanney by the whites: "Lanney – also Lanne, Lannie and Lannay – was the old Aboriginal verb of the western tribes of Van Diemen's Land (later named Tasmania) signifying to fight or strike" (11–12). McGarrity's *Once a Jolly Blackman* reaffirms this rejection of white association with orality in its ascerbic title which denies Mudie's claims about the inherent truth of the opening line, "Once a jolly swagman," of A.B. Paterson's "Waltzing Matilda"

(1895, *Collected*, 254). Orality cannot die to live in writing, as Ong sometimes suggests, if the indigenous orality becomes jingoist banality.

Yet there is a constant hope throughout all three literatures of achieving the oral, particularly the state of orality manifested in the indigene. The texts of two authors are of particular interest in this context, Keneally and Kroetsch. Both Kroetsch's *What the Crow Said* (1978) and Keneally's *The Chant of Jimmie Blacksmith* assert in their titles their attempts to subvert textual status and achieve orality. The potential "truth" of writing is constantly questioned in *Jimmie Blacksmith* and Kroetsch's *Badlands* and opposed by the validity of indigenous oral knowledge.

The latter two novels also present indigenous fears and confusions about photographs, as do *The Diviners* and Atwood's *Surfacing*. The indigenes are reacting first to the mystical potential in something which can capture a human image, and second to a white talisman, which is the way pieces of white writing are viewed by the indigenes in Dark's *No Barrier* and James Houston's *Eagle Song: An Indian Saga Based on True Events* (1983). But they are also rejecting that which erases the "natural" fluidity of orality, that which creates an "unnatural" stasis and uniformity. The narrator of *Eagle Song* dislikes the book because it "would not speak" (134), failing to achieve the illusion pursued by Domett, Muecke, and Ong. Anna Yellowbird in *Badlands* rejects the photograph because it encapsulated the image of the young white boy who died, and thereby prevented change. The photograph fails the test of natural mutability suggested by Ong: "Sound exists only when it is going out of existence. It is not simply perishable but essentially evanescent, and it is sensed as evanescent" (32).

Once again, orality is natural, as the indigene is natural. But speech is not the sole element of indigenous communication with this quality, as shown in Scott's image of Indian drumming. Even sound is not essential. *Burning Water* and Carr's *Klee Wyck* explicitly recognize "language" in totem poles (43, 51). Al Purdy's poem "The Horseman of Agawa" (1978) claims that Indian rock paintings will resurrect an Ojibwa ghost and "seize his voice" (*Being*, 146), although the text states that Purdy will fail to replicate this presence through his written poetry. Purdy's position might be interestingly contrasted with Ong's comment on Indian pictographs. He dismisses them as true writing because "the meaning intended did not come entirely clear" (86).

The assumption that any writing can make an intended meaning entirely clear must seem somewhat strange today in a world of polysemic readings. But that Ong should seek such meaning is also interesting. Ong is clearly attracted to orality not for meaning but for presence. It is phenomenology, not analysis, which drives him. Yet his text is "intended" as one of analysis. Ong establishes his bi-polar system on the theory that orality provides presence and literacy analysis. Thus he finds no attraction in a writing which is not analysis, a writing which is not White-ing. For a writer such as Purdy, whose work seems, like much creative writing, in pursuit more of presence than of meaning, the writing which implies voice in a very subjective way is the writing which attracts.

Poor Fellow My Country is able to follow this non-analytical writing to a further stage. The text finds the essence of Aboriginal rock paintings in the hand signs created by paint sprayed from the mouth. They are the oral perpetuated but their form explicitly acknowledges that they represent not what is painted but the emptiness described by the paint, the hand which is not there. They achieve the status of a metaphysical reference point, as do the rock paintings of *Surfacing*, only after the Indians themselves are gone. In the latter novel the narrator at first believes the essence of the land is to be seen through the Indian pictographs. No present Indians but Indian presence. Then she realizes, like Praed's Durnford, that the essence is rather certain metaphysical places the Indians recognized in their pictographs. In an apparently unconscious transference, Atwood is able to depict even the Indian presence as a temporary transition, unnecessary once the white metaphysics are of a sufficiently high order.

Yet there remains a sense of the Indian in this presence without sound. The silence of the indigene is as proverbial as the oratory, as noted by Parker's "How." The Indians in Evans' *Mist On the River* question why whites must talk so much. Stuart's *The Driven* observes of the Aborigines: "the gift most of them had of silence" (10). The absurdity of the inflated diction of representations of historical indigenes has often met its match in the taciturn indigene. Lighthall provides a delightful combination of the two in *The Master of Life*: "Thou sayest 'Ugh!'" (127). The potential of this cliché of the stage Indian was explored more extensively before in Richardson's *Wacousta*, which employs "The low and guttural 'ugh!'," "an assentient and expressive 'ugh!'," and an "almost inaudible 'ugh!'" within the space of three pages. These are said to represent "astonishment," "approbation," and "eagerness," respectively (113–15).

Beyond this apparently unintentional burlesque lies an even greater sense of a different consciousness. If the indigenous language presents barriers of communication which clearly delineate Other from self, how much more so silence, in which there is only presence, in which all is left not only unwritten but unsaid. Part of this is simply an extension of Ong's evanescent orality. In his oral world, silence is not a time for isolated reading but a time to hear the presences which echo. Many recent texts attempt to use this resonating silence to represent both the epistemological and political barriers of communication. The lack of indigenous words represents both what cannot be communicated and what is not heard. Foucault's *The History of Sexuality* provides an apt synopsis of the reverberations which this process suggests: "Silence itself – the things one declines to say, or is forbidden to name, the discretion that is required between different speakers – is less the absolute limit of discourse, the other side from which it is separated by a strict boundary, than an element that functions alongside the things said, with them and in relation to them within over-all strategies" (27). There is a sense of that "element," and the aporia which it produces, in *Reading the Country*: "In the Aboriginal-White encounter there are often long silences, an absence of words which speaks of the lack of common ground between Aboriginal discourses and White discourses. Perhaps it is important to record these silences also as we head out from Roebuck Plains Station with the key to the gate which will take us further east from the Old Sheep Camp" (Benterrak, 67). The aporia may not be a strict boundary but neither is it the key to the gate.

Mel Dagg's "Sunday Evening on Axe Flats" (*Truck* 1982) uses silence to represent the inadequacy of white/indigene dialogue and also to provide a metaphysical aura, this time as preparation for orality, for the telling of a legend:

> She wraps herself in layers of silence, travelling outside the day, outside herself, waiting. Then, her voice a monotone, she begins drawing the round slow words from within. So that in the silence before she begins I feel it entering the house, gathering in the folds of the medicine bundle that hangs in her bedroom, until she is filled with it, possessed by it, must speak it, is compelled to tell it. (44)

Yet the legend seems deflation, a diminution of the presence of silence. The greater level is maintained in Patrick's *Inapatua*: "Here Illuta knelt to pray. She didn't say the words, she drew the symbols – the feet of birds" (139).

Orality as defined by, and at times as exemplified by, Ong, is a major part of the primitivist attraction of the indigene for the white text. A part of this is simply primitivism, a desire for an earlier time, before the technology represented by writing. Ong constantly asserts the failed perception of us "deeply typographic folk" (32). But with this rejection of technology comes a belief in an additional human presence in a primary oral culture which eventually becomes a belief in a metaphysical presence. Direct associations with nature and even with something akin to a noumenal sphere are linked to or even emanations from primary orality. The standard commodity of orality is only very seldom the emblem of deficiency as suggested by Fanon. Rather it becomes, in Lévi-Strauss's term, totemic, an element with direct rather than representative connections to another realm. The indigene's orality provides contact with the powers which the indigene's orality perceives.

In Sid Stephen's "She Says Goodbye to Mr. Cormack" (*Beothuck* 1976) the presence of silence exceeds even the limits of time for the last Beothuk, Shawnandithit:

> her tongue
> is even now becoming stone,
> dense with silence
> and hard with meaning. (np)

Through the hardening comes the fluidity, the ability to overcome the restraints of linear, logical, white interpretation. Orality becomes the land, becomes presence, and mystically becomes the silent invocation of the consciousness, the vision, of Other.

CHAPTER SEVEN

Mysticism

Orality is a manifestation, a demonstration, of the Other. But the value of the Other, that different order of consciousness, lies behind the orality. Ong's claim that there is a direct association between orality and "magical potency" (32) agrees with Goody's assertion that "spells and other attempts to control the course of events are dependent upon the magic of the word" (1977, 149). Goody continues his consideration of incantation by once again emphasizing the consciousness of the speaker: "The magic of the spell is dependent, at least in part, upon the virtual identity of the speaker and spoken. How can one separate a man and his words? How can I imagine myself as destined to speak another language or in another way?" (150). Orality is presented as magic subjectivity through phrases which themselves seem to transform the text into subjective expression. The oralist text, however, tends to move from man and words to man in silence, a state which presumably offers minimal potential for communication. The texts seem to turn to silence *because* it is so incomprehensible to the outside observer. Even more than the strangeness of orality, silence comes close to representing the always unknowable, that which always lies veiled, the mystical.

Unlike "orality," "mystical" is a quite common word. Its basic philosophical premise, that there is a dimension other than the material one generally recognized as the real, is well-known to the average reader, regardless of how little that same reader has considered such noumenal elements. But also unlike "orality," mystical is far too commonplace to depict the expansive shape of this standard commodity. It would perhaps be better to use some overtly defamiliarizing term, such as "the unnameable," for at its most basic the mystical in the context of the indigene is the spiritual consciousness of the alien Other, that essence which seems beyond capture by a white semiosis.

The *Oxford English Dictionary* uses various phrases to define "mystic" and "mystical," many of which refer specifically to Christian mysticism. One entry explains "mystic" as "a sacred mystery," which seems an appropriate association with the indigene, but another definition given for "mystical" is perhaps still more appropriate, in spite of its layer of Christian monotheism: "Having a certain spiritual character or import by virtue of a connexion or union with God transcending human comprehension." The various other commodities are also part of a separation between the everhuman self and the nonhuman Other, but the mystical indigene, whether the valorization is positive or negative, signifies an even more absolute division of worlds. The mystical indigene represents the metaphysics, the belief system of Other, and thus, as in Plato's cave metaphor, the extra-phenomenal realm of Other. That text in which the primary emotional sign is fear will usually reject the indigene belief system. For such a text that realm is an extra-phenomenal error. It claims the indigene's spiritual dimension is false, either because no such dimension exists in this material universe or because the true cosmology is one defined by the culture – usually a Christian one – that has produced the text. That text which seems motivated by temptation will be drawn to the mystical indigene as a compelling glimpse of the noumenal.

The separation between human self and nonhuman Other can be seen even in the explorer's narratives, in Hearne's *Journey* and Thompson's *Narrative*, for example. Both texts expend significant heuristic energy on Indian belief although to opposite ends. Thompson explores indigenous views on immortality to justify his own Christianity. Hearne examines Indian conjuring to justify his own non-belief. Both treat their studies in relative theology as self-reflexive exercises. Overtly fictional texts display similar mirrorings. The most obvious rejections of indigene beliefs are in Christian texts. Egerton Ryerson Young's *Winter Adventures of Three Boys in the Great Lone Land* (1899) refers to the Indians' transformation from the "degradation and superstitions of a cruel paganism into the blessedness and enjoyments of a genuine Christianity and an abiding civilization" (79). Praed provides a less doctrinaire response in *Fugitive Anne*, in which the powers of indigenous orality are met by Anne's "Ave Maria," which joins with the Lord's Prayer to have great powers over the Aborigines and even over nature. Anne's "instinctively modern ideas" make her "revolted" by native "superstitions" (113) and yet the text asserts that her "religious instincts" are "interlinked by every fibre of her being with the primeval mysticism of the Australian Bush" (151). Anne's beliefs are aggressively Christian, but they are shown to have greater effect on the Aborigines because of her ability to shape the presentation of Christian ideology into a form which is semiotically meaningful in the context of Aboriginal mysticism, something quite different from the concrete Protestant-ism of Young.

Anne's powers can be linked to the generally shamanistic view of indigene mysticism presented in the majority of Australian, Cana-dian, and New Zealand texts. Mircea Eliade's *Shamanism: Archaic Techniques of Ecstasy* (1951) describes a process similar to that in Praed: "A first definition of this complex phenomenon, and perhaps the least hazardous, will be: shamanism = *technique of ecstasy*" (4). The next stage of Eliade's definition might not seem applicable in this context in that the novel represents Anne as manipulated by God rather than vice versa, but it still seems appropriate in its suggestion of how Anne uses her technique of ecstasy to control the indigenes: "It will easily be seen wherein a shaman differs from a 'possessed' person, for example; the shaman controls his 'spirits,' in the sense that he, a human being, is able to communicate with the dead, 'demons,' and 'native spirits,' without thereby becoming their instrument" (6). Thus *Fugitive Anne*, a text which specifically rejects the validity of indigenous mysticism, presents a Christian mirror of such mysticism as the ideal religious power. Like the shaman in Eliade's study, the Christian singer touches the spirit and uses it to guide those around her. Young emphasizes a quite different aspect of the Indian, one more suited to his own evangelical Protestantism than to the usual image of indigene as mystic. Like a very similar writer, Ralph Connor, Young often refers to the quality of the simple faith displayed by Christian Indians, a faith which is so much more devout than that found in whites. Such Indians resemble the Indian writer George Copway in his autobiographical persona who turned from "imaginary gods" (*Life* [1847], 11) to Christianity.

This unsophisticated approach to relative theology seems very different from the mystical Christianity of *Fugitive Anne*, but it suits the dominant ideology of Canadian (or Australian or New Zealand) culture of the period. Christian dogma was a given generally accepted as being on the same level of valorization as material reality. Fanon inadvertently comments on this view in his discussion of the tendency for indigenous religion to interfere with revolutionary action: "Mumbo-Jumbo and all the idols of the tribe come down among them, rule over their violence and waste it in traces until it is exhausted" (*Wretched*, 19). In his dedication to materialist change,

Fanon rejects the reality of any spiritualist ideology, including Christianity, as fact or even as of any epistemological value. But his absolutist dismissal of indigenous belief is like that of narrowly Christian texts; it is a similar iconoclasm in the name of truth, in his case, a vaguely defined revolutionary socialism. His rejection of the mystical indigene also provides a telling contrast with later white literature, which turns its iconoclasm on Christianity in order to "return" to a general embrace of the mystical indigene.

Most texts from the early nineteenth century show little acceptance of the validity of indigenous religious beliefs. There are glimpses of what might be called relative theology, but this form of gently ambivalent tolerance became much more popular towards the end of the Victorian period. At the beginning, those texts produced in the colonies, all in some sense a part of imperial policy, tended to reflect that policy in generalized progressivist claims. Howe's "Acadia" asserted that contact had defeated both Indian and Indian theology: "His dream of Gods and Spirits soon was o'er" (*Poems*, 16).

This view of native religion suits the standard commodity of the prehistoric, the indigene as remnant of the past. Goody encapsulates this position and then follows it with the alternate assumptions of a relativist analysis: "The notion of a shift of emphasis from magic and myth to science and history has been the commonplace of anthropological discourse since its very beginning. Moreover, there has always been a tendency to interpret these terms as descriptions or indices of modes of thought and action that one could dichotomize by words like primitive and advanced. However, another current of opinion has concentrated upon analyzing the technical achievements of simpler societies and calling attention to the mythical or magical elements of our own, though the former tended to be regarded as precursors and the latter as survivals" (148). In "Acadia" the spiritualism of the Indian is a past force which has no relevance in a progressive civilizing world. The text makes a clear although unstated division between indigenous beliefs and the God and Spirit of the missionaries which were so much a part of white civilizing. In *Honi Heki*, Dickson's support for the Maori leader's politics seems highly influenced by his perception of Honi Heki's solid Protestant faith. The pseudonymous Australian "Moan Bambi" describes Aboriginal converts in *Lili-Illa* (1923) as being so fervent as to scar their chests in the shape of a cross.

Such fervency was not likely to be approved of by *The Literary Garland*. Still, its Indian poems and stories seem almost obsessed with converts: the "Indian Nurse's Death Song" (1850) asks that her white charge be guarded by "He thy fathers worship" (106); the "Huron Princess" (Leprohon 1850) dies at the stake while testifying to "Thou Great and Glorious One, Protector of my race" (582). Some texts are overtly Christian; others use a monotheism built on a Christian pattern. The latter creates an acceptably "civilized" theology yet requires no specific conversion for an Indian to participate. Similar examples in other texts often use the phrase, "Master of Life," which easily moves into Christian discourse, whether in the simplistic form employed by Young or the complex excursions in relative theology found in Child and Cohen. Mair's *Tecumseh* and Lighthall's *The Master of Life* each pose a monotheistic Indian hero who effects the role of peacemaker in opposition to a polytheistic, hypocritical villain.

The superiority of the Indian Christian is partly explained by the greater response which comes from the innocent, childlike, unsophisticated indigene, but the primary cause is usually given as the Indian's closeness to nature. The Indian monotheism is almost invariably a species of Christian pantheism, at times with a transcendentalist overlay. The Christian Indian of Cheney's "Jacques Cartier and the Little Indian Girl" is resolutely opposed to "heathen ignorance and superstition" (521) but remains devoted to the "temple of nature's God" (525). In Thomas D'Arcy McGee's "Jacques Cartier and the Child" (*Poems*, 1870), the Indians, having no valid religion, are the "lost children of Adam" (390), but in "The Arctic Indian's Faith" (*Poems*, 556), McGee conforms to the usual claims for Indian pantheism.

Christianity is associated in these nineteenth-century texts with the scientific progress of civilization. There is little evidence of concern for specifically Christian beliefs. Rather than examining some theological principle, the emphasis is on the progressive, rational development of a white society in which the religion of the moment is an accepted ancillary. It provides no obstructions, if it provides no obvious support. The separation between the indigenous and Christian theologies in their relations with science are suggested by the various references to the indigene's assumption that white technology represents mystical powers. In William Hatfield's *Desert Saga* (1933), guns (52), the telegraph (102), and a barometer (212) are all viewed by the Aborigines as magic, as is a thermometer: "The stone-age witch doctor fondling the paraphernalia of modern medical science" (191). Yet in this and similar texts there is no discussion of the fact that Christian theology, obliquely acknowledged by the text to be valid, is also limited in its ability to account for technology.

On the other hand, the pantheistic Indian provides an alternative ideal for those who find the dynamics of progress to be too impure. In such examples, the Indian enmeshed in the semiotic field of nature joins with the dominant Christian ideology to provide a possible paragon. In the few instances in which the logical results of this blend are examined, however, the best that the native can expect is assimilation and resulting deindigenization. Yet even that is unlikely as the power of historicity makes the demise of the pure Christian savage almost inevitable.

With a few exceptions, early depictions of the Aborigine do not emphasize the Christian convert, although historically the missionary presence was reasonably similar. But in the presentation of traditional beliefs, there is a like devotion to nature as in this passage from Katharine Susannah Prichard's *Winged Seeds* (1950):

> The fruit had a sacred significance for her, Dinny told Pat, Kalgoorla believed the spirit of the dream ancestors, who created it, had entered into her mother before she was born at the place of the kalgurluhs. It was there she belonged; there her own spirit when she died would seek reunion with the kinsmen of her tribe, allied by this totem. (160)

In Ian Mudie's poem, "Underground" (*Corroboree* 1940), the "Alcheringa," the dreamtime, the essence of Aboriginal religion, *is* nature:

> Deep flows the stream,
> feeding the totem-roots,
> deep through the time of dream
> in Alcheringa. (4)

There is a clear break, however, between most such depictions of the power of nature within indigenous beliefs and that extolled in the Christian pantheism of converts discussed above. Texts which view indigenous religion as a positive emanation of nature tend to see the white values as anti-nature and thus reject them. The distinction between white and indigenous beliefs is akin to the distinction between pre- and postlapsarian, as described by Eliade: "In numerous traditions friendship with animals and understanding their language represent paradisal syndromes. In the beginning, that is, in mythical times, man lived at peace with the animals and understood their speech. It was not until after a primordial catastrophe, comparable to the 'Fall' of Biblical tradition, that man became what he is today – mortal, sexed, obliged to work to feed himself, and at enmity with the animals" (99). The pantheistic Christianity in the earlier texts carries hints of a prelapsarian paradise. Contemporary narratives make still greater claims for an Edenic sublime.

Fred Bodsworth's *The Sparrow's Fall* has been noted as a comment on Christian writing failing to equal Indian orality, but its major statement is on religious conflict: Christianity interferes with the natural order of the north in which the Indian, Jacob, must kill to survive. Bodsworth's analysis of the inaccurate portrayal of nature in Christian literature could be compared to the many instances in his work and elsewhere in which very similar accounts of nature presented through indigenous oral literature are immediately accepted as valid, as manifestations of natural presence. *The Sparrow's Fall* shows that, unlike the Christian, the Indian belief system can respond when Jacob finds himself far from home, as when he leaves a caribou skull to propitiate the local powers: "In this strange land there would be other spirits he didn't know, and they would be pleased at this respect for them that Jacob was showing" (151).

The distinction here is partly historicist, as Jacob's power is a remnant from before contact, from the time of the land, but it is also a claim for the holistic. Jacob's "strange land" is here a variant within a viable cosmology of the land, not the absolute alien confronted by Christian ideology. In addition, it presents one more reflection of the distinction between cohesive magic and fragmentary science, as in Lévi-Strauss's claims for *The Savage Mind*: "Seen in this way, the first difference between magic and science is therefore that magic postulates a complete and all embracing determinism. Science, on the other hand, is based on a distinction between levels: only some of these admit forms of determinism; on others the same forms of determinism are held not to apply" (11). Jacob's Ojibwa religion allows transference from one aspect of nature to another because it is able to determine all things. The religion of nature is valorized throughout nature, although as nature varies the practitioners of the natural religion must reshape their processes. White Christianity is valorized only as limited metaphor, something isolated from either the magic religion of the Ojibwa or the scientific truth which is the determining force on a number of levels of white culture. The text seems to suggest that indigenization of even the limited efficacy of white religion will require a complete overturning.

Brian Moore's *Black Robe* notes the impossibility of an Indian father accepting a young Frenchman as son-in-law:

Her father would say, "How can I give you as wife to a Norman? Everyone knows they are stupid as a blind elk. They do not know that this world is alive, that the trees speak, that the animals and fish are possessed of reason and will revenge themselves on us if we do not respect their dead. (81)

This indigenous animism is attractive for its holistic pantheism but also for its passion. Todorov considers various attempts to evaluate native religion in the Americas from a Christian perspective: "Religious feeling is not defined by a universal and absolute content but by its orientation, and is measured by its intensity; so that even if the Christian God is in Himself an idea superior to what is expressed through Tezcatlipoca (as is believed by the Christian Las Casas), the Aztecs can be superior to the Christians with regard to religious feeling, and in fact they are" (*Conquest*, 189–90). There is a clear appeal to such relative theology, what Todorov terms "perspectivism, in which each man is put in relation to his own values, rather than being faced with a single ideal" (192). But it is difficult to think of a text which achieves such "perspective": texts fall into either the class illustrated by the Christian denial of Young's *Winter Adventures* or that of the denial of Christianity in Moore.

Even in the many nineteenth-century texts which extol the virtues of Christianity as practised by native peoples the success of such imperial proselytizing is always modified by the subtextual recognition that assimilation or death are the likely results. As *The Sparrow's Fall* exemplifies, contemporary texts seldom allow even this limited success to Christianity. Cohen's *Beautiful Losers* rejects the unnatural chastity which the Roman Catholic Church imposes on Catherine Tekakwitha, in opposition to the mystical powers of Indian sexuality. Prindy, in Herbert's *Poor Fellow My Country*, combines his Aboriginal religion with Judaism but refuses to embrace the predominant faith of white Australians: "Christmas not our *yom-tov*" (796). Even the most positive contemporary portraits of the influence of Christianity on indigenes, such as Stow's *To the Islands*, show it as an alien and often dangerous imposition. The old missionary, Heriot, tries to find a suitable Christian orality in a song sung "to a corroboree tune:"

This ae night, this ae night.
    Every night and all,
Fire and fleet and candlelight
    and Christ receive thy soul. (77)

But as he explores indigenization he realizes the process – and the process of his own individuation – must be through Aboriginal belief: "my soul is a strange country" (126).

Lévi-Strauss's comments on scientific determinism suggest the limitations of Christianity here. Most of these texts reject the possibility of the Christian religion as holistic, of a Christian God who *in fact* sees every sparrow fall, and as a result Christianity is no more than one, very minor, level of determinism. Its valorization in these texts is akin to other elements of white ideology that are shown to be similarly constricted, or similarly false, such as the masonic order in *The Chant of Jimmie Blacksmith*. The hangman-butcher, with his illustrious masonic regalia, is an agent of the civilized violence which has made Jimmie a perverted form of the traditional, validated, natural violence represented by his uncle, Tabidji.

The masonic order, as one might expect, is not a general focus in these texts, nor are similar secret systems. But scientific determinism itself is often presented as a belief system that dominates white practice without providing the holistic cultural support of indigenous beliefs. Such a system is a contrast to that of Eliade's shaman or to the Christianity of Praed's *Fugitive Anne*. They use the spirits in support of themselves and of their cultures. In contemporary texts, the western ideology of technological progress is presented as a delusion, in which the practitioners believe themselves to be manipulators of a scientific version of the technique of ecstasy but are instead the puppets of demonic possession.

In B. Wongar's "Goarang, the Anteater" (1978), white technology is used to turn an Aborigine into first an echidna and then an ant: "Then it will be possible to feed a whole tribe with a single scrap of rotten garbage" (*Track*, 75). The mad scientist produces a perverse inversion of the animal transformation stories so often presented as typical of the natural indigene mysticism. Drew's *The Wabeno Feast* depicts the wabeno tradition as a strange yet perhaps necessary suicidal purging by a small Indian cult. They embrace the fires, that quintessential image of power and danger, of mystical insight and mystical destruction, in order that the culture as a whole may function. But the Indians deem the wabeno to be the essence of white culture: "You are all wabenos, you whites, maddened by fires. You flee the enemy within, and fleeing, burn the plains and woodlands" (218).

The rejection of white belief systems can be viewed in an historical context. The clear-cut Christian assertions of Young and Connor and the simple Christian pantheism of *The Literary Garland* seem unavailable to contemporary texts. They are unable to replace an indigenous spirituality with an assimilationist white one. This leaves two primary alternatives. One is that found in Herbert's *Capricornia* and Fry's *How a People Die* and throughout the short fiction of Nene Gare (*Bend* 1978) and Kinsella. In such texts, the indigene is employed as only an oppressed minority; few references are made to a mystical dimension and the emphasis on the indigene as part of the natural is similarly limited. Although orality is still often a significant force, its metaphysics is severely depleted.

The rejection of mysticism can be a sign of verisimilitude. It might also in certain contexts be part of an ideological choice, to avoid hiding the social problems of the indigene in contemporary white society under a layer of what Fanon called "Mumbo-Jumbo." But the tension of the semiotic field of the indigene is such that the deletion of this commodity seems to be part of a general avoidance of the primary questions of the quality of being for the indigene. These texts make few comments on indigenization, seldom even to the extent of examining land rights. The few times glimmers of an indigenous belief system appear in such texts, as in Kinsella's "Caraway" (*Dance*, 60–8) and "Parts of the Eagle" (*Moccasin*, 45–57), they are hesitant remnants with few suggestions of validity. The de-mystified indigene is a de-valorized indigene.

But this is the alternative adopted in only a small part of recent fiction. Most contemporary texts are less willing to be restricted to the material reality of the indigene of the present. Another novel by Fry, *Come a Long Journey*, uses an Indian storyteller whose explorations of his native and natural beliefs are a significant element in the indigenization of the white narrator. The children's novels of the Australian Patricia Wrightson follow a similar transition from *The Bunyip Hole* (1957), in which the title refers only to white children's playful naming, to *The Nargun and the Stars* (1973) and similar works, in which spirits from an Aboriginal religion, manifestations of rocks and streams, "the living earth" (48), are shown to have continuing power over the land. Wrightson's *The Ice is Coming* (1977) asserts that these spirits are "born of the land itself" (12), and thus recognized by the only slightly less indigenous Aborigines: "The People are dark-skinned, with heavy brows and watching eyes, and they belong to the land; it flows into them through their feet" (11).

The general concern for Aboriginal mysticism in *Poor Fellow My Country* is focused through the central white character, Jeremy Delacey. Throughout the text his personality and actions are presented as various tokens of the indigenous. An Aboriginal sage considers the appearance to Jeremy of an Aboriginal ghost to be an overt certificate of indigenization:

"Now properly you belong country. That *Lamala* belong to some old blackfeller before, finish now for good. He lonely. He grab 'old o' you. Now you all-same blackfeller ... belong country!" (1098)

The process created by this contact between man and ghost is very similar to that defined by Eliade: "'Seeing spirits,' in dream or awake, is the determining sign of the shamanic vocation, whether spontaneous or voluntary. For, in a manner, having contact with the souls of the dead signifies *being dead oneself*. This is why, throughout South America, the shaman must so die that he may meet the souls of the dead and receive their teaching; for the dead know everything" (84). If the indigene is of the pre-historic and is signified by death, as I note in the chapter on historicity, the white character becomes indigenized shaman through contact with the emanation of the dead indigene. An even more emphatic version of the process is found in *The Boys Who Stole the Funeral*. Murray's poem is one of a number of texts which present an association between indigenous orality and the orality of what might be termed "white savages," in this case the Irish. Watson's *Caledonia Australis* establishes the highlander as almost a mystical cousin of the Aborigine: "The Scottish Gaels were inveterate legenders and chronically superstitious. Legends and omens gave an intractable natural world a metaphysical dimension" (9).

The valorization of the standard commodity of mysticism in the semiotic field of the white savage of Britain, the Irish, the Scots, the Cornish, etc., made for useful transition figures. Thompson refers to the superstitions among the highland Scots in his employ and produces a geographic explanation:

> It is a sad weakness of the human character, and [one] which is constantly found, more, or less, in the lower orders of thinly populated countries; they all possess, if we may credit them, some superhuman power. (33)

Regardless of the source, Celtic mysticism is used to connect the spiritual consciousness of indigene and arrivant in a variety of texts from different places and different periods, including Traill's *Canadian Crusoes* and McLean's *Lindigo, the White Woman,* and the contemporary novels, Bodsworth's *The Strange One,* and Hulme's *The Bone People*. All of these texts suggest that whites of an Irish or Scottish heritage have an unusual ability to comprehend indigene mysticism and thus are unusually apt candidates for indigenization.

Margaret Laurence's *The Diviners* is one of the most interesting explorations of the Celtic-indigene combination. As the heroine, Morag Gunn, searches for her own Scottish past, she must deal with the past and present of the Métis Jules, father of her child. At one point, Jules asks, "I'm the *shaman*, eh?" (273). His primary contribution is as incubus, with a very clear emphasis on his sexual power, but his mystical potency extends through other commodities as well, particularly orality and the prehistoric. Whether sexually or otherwise, Jules is the master to whom the white initiate comes.

This process might seem to be inevitable. The text seeking indigenization turns to the consciousness of Other as the spiritual power of the land. What better way to acquire that consciousness than through the contact between white searcher and indigenous sage? Eliade points to the universality of this process in a comment on an Inuit ritual: "Here, as in so many other cultures, he alone is a shaman who, through mystical vocation or voluntary quest, submits himself to the teaching of a master, successfully passes through the initiatory ordeals, and becomes capable of ecstatic experiences that are inaccessible to the rest of mankind" (297).

Many of these masters are old men and women. They provide an image of the elder as the embodiment of the wisdom of the tribe, a figure found throughout white depictions of "primitive" peoples, but also, as noted above in *Poor Fellow My Country*, connected to the prehistoric and the dead. Texts often emphasize that the white initiate depicted might have the last opportunity to acquire the indigene shaman's window on the noumenal sphere. In some cases, such as *The Chant of Jimmie Blacksmith*, the old man can elucidate certain elements of spirituality, but his power is insufficient to protect himself from the evils of white intrusions. In others, most notably *Poor Fellow My Country*, the elder chooses to avoid the white world by removing his corporal entity to the other plane. As a result, the essence of Other in the indigene becomes ethereal manifestation, an aura of indigenous presence rather than the indigene as material reality.

Most explorations of indigenous mysticism have two primary dimensions. The first is a sense of another state, an altered consciousness. This has its own validity as an attempt to perceive that which hides behind the veil, the inside of Other. Its second dimension is both a reflection of the first and an extension of it as the process of consciousness alteration becomes a means of indigenization. Mysticism becomes the means of embracing what Herbert refers to in the Australian context as "the all-pervading *Mahraghi* [magic] of this ancient land, *Terra Australis del Espiritu Santo*. POOR FELLOW MY COUNTRY" (1463).

These last lines of Herbert's novel, incorporating the four words which the text uses as a tolling chorus of Aboriginal orality, might seem a major change from the many earlier texts in which the emotional sign for indigenous mysticism is more likely fear than temptation. Sayce's *Comboman* presents Aboriginal mysticism as a power which works on the white hero to "deaden his mind" (106). The rejection is based not on the attractions of an alien theology, such as Christianity, but on the repulsion of the indigenous manifestations of belief. A variant on this theme treats mysticism as evil through denying the value of the mysticism both within and without the indigenous culture. This approach might be called the witch-doctor as charlatan, in which the shaman figure is not custodian of the souls of his people but thief of their material wellbeing. *Tecumseh* uses a bipolar structure with Tecumseh, a significantly assimilated military leader, opposed to his brother, the Prophet, who employs a corrupt metaphysics to deceive the naive Indians who follow him. *Nemarluk* (1941), by Ion L. Idriess, assesses the situation very directly: "Each tribe had its witchdoctor, the cunning man who lived by preying upon the fears of the warriors, but who stirred up trouble only for his own gain" (12). Even a text which makes a significant attempt to be sensitive to the indigenous culture, Bowering's *Burning Water*, devalues the possibilities of an indigenous visionary process, the holistic determinism described by Lévi-Strauss, in the opening debate between two Indians on possible mystical meanings in the arrival of the whites. The voice of material reality triumphs: "You must never believe that you have seen a god when you have seen a man on a large boat" (17).

Yet elsewhere, the text assumes a more ambivalent position in judging George Vancouver's inadequate assessment of the Indians he encounters. His Roman Catholic friend, Quadra, tells the Indian chief, Maquinna, that Vancouver's problem is part of the general English failure to grasp metaphysical possibilities:

"They are without gods, and therefore ignorant when it comes to con-versing with those into whose heads the gods still speak."

"This poor coastal chief finds it difficult to understand what is meant by a people without gods. Who is it, then, that instructs them during moments of great decision?"

"It is a phenomenon called human consciousness," said Quadra. "Their chief, Mr. Vancouver, has a great deal of it." (168).

This balancing act between the new science of individual reason and the old collective spirituality is representative of the tension in many such texts. An absolute denial of the indigenous metaphysics is not possible in the historical novel as it does not allow the existence of a goal for the quest in the text, an epistemologically alien conscious-ness which must be embraced. Yet Vancouver, the new man, finds it impossible to accomplish the embrace. His failure to achieve even

a relative degree of indigenization shows that "human consciousness" is not the consciousness of this place.

A very large number of examples, from the beginnings of the
literatures, find an agent of positive entry into indigenous metaphysics not through the Celtic savage nor through an explorer who,
unlike Vancouver, is able to unhuman his consciousness but through
a white character who coincidentally has an already given role in
indigenous mysticism. This is the "sky-god," the "white goddess,"
the white fulfillment of indigenous legend. The belief that a "primitive" people should perceive these glorious agents of civilization
as gods perhaps was inevitable. Bowering's very practical Indian
was by no means the first to question such Eurocentric hubris but
neither are his fellow tribesmen the last literary indigenes to accept
the divinity, which they do in spite of the malicious bungling of
most of the whites in the text. Although anthropologists have questioned the general applicability of the theory, it is a commonplace
in Australian culture that Aborigines believed the whites to be the
spirits of dead Aborigines. The "jump-up whitefellow" motif is found
in many Australian texts, from the early picaresque of Tucker's *Ralph
Rashleigh* (1845?) to the sophistication of *To the Islands*. When an
Aborigine in the latter jokingly notes that Heriot is "white like devil-
devil or ghost," the missionary reverberates in his own white metaphysics when he replies, "I am a ghost" (68). Many explorers
believed that the indigenes viewed them as in some sense miraculous
on first encounter, and Hearne and Thompson describe incidents in
which they found Indian belief in their superhuman powers to be
of great use.

An obvious example of the white god is Praed's Anne who fits
the necessities of the Aboriginal legend. Variants run from the minor
reference in *Queen Trucanini*, by Cato and Ellis, in which Robinson,
the Aboriginal Protector, believes Trucanini sees him as "something
between a father figure and a god" (67), to Acheson's *Plume of the
Arawas* (1930), in which the red-haired Maori hero proves to be a
descendant of the Vikings. In O'Hagan's *Tay John*, the Indian legend
of a messianic "yellow-haired" leader is the guiding force of the text.
Tay John is an ambivalent figure like many mixed-race characters.
He fits neatly into the semiotic field of the indigene, although his
whiteness identifies his value for the Indians, as reflected in the
resolutely caucasian sign of his hair. Jackie, the white storyteller,
tries to deny the adjective used before, the overtly messianic "halo,"
but comes up with something similar:

"No, it was more like a torch, that hair, it seemed to me – a flame, anyway,
to light the hopes of his people, whatever they may have been." (101)

The similarly mixed-race Haddon Torquane fulfulls much the same role in Bartram's *Darker Grows the Valley*. His remarkable attribute is one blue eye. Both novels suggest an interesting interaction of values, as a white rape/seduction of an indigenous female creates a figure with a clear sign of his white forbears, a sign which fits an indigenous legend calling for a messianic saviour. Perhaps not surprisingly, both Tay John and Haddon Torquane are dead by the ends of their novels, an apt comment on a theology which seeks salvation through imperialist rape.

There are a number of instances in which the white leader has no mystical qualities and yet plays a "white-god" role, as in O'Reilly's *Moondyne* or in O'Grady's *Goonoo Goonoo*, in which the hero becomes "chief": "'Durunmi Murringu' means literally 'King of the black people'" (111). The terminology in Domett's *Ranolf and Amohia* and Connor's *The Gaspards of Pine Croft* link the devoted slave tradition of the indigene maiden to the elevation of a male white deity. Amohia looks at Ranolf's versions of the caucasian signifiers, his blue eyes and blond hair, and judges him "some high Being from another World!" (2: 87). Connor's vision is less metaphysical when he says of Oucanasta's love for her white husband that she had "worshipped him as a god" (31). Patrick's *Inapatua* shows the Aboriginal woman succumbing to her sexual urges at the sight of the Swede stoking the furnace: "She offered her body to the Sun God" (163). In Duncan Campbell Scott's story, "Expiation" (*Witching* 1923), the Indian trapper's "knowledge of heavenly powers was but dim and fitful," but he sees the Scot trader as "the greatest of all earthly powers" (103). Perhaps all of the skygods are simply a reflection of political and economic reality, turned into a metaphysics by white literature.

They are also very clearly emblems of indigenization. How could a "god" with overwhelming powers of orality such as Praed's Anne not be a part of the land of the indigene, not be indigenized? And as such, regardless of her feelings about superstition, she also participates in the mysticism, the altered consciousness which provides the metaphysical power of indigenization. Thus when Carlyle Sinclair joins in the chicken dance in Mitchell's *The Vanishing Point*, he becomes of the land but also of a completely different realm of being, in which the despairingly linear methods of civilized order are left far behind. The narrator of *Beautiful Losers* says, "I want to be consumed by unreason" (58). For the white cultures, the standard commodity of mysticism provides a sign for just such a consumption.

In the introduction to *Shamanism*, Eliade rejects the possibility that shamanism is just a version of insanity: "But one point remains (and it is an important one), to which the psychologist will always be justified in drawing attention: like any other religious vocation, the

shamanic vocation is manifested by a crisis, a temporary derange-
ment of the future shaman's spiritual equilibrium" (xii). The attraction to "unreason" in Cohen's text does not lead to indigenous
mysticism simply because the process of shamanic initiation is associated with psychic crisis. Rather, psychic crisis is presented as a by-
product when the shaman figure accomplishes a synthesis of that
which seems to the overdetermined scientific culture to be an irre-
solvable separation. The pursuit of unreason is a means of overcoming the alienation which reason is perceived to have caused: "They
[shamans] show us, in actual process as it were, the repercussions,
within the psyche, of what we have called the 'dialectic of hiero-
phanies' – the radical separation between profane and sacred and
the resultant splitting of the world" (Eliade, xii). The shamanic experience in contemporary texts is a participation in a synthesis which
at once erases the limitations of reason and indigenizes, but there
is still no reason to define this synthesis as sane. Gilman notes a
number of ways in which blackness and madness have been associated (*Difference*, 144). This image of the Other as unreason can be
seen as an associated paradigm for this synthesis. In one possibility,
white as sane subject can treat mad indigene shaman as a dangerous
vision of chaos. In the other, white as sane subject can treat mad
indigene shaman as an inspiring vision of liberation. The sanity can
be extolled or attacked but it need not be questioned at either end
of the seesaw.

The ability of the white self to participate in a standard commodity
through the agency of the Other is often a mark of indigenization.
In general terms it would be inaccurate to assume that the separation
between self and Other is a Manichean dualism that inevitably valorizes self as good and Other as evil, but it is a dualism. In contemporary texts the overcoming of this dualism by acquiring the quality
of the indigene can represent the breach of still larger epistemological
barriers, such as that of Cohen's unreason. The pursuit of orality
within the written text is one suggestion of the erasing of boundaries
and of a glimpse of the dark, of the mystical. A more obviously
profound connection is provided by the inner sign, the supreme
signifier of Jungian unconscious and of unreason, the dream.

The white Australian concern for the Aboriginal dreamtime falls
into two categories. The image of dreamtime as Aboriginal past is
part of the commodity of the prehistoric but the term also reflects
the mystical synchronic presence of unreason. As in Eliade's comment about the shaman's association with the dead, it seems to break
a number of the boundaries of scientific determinism. The two elements of the word, "dream-time," overturn the basis of technological

ideology by exceeding material reality and the reality of chronology. The Aboriginal religion, the indigenous metaphysics, is thus profoundly Other than the rational, linear, chronological white realm. Broderick's *The Dreaming Dragons* uses various ramifications of these mystical elements in a science fiction narrative which shows the Aboriginal beliefs to have a much more accurate assessment of space and time travel than white technology.

"Primitive" people have been represented throughout western culture as dependent on dream visions and the beginnings of such an association are probably lost in the mists of Delphi or before. Eliade views the dream as an essential part of the shaman's participation in the prehistoric: "It is always in dreams that historical time is abolished and the mythical time regained – which allows the future shaman to witness the beginnings of the world and hence to become contemporary not only with the cosmogony but also with the primordial mythical revelations" (103). Fraser's *The Blood Lilies*, a stereotypical Canadian western romance, begins with "medicine-dreaming" (1). Kelly's *A Dream Like Mine* asserts in its title the process which the indigenizing narrator is pursuing as he enters the Ojibwa sweatlodge. The preface to Lighthall's *The Master of Life* states of "the Red Man":

> He was a mystic; yet he believed one thing firmly, – that the whole world of objects was living: nothing to him was inanimate: he himself was but part of a living world, and so were his dreams. (vi)

Once again the white text implies the estrangement and disintegration of its own ideology through its assertions about the pure holistic system of the indigene. And, like the mystical indigene in general, the dream is one more manifestation of the natural world.

There are a number of texts which search for a specifically psychological base to the dream process of the indigene. Father Bernard, in Child's *The Village of Souls*, says of dreams, "What are they often but those memories hidden too deep in our minds for ordinary recollection?" (247). Price presents a similar scenario in *God in the Sand: An Australian Mystical Romance*. His hero, Errol, seeks what he terms the "pulsing life": "The Australian Aborigine, being a primitive or stone-age man, whose instinctive memories reach back to the world's very beginnings, knows and feels it" (14–15). These Jungian-like references to racial memory exemplify the division between the desire to maintain a technological ideology and the attraction of the unreason and anti-chronology perceived in the indigenous dream. Errol is a physical explorer, but his central expedition is a psychic one. He quite literally dreams of ways "of making contact with the emanations from that other and unseen world" (13). Again the pattern seems to represent the incorporation of scientific determinism within the shamanic process as defined by Eliade in response to an Amerindian belief: "In this example the grant of shamanic powers occurs after a deliberate quest. Elsewhere in North America candidates withdraw to mountain caves or solitary places and seek, by intense concentration, to obtain the visions that can alone determine a shamanic career" (101).

By entering their own dreams and by embracing the dreams of the indigenes, the white characters can enter the metaphysical Other and become indigenized. In *Poor Fellow My Country*, Delacey's black ghost is a part of his vision of a future Australia that he expressly calls "my dreaming" (1081). Mudie presents the process still more boldly as he wakes from a night in "Byamee's dream country":

> Thus wearily must wander nightly,
> as those of old-time wandered sometimes,
> the Doowees, the dream-spirits,
> of we that were warriors
> but fell down into death's pit
> and jumped up white of flesh. ("Morning," *Corroboree*, 17)

Many Aborigines have questioned the hubris of the Jindyworobak group in their attempts to transmute bourgeois white experience through simple evocation of Aboriginal signifiers. This must represent one of the more blatant examples.

Yet there are a number of instances in which white dreaming is given a more hesitant quality. In these the process of indigenization is only tentative, perhaps more at the level of participant observer than Mudie's reincarnation. The Aboriginal Justin in *To the Islands* recalls the importance of a white dream in revealing a massacre: "Then a good while after, Father Walton dreamed a dream. In his dream he saw the figure of a native getting shot" (28). Father Walton seems more of a receiver than the aggressive incorporators of the Jindyworobaks. In *A Dream Like Mine*, however, such reception proves too strong for a white and turns into the narrator's nightmare.

Robert Kroetsch's *Gone Indian* provides one of the most telling comments on the white impetus to gain the land through becoming one with the mystical insights of the indigene. The "hero" of the novel, Jeremy Sadness, an American graduate student, is a product of dream after dream. As a child, Jeremy learned of Grey Owl, the Englishman Archie Belaney who became a Canadian conservationist and author and passed as an Indian: "He gave me his dream of the European boy who became ... pathfinder ... borderman ... the truest Indian of them all" (94). Jeremy comes to believe himself "the last Stone Age hunter at the end of the great Hunt, dreaming his final prey" (103). Jeremy's academic advisor, Professor Madham, accuses him of vision theft, he who "would dare to dream *my* north-west" (101). But Jeremy's dream, like Belaney's, is an active embrace of Indian life. The professor admits that his dream was a dry academic exercise, not a true guiding vision: "But I am a western boy who ever dreamed east" (95). All these dreams remain at the level of dream as delusion. Jeremy's vision is a noble one but the pain he undergoes in its pursuit is pathetic rather than tragic. He is "gone Indian," but he proves that it is impossible to truly dream, to reach the mystical Other, to become Indian. For, in spite of Mudie's claim, the journey is much too long.

It is presumably impossible to provide even an approximately accurate psychological interpretation of the white need for any of the standard commodities of the indigene. Kovel's obvious excesses show that it is a field of study with many traps for the unwary. But the commodity of mysticism, with its still more overt assertion of the alien consciousness apparent in orality, with its attempt by the white text to reverse the soul-making agenda of the missionaries, seems to beg for at least some partial psychocritical answers. Various possible approaches could be taken. For example, one could follow Lacan and proclaim the mystical to be an attempt to overcome the limitations of the symbolic perceived in the other commodities. The mystical indigene is a reassertion of the imaginary in a search for a transcendental signifier, beyond the mundane semiotics of violence or of an unmystified sexuality.

I would suggest a simpler explanation, less associated with the symbolic than with the symbiotic. The need for mysticism is a mystical need. Eliade refers to the value of the shaman as restorer of the soul: "Only the shaman can undertake a cure of this kind. For only he 'sees' the spirits and knows how to exorcise them; only he recognizes that the soul has fled, and is able to overtake it, in ecstasy, and return it to its body. Often the cure involves various sacrifices, and it is always the shaman who decides if they are needed and what form they shall take; the recovery of physical health is closely dependent on restoring the balance of spiritual forces, for it is often the case that the illness is due to a neglect or an omission in respect to the infernal powers, which also belong to the sphere of the sacred. Everything that concerns the soul and its adventure, here on earth and in the beyond, is the exclusive province of the shaman" (216).

Whether because lost in an age of unfulfilling scientific determinism or because in a state of desire for indigenization which no material reality can fulfil, the white culture, through these texts, attempts a restoration of the soul, that holistic concept of power which has no position in the levels of contemporary technology. The central white characters of the texts, and the texts themselves, seek to atone for these neglects and omissions, not neglect of the infernal but of the internal, whether the internal soul of the self or the internal essence of the land, directly manifested through the mystical commodity of the indigene. At the end of Atwood's *Surfacing*, the alienated self of the nameless narrator is at least tentatively restored by her grasp of the essence of the land which the remnants of Indian mysticism have shown her:

> These gods, here on the shore or in the water, unacknowledged or forgotten, were the only ones who had ever given me anything I needed; and freely. (145)

The indigene shaman possesses the mystical land and through either his/her aid or the general assistance of indigene mysticism the white shaman initiate can also know the land as a spiritual restoration of the soul-less white consciousness. Eliade describes the shaman's exploration of the sky and the underworld in the search for ways of healing the soul: "The danger of losing his way in these forbidden regions is still great; but sanctified by his initiation and furnished with his guardian spirits, the shaman is the only human being able to challenge the danger and venture into a mystical geography" (182). The indigenized white is sanctified by indigenous mysticism and is able to enter the formerly forbidden regions of the alien land. He or she becomes, as in the case of Atwood's narrator, more and less than human, almost Other than human. It becomes possible for the text to move through mystical geography and thus to graph the geo which was before the possession of only the mystical indigene.

Yet this process which uses the power of the mystical indigene to restore the white soul at the same time denies the protective nature of that power. Eliade claims of the shamans: "This small mystical elite not only directs the community's religious life but, as it were, guards its 'soul'"(8). As the soul of the individual white initiate is restored and, perhaps, even the collective soul of at least a certain aspect of the white society, there is a sense in which the collective soul of the indigene is in decline. Regardless of questions such as that raised by Fanon about the validity of indigene mysticism within the indigenous cultures, indigene mysticism in the white text is devalued as it is emphasized. Throughout these literatures, the image of the indigene as guardian spirit proves unable to guard the spirit of the indigenous peoples from the acquisitory powers of the indigenizing text. Or, to put it in the terms of a blunt analogy, if the rabbit's foot were lucky it would still be on the rabbit.

CHAPTER EIGHT

Historicity

Each of the standard commodities might be seen in light of the others but none perhaps so productively as the prehistoric. For the semiotic field of the indigene is constantly both historical and ahistorical. It is historical because it always holds within it a sense of the indigene as an historical value, as a part of the development of the country. All indigene images contain at least a residue of a pre-white past. In this sense the Aborigine is to a modern white Australian what a castle is to a modern Briton. Lévi-Strauss asserts, "The virtue of archives is to put us in contact with pure historicity" (*Savage*, 242). This is no less true for any aspect of material culture which is clearly associated with a historical period. Similarly, the reified indigene is seen to put us in contact with pure prehistoricity.

At the same time – a phrase all too telling in this context – the indigene is ahistorical because the field is usually removed from historical necessity. The generally synchronic approach of the "present" study is open to many arguments from those more diachronically inclined. As Lévi-Strauss says of historians: "In their eyes some special prestige seems to attach to the temporal dimension, as if diachrony were to establish a kind of intelligibility not merely superior to that provided by synchrony, but above all more specifically human" (*Savage*, 256). But even historians should admit that the severely limited semiotic field of the indigene in literature has allowed diachrony little power – perhaps because it allows so few instances of the specifically human.

Such signs as the treacherous redskin and the Indian maiden have endured from the beginning of the literatures to the present. The temptress of the land in Richardson's *Wacousta* (1832) represents the same commodity as her sister in Moore's *Black Robe* (1985). In an examination of the image of the indigene, it is useful to deny diachrony primacy in order to demonstrate that the image itself is synchronic. Historical change is not the cause and the image the effect. Rather, the image provides the source, and historicity as commodity is one part of the product. The reversal of the usual system of causality associated with history is appropriate given the stasis of the "prehistoric" indigene. The unchanging indigene of literature reflects the unchanging indigene in literature.

Both *Wacousta* and *Black Robe* might be called historical romances. As such, they place the image of the indigene in a specifically historical context but the implications of the image are often more noteworthy outside that context. Overt statements about the indigene in history encounter the valorization of the image within the fiction. Dark's *The Timeless Land* is perhaps the best-known example of the historical romance as epic history, a genre which the Australians have made their own. *Wacousta* and *Black Robe* concentrate on specific periods and places but *The Timeless Land* fulfils its title as it, like many other Australian works, sweeps through time. It begins with the Aborigines just before contact with whites and continues through the development of white society. The third novel in Dark's trilogy, *No Barrier* ends with Billalong, his mixed blood emphasized, lamenting a future which seems to hold no hope of a continuing Aboriginal society. Prichard's goldfields trilogy opens with Kalgoorla as a vibrant young woman but it ends in *Winged Seeds* with little suggestion that another young Aboriginal woman might take her place: "Who could measure the grief and despair which had overwhelmed this primitive woman with the breakdown of her tribal way of life and the extinction of her people?" (377). In the final symbol of the novel, the kalgoorluh plant cracks open and releases its seeds but this assertion of hope seems to be for the future of the land which the Aboriginal woman expresses rather than for her Aboriginal descendants. As in so many such fictional histories, the sincerity of the guilt felt for the mistreatment of the Aborigine in the past does not allow the Aborigine to be other than of the past. The Aborigines are a base for Australian culture, not a part of its developing fabric.

The apparently unintentional irony of such a view of history is neatly depicted in the title of Rex Ingamells's *Of Us Now Living: A Novel of Australia* (1952). It begins with an emphasis on the validity of pre-white Aboriginal culture, a sentiment one would expect from the leader of the Jindyworobaks, but then the Aboriginal characters gradually disappear from the narrative, leaving the implication that they are not "of us now living." These works provide the logical conclusion of the narratives in McCrae's *The Story of Balla-deadro* or

Lighthall's *The Master of Life*, both of which depict indigenous life before significant contact with whites. Regardless of the authors' obvious intent to provide a positive image of the indigene, and in many cases even to lament the process of the white invasion, the semiosis presents the indigene as a sign for past.

The circumscriptions of the semiotic field seem to create a conflict in the historical novel between the synchronic tendencies of the fictional image and the narrative's ostensibly diachronic subject. It is not too extreme to suggest that the situation resembles that identified by Berger in his comment on the use of historical references in advertising: "The fact that they are imprecise and ultimately meaningless is an advantage: they should not be understandable, they should merely be reminiscent of cultural lessons half-learnt. Publicity makes all history mythical, but to do so effectively it needs a visual language with historical dimensions" (140). Each literary image of the indigene contains a residue of such cultural lessons half-learnt, the semiotic field of the indigene which lingers, in the white consciousness. This image is mythical in all the usual senses. It is mythical because it is false. It is mythical because it carries with it intimations of a standing truth from before history. It is mythical because of its implied theology; it carries within it the religious "truth" of self and Other. And it is mythical because it is a defining point of culture, a point on which pivots the essentialist question of indigenization.

Obviously, these images are far from meaningless, as are the remnants of history which Berger is examining. But Berger's point is that they are "meaningless" in the sense that their implied meaning of "historical truth" is not only false but quite alien to the effect of the signifier on the perceiver. Their meanings are instead defined by their function as commodities and by what they thus reveal about the semiotic economy in which they are at play. Similarly the implied history of the indigene has meaning in its validation of the various indigene standard commodities.

The overall statements of the different historical romances noted above do little to support their implied liberal ideologies. Such statements instead link them to the position of John Dunmore Lang's "Australian Hymn" (*Aurora Australis*, 1826):

> God of our Isle! a happier race
>   Far o'er the wave thine hand has brought,
> And planted in the Heathen's place
>   To serve thee in the Heathen's lot. (19)

Lang's vision resembles Frantz Fanon's interpretation of the settler's view in Algeria: "the native, bent double, more dead than alive, exists interminably in an unchanging dream. The settler makes history; his life is an epoch, an Odyssey. He is the absolute beginning: 'This land was created by us'; he is the unceasing cause: 'If we leave, all is lost, and the country will go back to the Middle Ages'" (*Wretched*, 51). It is all too easy to reject Fanon's applicability. The many works examined in this study show that the white Australian, Canadian, and New Zealander are all very aware of an indigenous people that came before. The white authors know that they cannot create the land because it predates them in a quite distressing way. But there is still that sense of white history vs. indigenous prehistory.

"Prehistory" might be seen as another "anachronistic deviant," as Ong terms "preliterate." If further examined etymologically, the word "prehistory," "before history," implies a story before story, presumably an impossibility. The distinction becomes useful only when story is the written story. In this perception, history is written documentation and is validated by its written form. Thus the prehistoric indigene is one with the indigene of primary orality, the indigene before writing. The indigene is before history in the sense of being before "the cause" in Fanon's phrase. Before the white is before the Middle Ages, because before historical time. Thus the "siting" of the indigene as absence of history is similar to the view of the indigene as illiterate. The equivalent to the oralist text presents prehistory as pure. Prehistory is before the cause as it precedes the white destruction of nature. Yet like the oralist position, the site of prehistorical purity combines "positive" assertions about the indigene with a limitation all too similar to that in the "negative" vision of illiteracy and prehistoric inadequacy. Both require that the indigene be before the Middle Ages, be not part of now. What the primitivist desires and the progressivist rejects is the same, the "time" of primary orality, something very like an "unchanging dream."

There is a sense of this dream in each of the recountings of indigenous legends in white texts. As in the reference to Berger above, the mythological is seen as inherently beyond time, an artifact of the prehistoric. And in the Australian, Canadian, and New Zealand contexts, the mythological is inherently oral. The old Indian woman in Dagg's "The Museum of Man" protests,

"I do not think you understand that when the legends and myths we speak, telling them through the night, through the years, telling them differently each time, are printed in your children's books, they change, they die." (*Same Truck*, 32)

This combination of orality and the paradox of a mutable permanence leads to a claim for the native narrative as primal. Roland Robinson introduces *Aboriginal Myths and Legends* (1966) with his rhetorical question, "Where does imagination start but from primeval images still known in Man's barbaric heart?" (ix). As in so many aspects of the indigene semiosis, primary orality becomes primal orality and blurs diachronic distinctions. So in Fry's *Come a Long Journey* the Indian storyteller produces the effect of mythology with a story from his own experience, to draw the following reaction from the white narrator: "Once again, beyond all my expectations, I had been taken into the river valleys of the past, on a long journey into the yesterdays of Dave's life" (208).

Johannes Fabian suggests in *Time and the Other: How Anthropology Makes Its Object* (1983) that the subtext of time manipulations, such as are at work in Dark and Ingamells, is a more subtle version of imperialist philosophy so obvious in Lang: "In short, *geopolitics* has its ideological foundations in *chronopolitics*" (144). Yet one might consider Ingamells's "of *us now* living" from a different perspective. The illiterate indigene sometimes represents only a deficiency in the acquisition of scientific skills rather than the epistemological barrier of orality. This deficiency then is not absolute but only a relative inadequacy, subject to change. The indigene is perhaps less different in kind than in time and is, in this relative sense, of "us" as we were then. One of the more sensitive whites in Hatfield's *Desert Saga* says to an Aborigine:

Your people are living now as mine lived many years ago, ages ago – and the tribal songs and customs of your people must be like those of mine in a similar age, and studying them may help us to understand our own beginnings. (163)

The Aboriginal present is here valorized as the white past. It becomes, like Robinson's legends, the start of white imagination.

Often the connection is more indirect, as in Cohen's *Beautiful Losers*, in which the Indians are likened to ancient Greeks (11), a comparison used in Dickson's *Honi Heki* for the Maori (10). Hume Nisbet's *Rebel Chief* (1896) presents the Maori as Greeks (12), Spartans, Egyptians, or Assyrians (19) and ancient Britons (91). The latter makes the most direct connection to whites of British descent, which is the predominant character of New Zealand, Australia, and Canada. Thus all three literatures are drawn to this analogy. Herbert's *Poor Fellow My Country* compares the Aborigines to "Ancient Druids" (24), as B.A. McKelvie's *Huldowget* (1926) does the Indians of Canada's west coast (196). The latter perhaps is not surprising in light of a contribution to *The Literary Garland*. G.J. suggests in "St. Lawrence" (1840) that the Indians "held wassail here!" (532). *Black Robe* encapsulates the various aspects of this process in the perception of one of the Jesuits: "The Algonkian leader's face made him think of the stone image of a dead Saxon king he had seen carved on a tomb in Bayeux" (93). The Indian is precursor, dead figure of a dead people, permanent unchanging stone. Just as modern Britain had inevitably superseded the Druids' wassail, so the indigene would, as Lang suggests, inevitably be replaced, whether because ordained by God or just in response to some uncontrollable cycle. *Time and the Other* lays at the door of anthropology a challenge which could be used to confront any discourse on "primitive" peoples: "Anthropology contributed above all to the intellectual justification of the colonial enterprise. It gave to politics and economics – both concerned with human Time – a firm belief in 'natural', i.e., evolutionary Time. It promoted a scheme in terms of which not only past cultures, but all living societies were irrevocably placed on a temporal slope, a stream of Time – some upstream, other downstream" (Fabian 17).

The power of chronopolitics permeates all three literatures. The Australian squatter novel typically has a discussion between someone of liberal sympathies and someone who maintains that white settlement necessitates the eradication of the indigene. Rolf Boldrewood, the ultimate squatter novelist, presents this case in an essay in *Old Melbourne Memories* (1884) in which he describes the end of the Tasmanian Aborigines:

> They pined away slowly, and but a few years since the last female of the race died. The prosaic, joyless prosperity told on health and spirits. It was wholly alien to the constitution of the wild hunters and warriors who had been wont to traverse pathless woods, to fish in the depths of sunless forest streams, to chase the game of their native land through the lone untrampled mead, or the hoar primeval forests which lay around the snow-crested mountain range. (98)

The people of "wont," "mead," and "primeval" are of the past. The people of "wild," "pathless," and "untrampled" would not be of the future.

The inevitability of the demise of indigenous peoples so permeates nineteenth-century images of indigenes that it is difficult to find examples which do not reflect the theory. At their most extreme they follow the lines of Kearney's *The Open Hand* which refers to "Our mighty Anglo-Saxon race,/The chosen of his hand" (35), or of Dora Wilcox's "At Onawe" (1900) which simply deems the Maori "a nation/Doomed, doomed to pass" (138). The assessment in Meredith's *A Tasmanian Memory of 1834* is more complex but more resolute:

> And of the tribes, with whose brute thirst
> For blood those early days were curs'd,
>   But three poor crones live on.
> The Saxon foot, with onward step,
>   Another race treads out
> Which scarce a vestige leaves to tell
> It ever was – or to dispell
>   The Future's curious doubt. (22–3)

The Tasmanian situation provides a very interesting commentary on the end of the indigenous race. It has become a part of Australian mythology that the genocidal attempts of the nineteenth century in Tasmania succeeded. Lyndall Ryan's recent historical study, *The Aboriginal Tasmanians* (1981), however, has pointed out what many anthropologists long before asserted, in less prominent forums, that the mixed-race descendants of Tasmanian Aborigines and sealers, who continue to live on islands off Tasmania, have every right to be considered Tasmanian Aborigines. There remains a tendency in Australian society, however, to deny them this right.

It is a perverse coincidence of imperialist history that a similar situation exists in Canada. Newfoundland is, like Tasmania, an island state/province with a much longer white history than the federation of which it is now a part, but it has similarly fallen on economic hard times and become the target of jokes from "the mainland." And it also was the home of a now extinct people, the Beothuks. Unlike the Tasmanian Aborigines, the Beothuks are truly gone. But again unlike the Tasmanians, according to Frederick W. Rowe's *Extinction: The Beothuks of Newfoundland* (1977) and a number of other studies, the Beothuks' passing was only partly a product of active white opposition and much more a reflection of the way white settlement interfered with the delicate ecology of an inhospitable environment. This of course does not deny that the results of a less overtly belligerent invasion were more successful than the openly genocidal actions in Tasmania. Wolf refers to the plagues brought to the Americas as "the great dying." He attacks suggestions that these diseases were somehow independent of the invaders who brought them: "The advent of pathogens, however, does not in itself furnish an adequate explanation of what happened. One must ask also about the social and political conditions that permitted the pathogens to proliferate at so rapid a rate" (133). Yet my concern here is not with historical cause but with the signs which that history has left. And the sign which resounds through the Beothuk and Tasmanian Aborigine is death.

The attraction of these dead races has many parts. At one level, they provide a way of avoiding the question of "indigene as social problem." Most images of the prehistoric indigene are constantly met by the fact that the indigene is a contemporary reality for Australia, Canada, and New Zealand. Each indigene speaking on the television for land rights represents a claim that indigenous peoples are more present politics than prehistoric artifact. It is a much simpler job to package the past indigene if there is no present. Another appeal of the Newfoundland-Tasmania package is the sense of both completion and cosmic moment. There seems to be an inevitable attraction in teleology, in providing an ending to the story. The ethnography of an extinct people is assuredly complete. The unchanging semiotic field of the indigene is no longer a problem because the dead cannot be expected to change. As well as being complete, moreover, the Beothuk and Tasmanian Aborigine provide moments of completion which can, in certain texts, become glimpses of the apocalypse. Fanon said of the contemporary Algerians: "The natives are convinced that their fate is in the balance, here and now. They live in the atmosphere of doomsday, and they consider that nothing ought to pass unnoticed" (*Wretched*, 81). The fictional accounts of these indigenes key on this point of doomsday. The prehistoric meets the beginning of history, as the white cause commences.

The rejection of the possibility of live Tasmanian indigenes would be less surprising if it were the sentiment of only overtly anti-Aboriginal factions. That it is not suggests the importance of the sign of the dead Tasmanian, particularly as depicted in Truganini, "last of the Tasmanians." As a symbol of both white guilt and of the Aborigine as figure of the past, not present, she has incredible power. She resonates as the individual sign of doomsday. In Hibberd's "Captain Midnight V.C.," a play with a virulent desire to wallow in white evil, the black activist will call his new homeland "Trugininiland." Reeds's dramatic trilogy *Truganinni* shows a similar need. Even while alive, Truganinni asserts her role as antecedant as she sings the lines of her dead mother; the third play, "King

Billy's Bones," splits its focus between the remains of the "last" male Aborigine and the death of Truganinni. The Popular Theatre Troupe's "White Man's Mission" (1975) seems well aware of the power of the Tasmanian names as signifiers:

> See King Billy dropping,
> See Truganini fall,
> Everyone for Jesus,
> He shall have them all! (15)

There is little to distinguish between these images and those associated with the Beothuks. Like the "A—s" of *Beautiful Losers*, their name has become a synonym for corpse, and a prime focus for liberal guilt. The last Beothuk was a woman, Shawnandithit, whose name has a similar poetic balance to that of Truganini, and like Truganini she has been a topic for many twentieth century writers. In Michael Cook's play, "On the Rim of the Curve" (1977), she embraces the end of her long suffering at the hands of the whites and calls for "the blessing of death" (49). The Newfoundland poet Al Pittman depicts her as having

> The eyes of a martyr,
> of one who waits patiently for death
> knowing that beyond all kindred deaths
> yours will matter most. ("Shanadithit," 44)

The poem ends,

> Lie easy in your uneasy peace girl
> and do not, do not, forgive those
> who trespass against you. (46)

It must be noted here that this death, like the death of Truganini in most of the texts above and the deaths of several other fictional indigenes, is intended as a statement of guilt and an expression of hope for changes that the guilt might produce in the future. Fanon states of the revolutionary's acceptance of death: "he considers himself as a potential corpse" (*Wretched*, 23). There is a sense here that while Shawnandithit's act of death was not revolutionary, the effect might be, as the symbol of the death undergoes a political transformation. There is also a sense of death as positive escape, as in Sid Stephen's Shawnandithit poem "She Says Goodbye to Mr. Cormack" (*Beothuck*, np). The transformation may not be from a "vale of tears" to a "far better world" in a simplistically Christian sense but there is something here akin to Foucault's view of the tradition of death: "In the passage from this world to the other, death was the manner in which a terrestial sovereignty was relieved by another, singularly more powerful sovereignty: the pageantry that surrounded it was in the category of political ceremony. Now it is over life, throughout its unfolding, that power establishes its domain; death is power's limit, the moment that escapes it; death becomes the most secret aspect of existence, the most 'private'" (*Sexuality*, 138). Death as pageant becomes a political attack on past white iniquity. Death as secret becomes, particularly in poetry, an attempt to award the martyr with a private peace.

The feelings which Truganini and Shawnandithit evoke in their respective countries, and even more particularly on their respective islands, cannot be overestimated. At the premiere of a film which tries to represent Pittman's relationship with Shawnandithit and with the land, there were a number of comments by historians and anthropologists about the inaccuracy of theories of active genocide. The reaction of the audience, however, made it clear that they wished to maintain their guilt; they did not want to be absolved or forgiven.

One of the central attractions for any creative writer who decides to write on historical material is a type of revisionism. Each such author usually presents a claim to historical accuracy, but very often it is the "truth which has not been told" or perhaps even "the felt truth which must replace the claims of documented evidence." The iniquitous encounters with indigenous peoples on which these white cultures are based present a prime subject for revision. The powers of the semiotic field are such, however, that while expressions of guilt are often loud and long, the image of the indigene remains unchanged. In the context of Tasmania and Newfoundland this means prehistoric and dead.

In Newfoundland this death enables assertions of white presence which exceed those usually made in Canada. There is a constant concern in Newfoundland with who is a "native Newfoundlander." This means in its essence that the individual was not only born in the province but is a product of generations of residents. The extinction of the Beothuks leaves no "native" contradiction. Recent attempts by Micmacs in Newfoundland to assert aboriginal tenure have been strongly opposed. The argument might be interpreted as "We had natives. We killed them off. Now we are natives." In a paradoxical equation, the claims of guilt allow a belief in the white as "indigenous" which has not been possible for other Canadians since the nineteenth century. At a recent academic conference elsewhere in Canada, a white speaking on a Native American topic was introduced as "a native of Ottawa." He said he was not "a native of Ottawa," but was "only born there."

The Beothuk and Tasmanian Aborigine become a superior means of indigenization through their absence. They are an indigenous past without a present, the indigene as corpse. They have an historical role but there is a sense that even in their earliest appearances in white documentation they are already remnants. They are Wolf's "people without history" but even more "people before history." The central character in Helen Hodgman's *Blue Skies* (1976) seeks to exorcise her suburban housewife angst by visiting the Hobart museum:

> Stuffed native creatures froze warily behind glass windows; a moth-eaten Tasmanian tiger had pride of place, snarling dismally into eternity. On display in a corner was an Aboriginal group – the extinct people – models, not stuffed, an attractive reconstruction, as accurate as could be made, of a family group. They stood in line on a replica beach. (92)

The reification of the Aborigines becomes complete as they become less and less "real." How appropriate that the indigenes should become "models," objects in a case, with no possibility of becoming subjects, although still, of course, "attractive," as they prove so often to white culture. There is no reason to question why the white subjectivity is the only subjectivity. And yet that subjectivity is, at this point in the novel, itself lifeless. Her dead feelings meet dead, packaged nature, which includes the dead indigene. The text rejects the forces which killed nature but this does not deny the death. In O'Grady's *Goonoo Goonoo*, an Aborigine philosophically remarks on the demise of his people:

> That was a fine song and this has been a great corroboree, the last which the Moonbi people will dance. For the sun is setting on the Moonbi people and on all of the tribes of Murri – but what does it matter? The sun does not sleep for ever, but sets only to jump up again, and it will rise to-morrow to shine on the Wundangu. It will shine upon the tribes of the white people. (270)

Regardless of white expressions of guilt, such as Pittman's rejection of forgiveness, the semiosis remains in which the indigene embraces martyrdom and becomes death, to become ever-present symbol but never present people, the perfect evocation of Cohen's title, *Beautiful Losers*. As George Bowering suggests in "Indian Summer" (1968), "The Indians I think/are dead" (75). Or perhaps rather dying as in the "lament for his tribe." Robert Herbert's "Trucanini's Dirge" (1882) uses the Tasmanian figure in a typical example. D.D.D.'s "The Last of the Indians" in *The Literary Garland* (1846) is quite similar with an emphasis on the *ubi sunt* motif. As a number of critics of Old English poetry have noted, the *ubi sunt* has an inherent assumption that the essence of the culture and the community are in the past, a perfect, legendary past, beyond the touch of the present, like the Maori maidens in Domett's *Ranolf and Amohia*: "Like nymphs that frolic reeled in Bacchic dance/In Nature's golden-aged exuberance" (2: 246).

At one point in *Orality and Literacy*, Ong examines the sense of history in the consciousness of primary orality: "Persons whose world view has been formed by high literacy need to remind themselves that in functionally oral culture the past is not felt as an itemized terrain, peppered with verifiable and disputed 'facts' or bits of information. It is the domain of the ancestors, a resonant source for renewing awareness of present existence, which itself is not an itemized terrain either" (98). In the *ubi sunt* texts, however, the present is clearly ephemeral. That unitemized terrain of the ancestors' domain is the voice of a culture which soon will be only ancestral.

Ong thus suggests that the elevation of the prehistoric and this praise for past dead are an inevitable part of the indigenous culture. Lévi-Strauss's comments on mythology support this view and reveal another aspect of the attraction which indigenous myths and legends have for white authors: "Mythical history thus presents the paradox of being both disjoined from and conjoined with the present. It is disjoined from it because the original ancestors were of a nature different from contemporary men: they were creators and these are imitators. It is conjoined with it because nothing has been going on since the appearance of the ancestors except events whose recurrence periodically effaces their particularity" (*Savage*, 236). Many accounts of the histories of "primitive" peoples show the error in this bipolar structure and in the complete dismissal of any importance which such peoples might find in their immediate past, but Lévi-Strauss's comment remains a useful assessment of the point of view which underlies the *ubi sunt* lament. According to Lévi-Strauss the indigenous culture itself defines the present indigene as trapped within a prehistoric consciousness of which that same indigene is at best a diminished remnant. Present is only past and an inferior version at that.

The "last of his tribe" lament can appear in many forms, as suggested by the passage quoted from *Goonoo, Goonoo* above. Mair's

"The Last Bison" (*Dreamland*, 148–53) continues the genre in a transformation of the speaker from Indian to buffalo, which suits the
indigene's role in the standard commodity of nature. It also conforms
to the tendency to see nature as synchronic. The indigenes are natural and so timeless, one with Dark's *Timeless Land*. In Stow's *To the
Islands*, one of the white characters "saw himself for the first time
as a stranger, cast without preparation into a landscape of prehistory,
foreign to the earth. Only the brown man belonged in this wild and
towering world" (58). In many works, the death of the indigene is
linked to the death of the land, most profoundly in Drew's *The
Wabeno Feast*, a paean to ecological despair.

The number of indigenes which represent the dying gasps of their
culture seems almost limitless. The songs of Jules Tonnerre are
laments for his tribe in Laurence's *The Diviners*, as are those of his
father, Lazarus. Of course, the Métis people still exist, but the
semiosis of the text is remarkably similar to poems which address
actual extinction, from the *ubi sunt* passages to the deaths of Jules
and of most of the primary Métis figures to the ironic signifier of
Lazarus's name. In Mason's *The Pohutukawa Tree*, Aroha is the figure
of the lingering past, with her ceremonial spear and her constant
rehearsals of the glories of Maori of an earlier age, until at the end
she declares, "I will die true to my past" (103).

The death of the individual indigene is equivalent to the death of
the race. This might seem an extravagant statement. Most of these
deaths present not the execution of the treacherous redskin but the
lamentable demise, in some cases the direct or indirect murder, of
a positive character: in Laurence, a "shaman," in Herbert's *Capricornia*, Tocky, a child of nature, and her own child. But the death
of the people usually receives exactly the same treatment: deaths of
both individual and group are ubiquitous in depictions of the indigene. The obvious references in the titles of Grace's collection of
Maori stories, *Tales of a Dying Race*, or James Devaney's Aboriginal
legends, *The Vanished Tribes* (1929), here labelled as artifacts of the
prehistoric, are matched by novels like Fry's *How a People Die*, and
Rose's *Country of the Dead*. Novel after novel, play after play, depict
the indigene as corpse or becoming corpse. In Laurence, Jules is but
a passing stage in the heroine's development, like the Indian base
for white Canadian culture. Dan in Musgrave's *The Charcoal Burners*
serves much the same role, but his death at the hands of unnatural
white forces is a precursor of the heroine's murder, both examples
of Cohen's "beautiful losers." These individual deaths have the same
feeling of inevitability about them as the deaths of the tribes or of
the races. When she is driven from her white love and from her

homeland, Prichard's Coonardoo must die. As people of the past there is no possibility of life in the present: an Aborigine suggests Stuart's *Yandy*: "For how could a man let go his dreaming, and still live?" (106).

The indigenes are more than people of the past, they are of a realm before past, before the extent of white knowledge. In some cases this prehistory seems to extend to Eden as in Kidd's *The Huron Chief*:

And I have often thought this spot to be
A type of that pure sanctu'ry,
Where, first repenting, man had trod,
When by some holy angel guided,
To talk in prayer alone with God – (53)

Roland Robinson perceives this resonance of a biblical golden age as a prime cause of the fascination with Aboriginal mythology: "We still carry within us subconscious desires for the lost Garden of Eden, or the Hesperides" (*Aboriginal Myths*, ix). The various "lost tribe" narratives, with their references to superior races of indigenes at the centre of Australia, trace similar patterns. G. Firth Scott's *The Last Lemurian* (1898) uses one of the secular Edens of western culture, Lemuria, while Meredith's "The Lost Tribe of Boonjie" turns to a better known dream paradise, Atlantis.

But of course the "dream" has many more dimensions in Australia. The term, "dreaming," allows a simultaneous incorporation of the indigene as mystical and the indigene as of another time. Ion Idriess's *The Red Chief As Told By the Last of His Tribe* (1953) makes a very similar observation to that of William Hatfield about the Aborigine as white past, which Idriess refers to as "the Dream Time of all of us" (29). The concept of the dreaming is primarily valorized in the standard commodity of mysticism but its "timeless" character is important, as a fulfilment of that desire for the "unchanging dream." In *Reading the Country*, Muecke attempts to deal with this assessment: "As long as Aboriginal cultures have the role of representing timelessness then the story of their more recent history will tend to be put to one side, or that too will be brought forward as more evidence of the continual struggle of an eternally oppressed people, always the same as they were from the beginning" (Benterrak, 127). Muecke would rather see the concept of "dreaming" as a part of orality: "There is no basis for seeing the dreaming as a mythological past (as in 'dreamtime') while it is alive as a *way of talking*" (14). Since the concept of orality is, however, closely related to the image of the indigene as prehistoric, Muecke's distinction is unlikely to make a significant change in the semiotic field at play.

Any standard commodity within the indigene's semiotic field can be linked to the prehistoric. Netta's sensuality in Hilliard's *Maori Woman* seems to come from "the origins of time" (208). In another example of dreaming as a part of both the prehistoric and mysticism, Broderick's *The Dreaming Dragons* presents the Aboriginal belief in the rainbow serpent as based on a lingering presence of dinosaurs in Australia, a prehistoric animal for a prehistoric people. Similarly, the archaeologists in Kroetsch's *Badlands* find the Indian girl Anna Yellowbird among the dinosaur bones: "her cabin of bones, her fossil tipi" (144). She might be linked to the title character in *Queen Trucanini* by Cato and Ellis and William Lanney in Drewe's *The Savage Crows*, each of whom is said to have been treated as a "living fossil" (2,13).

That oxymoron seems a good encapsulation of the indigene as past in present. But there is another aspect of the commodity more extreme than this and more extreme even than the indigene of Eden, of the golden age. This is the indigene outside of time. I noted at the beginning of this chapter how the indigene often seems ahistorical, beyond the necessities of historical change. Richard Howitt, in "First Approach of Civilisation to Australia Felix" (*Australia*, 1845), sums up this impression:

> Not uninhabited – not desolate –
> Age after age the same; from age to age,
> Tracked only by its native dusky tribes,
> In arts, in arms, in manners, and in mind,
> The same. (109)

Once again the timeless people of the timeless land. Howard O'Hagan in *Wilderness Men* (1958) claims that "For the North American Indian tomorrow was but promise of another yesterday" (9). Al Purdy in "Inuit" (1967) seems to neglect the fact that the large soapstone carvings now known as "Eskimo Art" are a quite recent innovation:

> these unknowable human beings
> who have endured 5,000 years
> on the edge of the world
> a myth from long ago
> that reaches into the past
> but touches an old man still living. (*North*, 33)

The indigene semiosis leaves the individual carver as personification of collective timelessness:

an old man carving soapstone
with the race-soul of The People
THE PEOPLE
Moving somewhere
behind his eyes. (33)

One white character in Hilliard's *The Glory and the Dream* attacks the absence of time in the Maori dance:

> To him it was all totally static, lacking a dynamic of its own to reflect change: frozen in history, inert, a museum piece; an effort to make the past live again by reproducing its expressions intact and unaltered and guarding them with what fierce loyalty, what intensity of devotion. (171)

The text seems to reject this attitude: the character's perceptions are shown to be, if not racist, limited and superficial. Yet this is an accurate representation of the ahistorical indigene throughout Australian, New Zealand, and Canadian literatures – and in Hilliard's novel as well.

And in the documentation of a variety of indigenous peoples throughout the world. Mannoni presents the synchronic mind of the Malagasy as in many ways an asset: "The source of paternal power is, for him, lost in the night of time, without, however, diminishing in strength in the process: rather the contrary" (59). Lévi-Strauss claims that the ability of "the people we call primitive" to overcome temporal barriers is their power: "native institutions, though borne along on the flux of time, manage to steer a course between the contingencies of history and the immutability of design and remain, as it were, within the stream of intelligibility. They are always at a safe distance from the Scylla and Charybdis of diachrony and synchrony" (*Savage*, 73). This assessment of a practical equilibrium might be compared to a similar one by Ong: "By contrast with literate societies, oral societies can be characterized as homeostatic. That is to say, oral societies live very much in a present which keeps itself in equilibrium or homeostasis by sloughing off memories which no longer have present relevance" (46).

Diachrony in white terms, as something other than just the dreaming, the domain of the ancestors, seldom appears in the literature, even in the limited sense posited by Lévi-Strauss. In one of the few instances in which an indigene diachrony is considered, in an

Aboriginal initiation song in Keneally's *The Chant of Jimmie Blacksmith*, it is a vague process: "The woman-stealing it recounted had taken place during the English civil war, two and a half centuries previously" (4). The reader is left with the simple reflection of how much *change* has taken place in European history in that time and how little in Aboriginal, except, of course, the change created/inflicted by the incorporation of the Aborigine into the white diachrony. Just perhaps the indigene is not timeless, but the indigene continues to be less of time, with at best a crude historicity, vague moments with large gaps unlike the minutiae of white documentation. Fabian suggests that "anthropology's efforts to construct relations with its Other by means of temporal devices implied affirmation of difference and *distance*" (16). He goes on to assert that the primary effect of such devices has been the *"denial of coevalness. By that I mean a persistent and systematic tendency to place the referent(s) of anthropology in a Time other than the present of the producer of anthropological discourse"* (31).

It would be easy to assert that the creative text does not make ethnographic claims for an accurate account of a contemporary culture. Often, as in the case of *Jimmie Blacksmith* and many other of the works noted above, the action of the text is overtly set in the past. The analytical accounts of Ong and Lévi-Strauss support a view of indigene semi-time as perhaps superior or at least equal to white time. Yet when Lévi-Strauss attempts to overcome the various assumptions of the prehistoric, he replaces it with an all-too-similar distinction: "the clumsy distinction between 'peoples without history' and others could with advantage be replaced by a distinction between what for convenience I called 'cold' and 'hot' societies: the former seeking, by the institutions they give themselves, to annul the possible effects of historical factors on their equilibrium and continuity in a quasi-automatic fashion; the latter resolutely internalizing the historical process and making it the moving power of their development" (*Savage*, 233–4). The normative "others" are those who "develop." The "cold" Others are a "quasi-automatic" "annul"-ment. The absolutist distancing of the Other from the culture in which the anthropological text is produced has the same effect as the "people without history" label. In a later volume, Lévi-Strauss makes some attempt to overcome this bipolar view when he proposes: "I ask the historian to look upon Indian America as a kind of Middle Ages which lacked a Rome: a confused mass that emerged from a long-established, doubtless very loosely textured syncretism, which for many centuries had contained at one and the same time centers of advanced civilization and savage peoples, centralizing tendencies and disruptive forces" (*Raw*, 8). Yet Lévi-Strauss's own commentary in this volume makes few such distinctions. The world continues to be divided into the hot self and the cold Other.

A variety of contemporary anthropologists such as Fabian have been trying to find a way out of this ethnographic absolutism which, as Fabian shows, prevails from the beginnings of anthropology and continues through and after the magnificent "change" of synchronic structuralism. It similarly prevails in literature. For the first white arrivals these places, Canada, Australia, and New Zealand, were spatially distant from what they felt to be their place, Britain, and also temporally distant. Even when the "explorers" encountered the indigenes, there was a sense of this denial of the coeval. Many early accounts imply that these voyagers were just as much time travellers. The meeting made them and the indigenes "in fact" contemporaries but the whites viewed the interaction as across a gap of time too great to be bridged. The difference of place had been overcome by white technology. But although self and Other could be both here now, they could not both be here in the now.

One might expect that contemporary literature, set in the present, in which the now is our now, would present a different image. But the indigenes continue on the other side of this atemporal temporal divide; they remain very much in the "cold." The alienated, deindigenized Aboriginal narrator in Patrick's *Inapatua* observes his brother's tribe:

> I suddenly knew that the group on Ah Fong's veranda were part of an ever present past ... They would not predict or discuss the future ... They lived entirely in the dreamtime of the Abunda and talked only of the present." (15)

The split between narrator and brother would be defined in the Australian context as the distinction between detribalized and tribalized Aborigine. Usually the term "tribal" is applied to those Aborigines who continue to live far from major population centres and are deemed by the white culture to have maintained "traditional" hunting-gathering patterns, rituals, and language. They are, in the view of the white culture, "true" Aborigines, unlike the more urban, "false" Aborigines. The effect of this separation is to add a spatial coordinate to the common temporal distortion. Those most Aboriginal are those furthest away in space are those furthest away in time – not unlike the situation for the first explorers. Those nearest in space are those nearest in time but also least Aboriginal – the approach to the coeval leads to a decrease in Aboriginality. Fabian's chronopolitical slope continues to be an impossible climb.

The positive role of the indigene is often a precursor of the white, either simply historically or in evolutionary terms. As in the reference to Druids, some indigenes become less self opposed to Other than pre-self opposed to self. Metaphorically this often leads to words which place the indigene not at the beginning of human time as a whole but at the beginning of individual human time. One might think of a phrase such as "The child is the father to the man." But we do not of course expect the child to be cotemporal with the adult he or she will become. How then could we expect the white to be one in time with the "children of the human family" (130), as Dark's *The Timeless Land* refers to the Aborigines. Even the elderly in Conrad Sayce's *Splendid Savage: A Tale of the North Coast of Australia* (1927) are "grave, aged children" (200).

Such, of course, was not very different from their legal position. Duncan Campbell Scott as Canadian poet presents the Indian as pathetic remnant, the dying race in poem after poem. As Superintendent of Indian Affairs, however, Scott also emphasized their child-like status, "minors in the eye of the law" (1931 *Administration*, 5) and praised assimilation as a process of cotemporalizing maturation, "weaning the Indian from his primitive state" (25). The policies might be different but the semiosis is similar to that employed by Scott's poetic antecedant, Adam Kidd, who refers in *The Huron Chief* to "Nature's humble child" (105).

In many works, as in Kidd or in Idriess's reference in *Nemarluk* to the "untamed child of the wilds" (51), the term "child" means progeny, once again raising the image of indigene as nature. But "child" also implies an infantile state, as in Dark's comment. The prehistoric is nature's child, the barely developed human, the *tabula rasa* awaiting civilization. Gilman states that Hegel described African blacks "not only as 'pre-historic,' that is, outside of the concept of history, but also as an 'infantile nation'" (*Difference*, 195). In Gilman's interpretation, the appearance of Hegel's prehistoric within the period of history becomes the ahistoric, and thus an appropriate realm for the permanent child.

Contemporary texts maintain this image but with the observation that civilization has not written well on this blank slate. The Aborigines in McGarrity's *Once a Jolly Blackman* seem "God's abandoned children" (15). A similar assertion is found in the title of Sheppard's *Children of Blindness* – nature's child has become degenerate child of white paternalism. But although both seem to be children, they are often viewed as quite separate peoples. The situation once again reflects the ahistorical indigene. The indigene should be beyond time, should be prehistoric. As Lévi-Strauss acclaims, "The characteristic feature of the savage mind is its timelessness" (*Savage*, 263). When the indigene enters history, a problem arises because there must be change. The common result is a rejection of the indigene who has changed. At one level, this is simply an aversion to decay, as in Simpson Newland's portrait of an old man in *Paving the Way* (1893):

> In this sketch some will doubtless imagine they detect exaggeration; but, if so, they cannot have seen the aboriginal of Australia in the last stage of decrepitude and misery, when all the joys of his merely animal existence have flown, leaving him, however, still clinging to life through the mere base brute-fear of death. (292)

But of course what can one expect from the aged indigene, who is almost always employed as the past in the present, as an incongruous artifact who offends the process of natural time? The limited ability to approach a coeval state parallels the degeneration one might expect from any other surviving object of an earlier age. The indigene finds not a new birth at the end of prehistory but only a slow death. Drew's *The Wabeno Feast* eulogizes the past Indian but begins and ends with a contemporary Indian drunk. The only present Indian in the rest of the work is a prostitute.

Often this degeneracy is placed within a heightened version of the familiar literary theme of the generation gap – or perhaps better, degeneration gap. Hugo Muller's "Culture" (*Waswanipi* [1976], 54) shows a young couple looking at pornography, unlike the old woman of "Nannish" who is properly beyond history:

It's all there
within her
as she sits
motionless as time,
only her eyes blinking.
It is her –
strange, sweet
mellowed, strong
unfathomable. (22)

In Jill Shearer's *The Foreman* (1976), the Aboriginal hero is attacked by his progressive wife for "looking into the eyes of dreaming old men. Back over your shoulder to the Dreamtime" (65–6).

The degeneration gap is a pseudo-diachrony quite equal to the lament for his tribe as a morbid attraction, as a statement on the impossibility of crossing from prehistory to the coeval. The conflict between an elder with indigenous values based on a natural pre-historic life and a deindigenized youth engaged with the possibilities of development and change is ubiquitous, from the Indians in Evans's *Mist on the River* to the Aborigines in Rose's *Country of the Dead* to the Maori in Mason's *The Pohutukawa Tree*. The text usually reveres the elder figure and sympathizes with the younger, but there is seldom any potential for synthesis. The best hope for any indigene caught between heroic past and decayed present is the ironic recla-mation represented by Joe Lightning in Kroetsch's *What the Crow Said*: the Indian warrior become shuffleboard shark. The prehistoric indigene who makes the error of living into contemporary society soon dies. As Aroha says in *The Pohutukawa Tree*: "My tribe had rotted, rotted away" (23).

There are, of course, some Indians who are not dead. But are they Indians? The prostitute and the drunk in *The Wabeno Feast* are not just a diluting of the indigene. Beilby's *The Brown Land Crying* sees no Aboriginal quality in a casual contemporary group:

> Such conclaves were in no way tribal because there were no tribes, no rituals, no longer any strict taboos, only a miserable little mixed-race circle bound by a common wretchedness, invoking the degrading magic of the bottle (3).

The situation is akin to that in Peter Weir's film, *The Last Wave* (1974), in which one white lawyer maintains that urban Aborigines are detribalized, that innately chronopolitical term. The other lawyer proves that they still have a mystical tribe with all the appropriate prehistoric resonances. Unlike white Australian society, which is assumed to be diachronic, Aboriginal society is allowed no room for the flux of history. The prehistoric Aborigine is Aborigine; the pres-ent Aborigine is not. The indigene who wishes to cross the temporal and temperature barriers, to become coeval, to become "hot," either dies with the prehistoric indigene or becomes no longer indigene. So whether or not the indigene in body dies, the indigene dies.

The indigene of today continues to be a deviant, the drunk and prostitute of *The Wabeno Feast*, but loses the metaphysical resonance of the Other. The present indigene is deindigenized, no longer valid, so the focus of indigenization must be the "real" indigenes, the resonances of the past. In Atwood's *Surfacing* contemporary Indians are vague glimpses, with none of the visionary power of the rock paintings which their ancestors left. In Hodgman's *Blue Skies*, Aborigines are little more than aura: they express nature, express The Land, in a way that the drunk of *The Wabeno Feast* cannot. The Beothuk of Newfoundland, in their absolute absence, provide the ultimate resource. Such refers to them in the preface to *Riverrun* as people "I met in dreams" (ix). The Newfoundland poet Tom Dawe captures the vague symbolic entity, the corpse's absence of corporeality, in his title: "In There Somewhere" (1981). But never out here.

The image of the indigene is often spectacle, particularly in works which concentrate on the grand view of history. But the indigene can also be seen as the refraction of a different type of spectacle, as the image is manipulated to suit the focus of white cultures, a long distance gaze which provides us with a subtly comforting astigmatism. The convex lens draws the disparate indigenous cultures together to a prehistoric point, a tightly circumscribed locus at the beginning of Fabian's temporal slope.

CHAPTER NINE

Theatre

If Aboriginals suitable to play the respective parts are not available, it is advisable that others cast for the parts should concentrate on a suggestive portrayal of Aboriginal features and behaviour rather than attempt complete authenticity. (Dann, "Rainbows Die at Sunset" [c. 1970])

It is a commonplace in the study of dramatic literature that the play on the page is only a partial outline. In fiction, the reader who lifts the words from the page is controlled only by the interaction between imagination and text. The reader of the drama must also posit limitations to the imagination, the limitations of stage and actors.

Without seeing a staged version of George Dann's play, it is impossible to have a precise impression of the effects of the production note quoted above. But it neatly encapsulates a factor which clearly separates the indigene on stage from the indigene on the page. If, as in most instances, the indigene is played by a white, there is an apparently wayward signifier interfering with the sign of the indigene character. Depending on one's view of the semiotic process, it could be possible for a reader to remove the indigene from the text of a novel and recreate something within the imagination which closely represents the referent. For a theatre audience, however, the adequacy or inadequacy of the performance cannot deny the interference of non-Other portraying Other.

This process is doubly important because of the unusual semiotic power of the theatre. Keir Elam in *The Semiotics of Theatre and Drama* (1980) supports the claim of the Prague school that theatre presents the *"semiotization of the object"* (8). As Elam notes, this process was explored in Petr Bogatyrev's "Semiotics in the Folk Theatre" (1938): "on the stage things that play the part of theatrical signs can in the course of the play acquire special features, qualities, and attributes that they do not have in real life" (35–6). Stage conventions play an important part in the response to that signifying power, particularly that of the actors' bodies. Suspension of disbelief does not imply that the audience forget that they are watching actors. The point is often made by students of Elizabethan theatre that the audience was under no delusion that the boys playing women were anything other than boys. Or, to put it more generally, all audiences know long before the epilogue in *All's Well That Ends Well* that "The king's a beggar, now the play is done" (5.3.328).

But what kind of king during the play? The generic power of the semiotization of the object is particularly important in the context of the indigene. Elam makes the following analysis of the stage prop: "It is tempting to see the stage table as bearing a direct relationship to its dramatic equivalent – the fictional object that it represents – but this is not strictly the case; the material stage object becomes, rather, a semiotic unit standing not directly for another (imaginary) table but for the intermediary signified 'table', i.e. for the *class of objects* of which it is a member" (8). It might seem extreme to view an individual character of a play as such an object but this is the case for the indigene, a role which "embodies" the circumscriptions of the semiotic field established throughout the white semiosis. Thus each stage indigene is perceivable as generic, as standing for the intermediary signified, the Image. Through this process the stage indigene goes well beyond the equivalent in prose fiction or poetry. Elam notes: "Theatre is able to draw upon the most 'primitive' form of signification, known in philosophy as *ostension*. In order to refer to, indicate or define a given object, one simply picks it up and shows it to the receiver of the message in question" (29). Elam makes the point that the object is not the actual referent but once again the representative of the class: "the thing is 'de-realized' so as to become a sign" (30). The semiotization makes the indigene a more precisely defined image because of its de-realization and yet at the same time a more powerful image because of its verisimilitude which, in the case of indigene actor, appears to be ostension.

There are many examples of representations of indigenes on the British stage long before any definably Canadian or Australian versions. *The Indian Queen* (1664), by John Dryden and Robert Howard, and Dryden's own *The Indian Emperour* (1665) are but two of the better known ones. That there was an established mode of presentation is suggested by the comments of the Australian explorer, T.L. Mitchell, in 1839, on encountering four Aborigines, painted in a manner "giving their persons exactly the appearance of savages as I have seen them represented in theatres" (2: 108).

This conformation to theatrical expectations represents the power of the de-realized sign over the encounter with the ostensible referent. The limited verisimilitude which Mitchell is likely to have encountered is suggested by the musical *Van Dieman's Land: An Operatic Drama* (1830s) by Mitchell's contemporary, W.T. Thomas. The script gives the following description of costumes in the London production: "Ben-ni-long – White shirt – short trunks – brown legs and arms – scarf – Indian head dress. Kangaree – Indian striped dress. Bedia – Indian dress." The costume seems absurd for either Aborigine or Indian but it fits the need of the nineteenth-century theatre for spectacle in costume. Any history of theatrical design includes drawings very close to the costumes which this suggests, most of which make no clear representation other than a generalized exoticism. Yet the terminology, with "Indian" as a generic description, suggests an existing indigene convention to which the production was conforming. The same convention is obvious in the rhetoric of the piece. Ben-ni-long intones:

> Aye, let the colourless strangers fear! that have usurped our plains, and would fain extirpate our race! – let them beware the Caffre's just revenge! – . (37)

Such inflated diction shows little concern for the ethnicity of the character, which should be no surprise given the reference to "Caffre" by this character in "Indian head dress." Ben-ni-long's assertion follows a song by Kangaree and other natives:

> Softly tread, lest white man spy,
>   Olla loo! Olla loo!
> Pale-face him have cunning eye,
>   Caffre man to view! (36)

Thomas's play seems ludicrous in the extreme but it incorporates a number of elements often found in nineteenth-century Canadian dramas. Mair's *Tecumseh* is one example. The carefully contorted grammar of Kangaree's song employs a nonsense call and the word "pale-face," both general signifiers for indigenes. And the maiden song itself is de rigeur, although it need not be limited to the stage, as shown in Domett's Maori poem, *Ranolf and Amohia*. The art of Ben-ni-long's speech is no less than that exhibited by an Indian runner in Mackenzie's *Thayendanegea* who exclaims, "Woe! woe! the hour; the French have given way;/And Butler's Mohawks speed their frenzied flight" (37). Some lines later Thayendanegea himself displays one of the most extreme examples of the pseudo-Shakespearean inverted syntax with which so many of these noble savages are plagued:

Fails oral note to syllable the thanks;
Pay ne'er could gratitude, though drained its hoard,
Thou zealous teacher, friendly monitor –
Of Truth the pure-browed, radiant messenger –
For train of love-spurred efforts to promote
My people's inner weal. (39)

The ethnological assumptions which lie behind this inflated rhetoric reflect the standard commodity of orality. The existence of the indigene as rhetorician is established in all genres but he is particularly appropriate for a certain type of nineteenth-century drama which gloried in its flamboyant eloquence and placed verisimilitude or even intelligibility at a much lower value. When such speech was linked to the pictorial element of exotic dress and the other aural presence of song, the stage indigene became a useful ingredient for theatrical spectacle, useful enough to establish a recognizable genre – the Indian heroic tragedy. An anonymous reviewer of John Hunter Duvar's *De Roberval, A Drama* (1888) in *The Toronto Mail* concludes: "There is only one suggestion that we would wish permission to make, and that is, that the 'Indian maiden' – the Ohnaiva [sic] of the tale – is already too hackeyed a type to set side by side with the 'King of Vinceux' – Roberval himself. But, as to many readers a Canadian drama without the 'Indian maiden' would be as 'Hamlet' *sans* Hamlet, the suggested suppression will doubtless be considered hypocritical" ([1888] 8).

If parody often provides an apt definition of form, one might look to Stephen Leacock's "Mettawamkeag: An Indian Tragedy" (1923). Leacock observes in his preface:

Few people perhaps realize that no less than seventeen first class tragedies, each as good as Shakespeare's, and all in blank verse, have been written about the Indians. They have to be in blank verse. There was something about the primitive Indian that invited it. It was the real way to express him.

Unfortunately these Indian tragedies cannot be produced on the stage. They are ahead of the age. The managers to whom they have been submitted say that as yet there is no stage suitable for them, and no actors capable of acting them, and no spectators capable of sitting for them. (143–4)

A still more innovative manipulation of the rhetorical devices used by the oratorical Indian is found in S.G. Bett's *The Eyewash Indians* (1939), in which the parents speak in verse of the same metrical pattern as that used by Longfellow in *Hiawatha*. Their daughter, Pocahontas, a very contemporary young woman of the nineteen-thirties, is unable to establish even a limited level of communication with them. The standard commodity of orality as defined by the heroic poem becomes a comic signifier for the generation gap.

The limitations of the Canadian heroic tragedies seem to make them very much a genre of the closet, to be considered as poetry, but their style is still representative of the elevated, at times pompous, verse drama sometimes produced, although seldom successfully, on nineteenth-century stages. Mair expressed interest in a possible production (a modern reworking of *Tecumseh* played in Toronto in 1971 as *The Red Revolutionary*) but none of the Canadian plays mentioned here was ever performed before contemporary audiences and thus they are a limited source for comment on stage conventions. An earlier Canadian play, Rogers's *Ponteach: A Tragedy* (1766), similarly had theatrical intentions but no productions, although it uses fewer overtly emblematic stage Indian terms and its rhetoric is less florid.

But Thomas clearly shows that it was possible to place a very similar view of the Aborigine on the stage. J.R. McLachlan's "Arabin" (1847) was "freely dramatized" from Thomas McCombie's "recent popular work," *The Colonist in Australia; or, The Adventures of Godfrey Arabin* (1845). McLachlan adds to the rather generalized Aborigines in McCombie an individual, Warren Warren, described in the list of characters as "an Aboriginal Chief … in travelling costume." Early in the play his primary role is as trickster, fooling gullible whites. His star scene centres on a song which includes the verse:

> Merrijig, me sing –
> Mr. Robinson him bring
> Me backy, and me flour and me tea;
> Would him bring a leetle rum,
> Wah! – den me would have some;
> And me dance round and round about de tree,
> Merrijig, me sing – Wah! Wah!
> Chorus all – Merrijig, me sing – Wah! Wah! (41)

Warren Warren's description and his need to sing make him not unlike a variety of other indigenes in poetry as well as drama in the nineteenth century. As suggested above, the assumptions of musicality in the semiotic field of the indigenes made them perfect secondary characters in an era enamoured of the musical setpiece. Warren Warren's comic manipulation of whites, however, and the dialect he employs, such as the "backy" reference, place him in quite a different tradition.

Particularly in the late nineteenth and early twentieth century, the stage Aborigine, as distinct from the more generalized stage indigene, might be linked to the stage black of the nineteenth-century American theatre. Like the indigene, he is prone to outbursts of song but lacks the former's rhetorical speech. He is more actively involved in the activities of the central white characters than the usual indigene, often in the capacity of servant. His dialect is not the elevated diction of a Tecumseh, a Ponteach, or a Ben-ni-long but instead approximates the jokey pidgin of a Brunton Stephens poem. He is by no means a powerless figure, however, in that he often aids the hero by tricking evil whites, as does Geebung in "To the West" (1896) by Kenneth MacKay and Alfred Dampier, and Nardoo in "Coo-ee or Wild Days in the Bush" (1906) by E.W. O'Sullivan.

One of the most interesting facets of these stage Aborigines is their romantic involvements. In nineteenth-century poetry or fiction there is almost no inkling that a male Aborigine could have a sexual interest in a white. Such a connection was limited to the ethereal Aboriginal maiden. But on stage, there are a number of instances of just such romantic inclinations. In Henry Melville's *The Bushrangers; or Norwood Vale,* (1834) the Aborigine's sad tale of white savagery and the death of his love, his "poor mistress," draws the following reaction from a white woman:

"Poor fellow! You make me pity you. [*Eyeing him*] What a sad thing it is your skin is black – you have a good soul – I will get you a blanket off my own bed" (86).

Later works which treat the interaction as humour are far less subtle. "Coo-ee" reaches the point that the sexual banter between Nardoo and Paramatta Polly serves as a comic subplot to make Paramatta Bob jealous.

The acceptability of such a scene suggests a stage convention that left the audience well aware of the white actor playing the part, which contributed an ironic subtext to any action. The Australian drama of the period generally denigrates the Aborigine in a "playful" manner. Even when that familiar element of the standard commodity of violence, cannibalism, is highlighted in J.W. Wallace's *Drift* (1882), it remains at the level of comic relief. The Aborigine tends to leave the scene when the play turns more weighty. There is no room for Geebung or for the "cutely" named Cinderella, in Jo Smith's "The Girl of the Never Never" (1912), once more serious concerns for crime or romance take over the stage.

This extreme difference between the Canadian and Australian situations, in light of the many similarities in other genres in the period, could have many explanations. Not the least likely is the greater vitality of the Australian popular theatre and the greater concern to produce material on local subjects. As well, the stage conventions established by the American popular theatre seemed applicable to the Aborigine in Australia, and their generally comic tone gave them audience appeal. Margaret Williams, in *Australia on the Popular Stage: 1829–1929* (1983), suggests that the stage Aborigine suited a generic role in "the comic by-play, traditionally the function of farcical servant characters": "Two Australian figures fitted readily into this slot: the bushman and the Aboriginal, both at the bottom of the social ladder. The Aboriginal who comes to the rescue of the heroine in extremity occurs in the earliest play written in Australia, Henry Melville's *The Bushrangers*. And for another century a succession of nimble Aboriginal characters leap to the rescue of a series of very dim-witted Anglo-Saxon heroes and heroines in the role of faithful servant-clown. The Aboriginal is certainly a figure of fun, grotesquely attired in hand-me-downs and with a good deal of the caricatured quality of stage American black-face types (a similarity reinforced by the Aboriginals of Australian melodrama being played by white actors made up in something of the style of the minstrel show). But his generous share of colonial impudence and the teasing affection in which he is held by the household gives him a natural affinity with the other local characters, which puts the immigrants, especially the new chum, very much on the outer" (267).

It is difficult to see characters such as Cinderella as less than "outer," but Williams has an accurate view of the appeal of the figure. In the manuscript for "Robbery Under Arms" (1890), an adaptation by Dampier and Garnet Walch of Rolf Boldrewood's novel of the same name (1889), the minor part of "Billy the Boy" is cut in order to give more lines to Warrigal, allowing more frequent repetition of his comic catchphrase: "Quick like wallaby – my word." The heroic Aborigine in McCrae's poems, like the heroic Indians of Mair and Rogers, central figures with elevated speech, had much less appeal for a theatre concerned, as "To the West"'s blurb proclaimed, with "realistic and sensational drama." It almost seems as though Aristotelian conventions were being observed, in this clear demarcation between the aristocrat of the heroic tragedy and the rustic clown of the comedy.

There was some continuation of the separation between Australian and Canadian modes in later plays. Richard Diamond's "In the Shade of the Coolibah Tree" (c. 1950), in spite of the title's reference to Paterson's "Waltzing Matilda" (*Collected*, 254), is very much American inspired. Set on a paddlewheeler on the Darling, its singing Aborigines seem to have escaped from a rather amateur version of the musical, *Showboat*. The poetic Indians of Carroll Aikins's *The God of Gods* (1919) bear many resemblances to those in Mair and *De Roberval*. Still, the general picture of the indigene became much more uniform and much more in accord with the image as presented in other genres.

The primary mode for twentieth-century Canadian and Australian drama, and, more specifically, for plays about indigenes, has been realism. The most common scene is a small set which represents a living room or kitchen, or perhaps a confined outdoor space close to the same type of humble rural dwelling. The tendency is to confine the cast to a group similarly small, usually a family. Miscegenation and assimilation are recurring themes, with either a white family, one member of which has a relationship or potential relationship with an indigene, or an indigene family in which the generation gap is heightened by a daughter attracted to white culture and a white man or a son attracted to white culture and white ideals of success. This provides a reasonable summation of, in Canada, Fairbairn's *A Pacific Coast Tragedy* (*Plays*, 57–84), Gwen Ringwood's *Lament for Harmonica (Maya)* (1959 *Collected*, 339–53), and Bonnie LeMay's "Hit and Run" (1967); in Australia, three plays by George Dann, "In Beauty It is Finished" (1931), *Fountains Beyond* (1942), and "Rainbows Die at Sunset," Louis Esson's *Andeganora* (1937), Drake-Brockman's *Men Without Wives*, Oriel Gray's "Had We But World Enough" (1950?), Ireland's *Image in the Clay*, Barbara Stellmach's *Dark Heritage*, (1964), Bec Robinson's *Dark, Out There* (1967) and Shearer's *The Foreman*; and in New Zealand, Mason's *The Pohutukawa Tree* and Fiona Kidman's *Search for Sister Blue* (1972), a radio play. A number of other works differ only slightly. Fairbairn's *Ebb-Tide* (*Plays*, 5–29) and Carol Bolt's *Gabe* (1973) use small casts of whites and Indians in rural settings but not family groups, and Katharine Susannah Prichard's *Brumby Innes* (1940), does the same with Aborigines. There are a number of notes which parallel Dann's attempt to avoid the stage indigene. Stellmach directs, "Care must be taken with makeup. It must be remembered that Neil Harrison is only quarter-cast [sic]" (3). Language is a similar consideration, as the Australian texts try to avoid Stephens' pidgin and the Canadian Mair's oratory. LeMay asserts, "No attempt should be made to have Louise and Joe 'sound like' Indians. This is portrayed in their speeches."

The possibilities of verisimilitude in the theatre create an attractive genre for "objective" portrayals of the indigene as social problem. Elam refers to John Searle's "The Logical Status of Fictional Discourse" (1975), in which Searle attempts to differentiate between the ways in which actor and playwright create the real: "The actor pretends to be someone other than he actually is, and he pretends to perform the speech acts and other acts of that character. The playwright represents the actual and pretended actions and the speeches of the actors, but the playwright's performance in writing the text of the play is rather like writing a recipe for pretense than engaging in a form of pretense itself. A fictional story is a pretended representation of a state of affairs; but a play, that is, a play as performed, is not a pretended *representation* of a state of affairs but the pretended state of affairs itself, the actors pretend *to be* the characters" (328). In the case of the indigene, this stage "being" creates a still greater slippage for the observer. Elam observes of the dramatic world: "Clearly, with respect to the 'real' world of performers and spectators, and in particular the immediate theatrical context, it is a spatio-temporal *elsewhere* represented as though actually present for the audience" (99).

The relation between Elam's "elsewhere" and the bourgeois audience is an interesting one. In most instances, no one watching the play would have had more than fleeting contact with the social situation seen on stage. Elam makes a distinction between "sociofugal space" and "sociopetal space." In the former, which Elam believes describes the proscenium theatre, the structure and the social expectations associated with that structure work to separate the audience members from each other; in the latter, as in an informal or avant garde environment, the audience members are made to feel part of a collectivity.

Yet such a distinction seems of limited applicability in the present context. If the illusion of a "sociopetal space" is created, there might be a greater apparent communality within the audience and even an illusion of communality with the indigene characters of the play, but the separation of experience at the same time maintains a distance much larger than that created by theatre apron or proscenium pillars. The delusion involved in the acceptance of the performers as ostension becomes even greater than it would be in a performance on another subject.

A more general argument with Elam's division of audience could be made. All theatrical spaces are to a significant degree sociopetal. Anyone who has ever attended a theatrical performance knows how much the audience provides the primary context for the process of eliciting meaning. Such essential factors as the evaluation of individual character, a central aspect of assessing the meaning of dialogue, are closely shaped by the reaction of other observers. For example, ironic recuperation, the interpretive mechanism which decides that a passage should be interpreted as meaning the opposite of its most obvious denotation, is a very difficult process in prose fiction. The individual reader must examine often enigmatic markers hidden within the text. In general, similar irony is established in the theatre collectively through audience reaction. Sometimes the same production of the same play is accepted ironically one night and "literally" the next.

This returns us to the question of verisimilitude, a central concern of representations of the indigene in all genres, at least since the "information" documents of the explorers. In the theatre, decisions on the success of verisimilitude are similarly a result of collective valorization. The white audience, as participants in the general white semiosis, collectively assess the semiotization of the indigene object on stage, in a process which, by making the signifier seem closer to the referent, reinforces the signifier's limitations. The contradiction is reminiscent of Brecht's famous assertion that his epic theatre was the most realistic form of theatre because what could be more realistic than actors admitting to be actors.

All of these plays employ many standard commodities of the semiotic field of the indigene, besides the obvious ones of "realistic" sex and violence. In fact, physical violence is more often a reference than a part of the action. The theatres of Canada, Australia, and New Zealand have been no more likely to accept explicit violence than explicit sexuality. Thus, the gruesome scalping scene of *Ponteach* or the attack of three hundred Indians in *Thayendanegea* are quite unlike the offstage murder which provides the climax of Dann's *Fountains Beyond*. But in "Rainbows Die at Sunset," Dann is able to use contemporary involvement by Aborigines in professional boxing as a means of reworking indigene violence on the stage.

A more common theatrical device is the use of indigenous song and music. In *Andeganora, Men Without Wives,* and *Brumby Innes,* the sound of the corroboree is a sign of developing passion and potential violence. In *The Pohutukawa Tree* the Maori chant serves a similar purpose, reinforcing the image of Aroha's decline. Despite the far greater subtlety, these expressions of indigene orality play a similar role to that of Warren Warren's song and the "Indian shout" in Thomas. As in those cases, attributes which have only a philosophical "resonance" in a novel or poem literally resound in the theatre. A genre always searching for elements which fill the gaps, both thematic and theatrical, left by the limitations of spoken dialogue finds commodities which are perfectly suited to the economy of the theatre.

Such devices become more fluidly employed in plays with less overt concern for verisimilitude. Even more than indigene songs, various non-vocal forms of indigene sound provide potential for a general presence. Reed's *Truganinni* employs rhythm sticks. In Leonard Peterson's historical drama, *Almighty Voice* (1970), the death of the hero is mystically elevated by the chanting and drumming of his mother:

> In empty despair she trails a hand over the drum that has spoken so often of the unspeakable. And under her hand it stirs once more, murmurs, cries out, possessing her. (48).

By the end of the play, the drum, which has been a presence throughout the play, "possessed and possessed, thunders up full and defiant, and cuts" (49).

Both *Truganinni* and *Almighty Voice* use the potential of theatrical sound to create an enclosing atmosphere. In some cases the effect of indigenous sound becomes analogous to that of white noise, the ambient sound which defines a culture but is seldom observed by most within that culture. As Elam notes: "It is an essential feature of the semiotic economy of the theatrical performance that it employs a limited repertory of sign-vehicles in order to generate a potentially unlimited range of cultural units, and this extremely powerful generative capacity on the part of the theatrical sign-vehicle is due in part to its connotative breadth" (11). While such indigenous sound is certainly part of a "limited repertory," it adds much to connotative breadth by acting to underscore any part of the production. In many plays on indigenes the sound begins as ambient noise, perhaps noticed by neither audience nor characters, and then is tranformed. Fairbairn's *The Wardrums of Skedans* (*Plays*, 87–111) pushes ambient sound well beyond underscoring to become active subject, equal to the indigene as character, as the Haida Indian drums build to the point at which a Spanish archaelogist dies from their mystical power.

Ritual movement is used in very similar ways. In the context of verisimilitude, *The Pohutukawa Tree* resorts to something not unlike the common assumption that "primitive" peoples have inherent rhythmic talents to explain the ability of the young Maori, Queenie, to dance to the sounds of Glen Miller. *Almighty Voice* uses a similarly undifferentiated but more ethnographic action in the recurrent dancing of the Indian characters. In some Australian plays the corroboree goes beyond presence as sound to a setpiece of spectacle. *Fountains Beyond* suggests a corroboree as an interlude:

> It is not essential to the play but may help to establish atmosphere.
> Should the producer favour its inclusion, there should be no attempt
> made to stage a real corroboree, as that would incur considerable diffi-
> culties. (32)

The apparently unintentional irony of the last phrase in this note nicely underlines the question of verisimilitude throughout stage portrayals of the indigene.

Ron Kimber's "Run Run Away" (1979) is generally oriented towards verisimilitude and could thus be considered as within the genre of realism, except for the opening and closing scenes of an old Aborigine playing a gum leaf, which provide a frame of both culture sound and nature sound. The manuscript notes that in one production the final speech, in which the deindigenized hero reasserts his allegiance to his past, was spoken by the gum leaf player. The character established through various techniques of verisimilitude as ostension is transmuted into the overtly symbolic figure who to this point has served primarily to establish the Aboriginality of the performance. As the "real" Aborigine is "de-naturalized," in the sense used by Artaud, in other words given a more overtly symbolic value, he is also made more clearly a part of the semiotic field of nature, which is represented by the old Aborigine, the already "de-naturalized" gum-leaf player, who is outside the frame of the realist presentation. And yet this same association draws the old Aborigine into the "natural" verisimilitude of the play. This production thus would have encapsulated the process throughout contemporary plays on the indigene. It makes claims for the symbolic value of the "real" and at the same time asserts the "reality" of the symbol.

Indigene material culture is similarly used for its symbolic power, particularly in sets. *The God of Gods* emphasizes a large stone god, which, from contemporary photographs, appears less inspired by the Indians of Canada's west coast than by some of Edward Gordon Craig's stage designs. Like the latter's creations, it dominates the stage to an oppressive degree and likely became, as Craig often wished of his designs, the primary sign-vehicle of the production, a situation in which cultural and natural ambiance would define Indian much more than the appearances or speeches of the individual Indian characters as represented on stage. The stylized igloo of Leonard Peterson's *The Great Hunger* (1960) and the Medicine Wheel in Sharon Pollock's *Walsh* (1973) perhaps could not be termed oppressive but they are certainly dominant. The latter is presented as mandala-like, incorporating all aspects of the universe within a single Indian vision. Its manifestation on the stage is a dogmatic assertion of the standard commodity of mysticism in a play otherwise primarily concerned with the material reality of history. Thus the theatrical economy is significantly different from that which might be assumed from the dialogue and action: verisimilitude is "watched-over" by indigene mysticism. Similarly, the massive presence of the title figure in *The Pohutukawa Tree* is a claim for the Maori's place within the semiotic field of nature and a definition of mystical nature firmly planted within the verisimilitude of the narrative.

Props might seem a more minor element, lacking the overall power of such massive setpieces, but they often achieve a similar ambiance simply through constant emphasis. Aroha's spear, in *The Pohutukawa Tree*, demonstrates both the past in the present and the validity of a noble violence. A similar spear in *Image in the Clay* presents the same commodities while the clay figure of the title permeates the play with mysticism. Duncan Campbell Scott's "dancing-mask" in "Joy! Joy! Joy!" (1927) turns from object into subject as its presence is sufficient to kill. Thus, as in the Fairbairn example, ambient culture becomes dynamic mystical violence. All of these examples conform to the one general rule for such devices, that they suit the theatrical metaphors of the period and genre and that they appear to be indigenous. Beyond this, they run the gamut in terms of ethnographic justification.

In contemporary theatre, the residues of realism are often stridently rejected, a highly appropriate decision in the case of the indigene which has maintained its semiotic field in spite of the various attempts at verisimilitude. Davies' *Question Time* employs a set which is an overtly emblematic vision of the north. The two Inuit characters are similarly symbolic, particularly the shaman who asserts the mystical indigene by covering the Canadian prime minister with the skin of a polar bear, the spirit of the north, which proves to be for him "*a wholly alien mode of being*" (26). The shaman is the mystical indigene of nature, but carefully shaped to suit the value of indigene ritual as theatrical device. Rodney Milgate's *A*

Refined Look at Existence (1966) presents very different values from most contemporary Australian plays: it depicts urban Aborigines in "a modern reworking of the *Bacchae*," with decidedly Christian overtones. Still, it can be conceived as another representation of the overtly theatrical indigene. Milgate's Aborigine is Artaud's de-naturalized symbol, only signifier, not the individual Aborigine somehow transported from reality to the stage.

A number of Australian plays from the seventies demonstrate such free theatrical symbolism but with the political energies often found in collective companies. One such group, the Popular Theatre Troupe, begins "The White Man's Mission" (1975) with an epigraph from Frantz Fanon and an introduction in which the performers refer to themselves as "descendants of mass murderers and slave drivers" (5). The play has the aggressive ahistoricity of many similar works, with the frame of a missionary service incorporating various political skits about the mistreatment of kanakas, indentured ser-vants brought from the Pacific islands to Australia, and Aborigines. A somewhat similar script about the Beothuks of Newfoundland, created by an individual playwright, Cook's *On the Rim of the Curve*, follows a comparable pattern but with a circus as frame. The Ring-master spiels:

> There'll also be songs and dances and, yes, even a few prizes. So stay with it folks for we also have an Indian or two present and if you're good, you can all help pull the trigger ... (*Europeans applaud.*) We'll trek up to Heaven and down to Hell, boys, but first, a word from our sponsor ... the Beothuk Indians. (11)

The ideology of these scripts might make them seem wholly posi-tive but their power must at the same time be questioned because of the "sociopetal" illusions of this form of theatre. Elam claims "this movement towards the opening up and loosening of proxemic rela-tions in performance, in order to escape from the tyranny of archi-tectonic grandeur and its aesthetic and ideological implications, looks back to earlier and non-institutional forms of performance" (63–4). Once again the audience combines with performance in a manner which creates an illusion of overcoming divisions between indigene and non-indigene. The ideological assertions of descent from past iniquities are valorized primarily in a version of the pro-gressivist hubris so often attacked by Foucault.

Contemporary theatre has explored many ways of employing the semiotization of the indigene. The one Aboriginal figure in Alex Buzo's *Macquarie* (1971) moves freely, portraying Bennelong, that primary signifier of Aboriginal contact with the first whites, then a history tutor, signifier of black achievements in education in a liberal world, then a journalist, the trace of the Aboriginal activist. Hibberd's "Captain Midnight V.C." is still more unfettered in its approach to chronology, moving from the beginnings of Australian white settlement well into the future. The opening prologue establishes the theatrical conventions and underlines the harsh satire which is to follow:

SPEAKER: This evening, ladies and gentlemen, we present the story of a half-caste aboriginal. As you are probably aware, we are all students from Melbourne University. Unfortunately we haven't been able to use aboriginals as actors in this play as there aren't too many to be found at our university, or any other university we suspect. Doubtless this is due to the feeble intellects of these yam-brained and mulga-skulled savages. So, we have had to make do with a few tricks of the theatre: some make-up for our half-caste parasite, and some masked wiggery for the fullbloods. Ahh, here is our hero now. He's just completed the finishing touches to his tan.

MIDNIGHT enters.

Note the murky discolouration of his ugly dial, neither copper nor coal, just dung dull. Notice also the pink palms, quite typical, and the black on the back.

MIDNIGHT displays his colour scheme to the audience.

No trouble picking him in the street.

BLANCHE and ROSE enter wearing black head stockings and wild pigs[sic] along with black gloves. They play up to the men in the audience.

And here are a couple of his half-sisters. Take a geek at them. Pretty high in the tar content don't you reckon? The sort of people you collide with on a dark night. One hundred per cent soot. The real thing, eh chaps? (1)

Hibberd's script comes much closer to the disruptive theatre described by Tzvetan Todorov in "Art According to Artaud:" "Stage language, if it exists and if it is to be formed, will be by nature destructive, threatening, anarchic, it will evoke chaos" (*Poetics*, 208–9). The text makes no claims to verisimilitude, to the presentation of a signifier which accurately depicts the referent, but instead recognizes the symbolic value of the image of the indigene and makes an anarchic dissection of its representation. The process is not unlike Todorov's analysis of Artaud: "The signifier must be simultaneously various and single; we might describe the specific feature of symbolic language as the *overflow* off the signifier, a super-abundance (and an overdetermination) of what signifies in relation to what is signified" (210). Through identifying the overdetermined image of the indigene, Hibberd creates a resonant metatheatrical device.

The various realist scripts above present the white actor playing the indigene as a problem rather than a problematic. Here, Hibberd uses the deictic possibilities of theatrical performance to make what could be the ideological moment, in all the possible meanings of that phrase. Elam states, "Spatial deixis, finally, takes priority over the temporal. It is above all to the physical *here* represented by the stage and its vehicles that the utterance must be anchored" (143). The ostension of a play in which the character claims *to be* indigene, in which the deictic nature of the theatre is delusionary, is reversed. The white actor who plays the Aborigine, a wayward signifier in the realistic play, becomes the most important element in a Brechtian semiosis.

The best-known examples of the indigene on stage in Canada and Australia are probably Ryga's *The Ecstasy of Rita Joe* and Keneally's *Bullie's House*. Both make significant use of techniques of verisimilitude but both also use overtly theatrical elements. Ryga's play in some ways seems expressionistic, not in the extreme sense of the German expressionists but as the expression of a single character's vision, that of the young Indian woman, Rita Joe. The play begins with a courtroom scene in which Rita is on trial and the rest of the play seems to be a combination of flashbacks and reveries from the point of view of Rita Joe. The theatrical focus on Rita Joe, in terms of both staging and point of view, creates one of the most emphatic examples of indigene as pathetic puppet of white society. In "Drama and the African World-view," Wole Soyinka looks at the way modern European theatre attempts to become "a paradigm for the cosmic human condition": "The spectacle of a lone human figure under a spotlight on a darkened stage is, unlike a painting, a breathing, living, pulsating, threateningly fragile example of this paradigm. It is threatening because, unlike a similar parable on canvas, its fragility is experienced both at the level of its symbolism and in terms of sympathetic concern for the well-being of that immediate human medium" (*Myth*, 41). If seen as in some way Soyinka's "cosmic human," Rita Joe, the pitiful female indigene in a world of white patriarchal power, becomes a representative for existentialism, like the dead in Sartre's *No Exit*.

Keneally's play does not similarly make use of non-realistic modes of presentation, but it exceeds material reality thematically and thus theatrically in its apparent acceptance of mystical elements, from the power of the wind to Doolie's ability to capture Bullie's love by "singing" him. Keneally uses indigenous culture as theatrical devices in the same way as other plays examined above. The "singing," which combines orality and mysticism, creates the appropriate Aboriginal atmosphere, which interweaves with the wind to show the mystical powers of nature to be part of the same spiritual dimension as the "supernatural" powers of the Aborigine. Like Aikens's *The God of Gods*, the set employs a dominant figure which proves to be an oppressive Aboriginality for both whites and Aborigines. The overwhelming presence of the sacred *ranga*, the material expression of secret Aboriginal beliefs, makes a visual impact even greater than the aural one of Doolie's chant. As well, its tangible reality serves as omnipresent validation of Aboriginal spirituality, at least within this exotic context, in opposition to the ineffectual reaction of the professor, who tries to find an element of the "white *ranga*" which it is in his power to give and which in any way compares with the importance of Bullie's gift.

He is like the other white characters in the play, and like the white characters in Ryga's play. Each one is only a manifestation of position, the administrator, the teacher, the judge, the minister. In the case of *Rita Joe*, the caricature can be justified by interpreting the various figures as being seen through Rita Joe's perception. In this way, they might be seen as one more example of the defamiliarization which is an important part of the representation of indigenous points of view in other genres. Still, there is no similar explanation for the two-dimensional white characters in Keneally. Although both plays make many gestures towards verisimilitude, they rework the values of the past not by overcoming the semiotic limitations of the stage indigene but by meeting the stage indigene, defined by such standard commodities as the natural, sexuality, violence, orality, mysticism, and the past in present, with confined signifiers of white control.

By the time of the productions of these two plays, the convention of whites as indigenes in "realistic" theatre was no longer acceptable. The lack of professional indigene actors meant that some whites were used to portray indigenes but both used a number of native actors. Not that they represented the first examples of indigenes on stage. The first productions of *The Pohutukawa Tree* used Maori actors. Almost since the first contact with whites, indigenes have been exhibiting aspects of traditional culture in reshaped versions. These have been – and are – viewed as indigenous theatre by many in the audience. In Canada, records show that Marc Lescarbot's *Neptune's Theatre* (1606), often asserted to be the first play in North America, included Indians in the cast. Eric Irvin's *Australian Melodrama: Eighty Years of Popular Theatre* (1981) notes an interesting cross-cultural example in the activities of Robert P. Whitworth:

> Whitworth, who had five plays produced between 1862 and 1867, first came before the public as a dramatist as the author of a drama written to provide an excuse for performances by a group of Maoris. They were brought to Australia by Whitworth and a "Dr McGavan," with the intention of demonstrating to Australians the habits and customs of the New Zealand natives, against whom some Australians had fought in the Maori War of 1860–61. They were said to be warrior chiefs, and instead of unimaginatively presenting them in a series of dances, war chants, sham fights, and other activities, it was no doubt Whitworth who hit on the idea of putting them in a play in which English as well as Maori characters were introduced. (22–3)

Louis Armstrong's two plays entitled *Hiawatha* (1904, 1909) used all-Indian casts in summer productions designed to attract tourists to Desbarats, Ontario, but his mixture of historical inaccuracies, both his own and Longfellow's, and extreme noble savagism suggests the cast could give little shape to the portrayal.

The importance of the indigene actor in questions of verisimilitude cannot be over-rated. Various comments in Elam's study suggest this, for example, his observation on the star actor: "The individual actor as recognized figure or 'personality' will bring to the performance extra-textual connotations which play no small part in the audience's decoding of the text" (86). The actor known as indigene is perhaps an even more important factor in that decoding than the actor known as "individual," especially if one considers the indigene actor as ostension, and as thus a presentation of that "class of objects," a generic validation of whatever lines spoken by the character or whatever actions performed.

The deictic nature of the theatre is also a validating element: "It is important now to note that the drama consists first and foremost precisely in this, an *I* addressing a *you here* and *now* ... Deixis, therefore, is what allows language an 'active' and dialogic function rather than a descriptive and choric role: it is instituted at the origins of the drama as the necessary condition of a non-narrative form of world-creating discourse" (Elam, 139). Elam's comment about the dialogic function suggests the Bakhtinian incorporation of another "voice" within the text. As I have noted in discussing form, Bakhtin's analysis in the case of the indigene in fiction claims a validation which the reader might all too easily accept but which the texts in the end cannot support. If in the theatre, the voice, the human sound actually heard, is from an indigene throat, how much more difficult for the audience to recognize the distance between "voice" and referent voice. The general question of deixis, of the "I" using an indexical expression which refers to the body being perceived, can be extended. Elam is discussing communication within the performance between two characters but one might see a deictic presentation by the performer to the audience. In the absence of the metatheatrical deixis of the white performer in "Captain Midnight, V.C.," the indigene actor becomes a naturalizing force.

In *Rita Joe* and in *Bullie's House* there were aggressive attempts to suit the indigenes in the cast. In the published text of Keneally's play, there is a lengthy comment by Bob Maza, one of the Aboriginal actors in the original production. He states that he overcame his rejection of a white-authored script when a young Aboriginal girl pointed out to him, "If it's true and it's about our people, does it matter who writes it?" (xiii). There are various possible refutations of this statement but one brief quotation from Foucault's "Two Lectures" will suffice: "I would say that we are forced to produce the truth of power that our society demands, of which it has need, in order to function: we must speak the truth; we are constrained or condemned to confess or to discover the truth" (*Power*, 93). The girl's simplistic view of the possibilities of an Aboriginal "truth" in the theatre shows no recognition of the theatrical power/truth which constrains it within a certain semiotization or of the power/truth of white semiosis which condemns it.

Maza follows his very subjective assertion of truth with a comment on the feelings of the "detribalized" cast:

We Black members of the cast were all urbanised and our tribal affiliations long distant and age old. Yet each of us felt the presence of that past – of the Ranga amongst us. (*Bullie's House*, xiv)

For this reason, they were concerned about the reaction of some Aborigines in the audience. Keneally's story is based on accounts of an actual event, and these Aborigines came from the area where the event took place. Maza admits that the ranga is a concoction of white ideas, created only to suggest that which the uninitiated must not see within the play. But he still fears the visitors might find it inappropriate to reveal something presented as ranga to white eyes. This comment on symbolic representation and meaning has wide-ranging philosophical implications for most of the texts considered throughout the present study. A misrepresentation of a culture lies about the culture but at the same time steals from it by attempting to apportion the original meaning to the misrepresentation.

There is no suggestion of whether the visiting Aborigines made such distinctions, but their reaction was negative. Maza provides the following comment on their response: "To me this is a pity. But then again I am not an initiated man" (xv). The Aboriginal actor here seems trapped within the white theatre, and within the white-defined concept of detribalization, for the concept of "initiation" functions only within the pattern defined by an Aboriginal culture, in which it represents a status of gender and maturity, not a quality of being Aboriginal or non-Aboriginal. Maza's feelings of exclusion are more a result of his identification with white limitations.

Yet it is difficult for me, as a white Canadian, to make such assertions. I have less trouble making the more theatrical observation that Maza seems to fail to recognize the distance between actor and role. This is particularly important for the Aboriginal presence within the white-defined indigene sign. A comparison might be made to the character of David Joe, Rita Joe's elderly noble father, a devotee of stylized rhetoric and natural metaphors. The late Canadian actor Dan George, interestingly always referred to in publicity as Chief Dan George to emphasize his position as *Indian* star, began his rise to fame as David Joe in the first Vancouver production. He consolidated his star status in the film *Little Big Man*, from which his line, "My heart soars like a hawk," became a new catchphrase of noble savagism. Somehow his race, as a "real Indian," erased the general awareness that he was hired by white producers, directed by white directors, and spoke white-written lines in white-written narratives. The result was a perpetuation of a noble savage stereotype of an order seldom seen in contemporary white culture.

Various extracts from Elam above reflect on the complications created by the apparent reality of the theatrical performance. An additional important element is the elision of the narrator to a far greater extent than in the most apparently "objective" novel, as Ong notes: "It is significant that dramatic presentation lacks a narrative voice. The narrator has buried himself completely in the text, disappeared beneath the voices of his characters" (148). With this disappearance of the narrator goes the disappearance of the author, hiding one more suggestion of how the semiotization of these performances is controlled by the white culture.

The separation between actor and the role played is seldom an absolute distinction for the audience. In "Dynamics of the Sign in the Theater" (1940), Jindrich Honzl states "the actor is usually a person who speaks and moves about the stage. However, the fundamental nature of an actor does not consist in the fact that he is a person speaking and moving about the stage but that he *represents someone, that he signifies a role in a play*. Hence it does not matter whether he is a human being; an actor could be a piece of wood, as well. If the wood moves about and its movements are accompanied by words, then such a piece of wood can represent a character in the play, and the wood becomes an actor" (75). But of course the actor is not a block of wood. As the actor makes the role a function of a living, human, subject, the effect is to validate the speeches and the actions of that role and thus also the story in which the role participates. In the case of Chief Dan George, Indian star, or of the indigenous cast of any white play, the effect is to justify the semiotic field and its standard commodities in a way which prose fiction cannot. A novel by a white author can only attempt the Bakhtinian illusion of representing "another's voice." The dramatic text makes it possible for another's voice to speak the Other as described by the white self. The perhaps surprising result for David Joe and thus for Ryga's play has been the acceptance of a character more clearly circumscribed within the semiotic field of the indigene than those in most recent prose fiction. And it will take much more than indigene actors to reshape it. In many ways, their role as signifiers of "reality" just makes the fences of the field that much stronger.

CHAPTER TEN

Rudy Wiebe and
Patrick White

The other chapters of this study examine a wide range of texts to consider the variety of ways in which the semiotic field of the indigene has shaped the literatures of Australia, Canada, and New Zealand. There the emphasis is on glimpses of the image, brief slices of text. No texts are given extended individual consideration, even those which might be considered major examples, such as Kroetsch's *Gone Indian* or Herbert's *Poor Fellow My Country*. The present chapter employs the methodology defined by the slices of the general and applies it to larger cuts of the specific, to a few texts written by Rudy Wiebe and Patrick White.

This limitation of scope presents an opportunity to examine the semiotic field as it appears in various aspects of these narratives, to provide a suggestion of how different commodities modify each other in individual texts. These are chosen because they are both significant representations of the field and considered to be among the most important novels of their cultures on any subject. White's *Voss* (1957) and Wiebe's *The Temptations of Big Bear* (1973) are particularly canonical, often used as representative in brief lists of Australian or Canadian fiction.

Wiebe and White are two of the most acclaimed novelists of their respective countries. Like much of twentieth-century fiction, their texts are often introspective, explorations of personal values. Yet, as might be expected in such post-colonial societies, that introspection is linked with what might seem a quite "extrospective" impulse, the definition of a nation. Most of Wiebe's writing is overtly nationalistic. Even a text with as varied a geography as *The Blue Mountains of China* (1970), a consideration of the diaspora of the Mennonites around the world, contains many comments on the importance of being Canadian. Despite constant attacks on them for being un- or even anti-Australian, Patrick White's novels show a similar search for country, as in *The Twyborn Affair* (1979), in which an expedition into gender identity pulls the central character between icons of decadent empire in England and icons of the bush in Australia. With this, in the texts of both authors, goes a search for individuation, usually traced along mystical patterns. It should not be surprising, then, that Wiebe and White have often turned to the semiotic field of the indigene with its long established signifiers for the spiritual and the national.

This study emphasizes texts rather than authors, partly as a response to the philosophical assumption explored by Foucault in "What is an Author?" (1979) that defining a text by its author limits a reader's understanding of the complexity of discourse, but even more as a response engendered by the specific objects examined here. The semiotic field of the indigene is so circumscribed that the obvious intentions of some authors to write in support of the indigene or to create "realistic" images are even less likely to be fulfilled than other attempts to liberate textual representation. White and Wiebe have both frequently expressed what might be called liberal values. In his strong support for the anti-nuclear movement, White has also spoken for the right of Aborigines to control mining on their land. Wiebe's concern for native causes in Canada is well known, and there can be no question as to the sympathetic intentions of his fiction. Yet the standard commodities remain the same, no matter how subtly they are presented. The possibility is open for an author, or, more precisely, for a text, to support or oppose the signifier presented; each text shapes the signifier according to its individual values and needs, but the commodities of the semiosis remain the same.

The fiction of Wiebe and White, particularly their historical novels, is arguably the most resonant literature on the indigene. Wiebe's *The Temptations of Big Bear* describes attempts by one Indian leader to maintain peace with the whites in the midst of the war between the provisional government of Louis Riel and the Canadian government. In "On the Trail of Big Bear" (1974), Wiebe quotes from an introductory chapter he later rejected: "To begin with, every individual who will appear in this story is an historic person. Not one name has been invented. Every person (and a fair number of the animals) who has a part was once, literally, a living being and there is documentary historic evidence available for each, if you care to look for it" (47).

White's *A Fringe of Leaves* (1976) depicts a shipwrecked Cornishwoman held captive by Aborigines. Jill Ward's "Patrick White's *A Fringe of Leaves*: History and Fiction" (1978) notes: "Ellen Roxburgh, around whose life the book is written, has a historical counterpart in Eliza Fraser, an unfortunate Scotswoman whose shipwreck amongst the aborigines of what is now Queensland, and ultimate rescue by a convict, has been the subject of much biographical recon-struction. Further than this, the novel is remarkable for the fidelity with which it clings to the minutiae of Eliza's daily existence" (402). Similarly, Wiebe's *The Scorched-Wood People* (1977), about Riel him-self and his Métis followers, and White's *Voss*, modelled on the nineteenth-century German biologist, Ludwig Leichhardt, who dis-appeared while exploring Australia, are both closely tied to history. Wiebe's *My Lovely Enemy* (1983) entwines history and the present as a contemporary historian attempts to understand the Indian of the nineteenth century. Wiebe's *First and Vital Candle* (1966) and White's *Riders in the Chariot* (1961), which explore mystical experi-ences of indigenes and whites in contemporary society, are the exceptions among the major texts.

Wiebe's novels use a variety of narrators. *First and Vital Candle* is primarily in the third person, with one white character, Abe Ross, a northern fur trader, as centre of intelligence. It is similar to *My Lovely Enemy* as an account of one white man's individuation and the role of the indigene as part of that individuation. In the latter text, James Dyck's historical research is a part of his deepest psychic order. The novel begins in the first person, in which James states that "to be an historian is to be a time-traveler and a voyeur" (2). He describes himself, "my mind poised to hook at anything that has to do with Indians" (38). Yet he recognizes that he must "poise" much more than mind, and his experiential research creates a much larger impact on his self than that implied by "voyeur."

The Temptations of Big Bear employs a great number of narrators but the primary centre of intelligence seems to flow from a general Indian mind to various individual Indian perceptions, often without definition. In a typical section, an apparently omniscient, panoramic description of landscape moves toward an Indian sense of the black hills and then enters the consciousness of Big Bear's son:

Almost as black as the buffalo feeding on the hollow below, tiny blobs on the immensity of land.

"Poor *mus-toos-wuk*," said Big Bear. "Just sixteen."

It was not really a comment on the smallness of the herd; Kingbird understood that as he scratched himself behind his ear where an ant had crawled. (124)

The Scorched-Wood People uses a specific historical figure, the Métis songwriter Pierre Falcon, as narrator, but he clearly has knowledge which is beyond his personal experience and even beyond his death. The "voice" of the text thus becomes a free-floating Métis hero, fitting the pattern noted by the narrator when he calls to his Roman Catholic God for "this song of Riel":

> Give me this song too so that when in the century to come our people lie in the miserable trenches of poverty and humiliation and disease and perhaps despair, when troubles surround them like automatic rifles they can sing a song of faith, of belief in vision for which the mud on their feet gives them no evidence. (140)

Falcon questions whether he ever fully received this vision but the novel seems to be the "song" for which he prayed.

These three novels by White effect the powerful third-person probing of individual minds so often found in his works. *A Fringe of Leaves* invades the confusion of Ellen, always at least partial outsider whether with English gentry or Australian Aborigines. *Riders in the Chariot* does the same, person by person, through four such alien psyches, the four "riders," two white Australian women, a male Jewish immigrant, and Alf Dubbo, an itinerant Aboriginal artist. *Voss* presents a bi-polar version. Voss's contemplation of his journey is parallelled by an account of the static life of his friend, Laura, who is trying to survive in the desert of Sydney society. Their various severe alienations are counterpointed by their visions, both separate and shared, and by their extremely limited contact and yet very real devotion to each other. This duality, however, a division by gender which carefully reflects the realities of male and female experience in the Australia of the period, is undercut at the end of the novel by a suggestion of a third narrative. The reader learns that Jackie, Voss's Aboriginal companion, "became a legend amongst the tribes. Of the great country through which he travelled constantly, he was the shifting and troubled mind" (421). Yet it is a legend which the text does not tell.

This concern for legend suggests one element of these texts which enables them, at their best, to make from the semiotic field a creative tension. This is the genre employed, sophisticated forms of the historical romance. White especially seems to follow Nathaniel Hawthorne's dicta on the romance, rejecting "the probable and ordinary course of man's experience" in favour of "the Marvelous," not as overt fantasy but as a glimpse of an Other, visionary realm. As Hawthorne explains in *The House of the Seven Gables* (1851): "The point of view in which this tale comes under the Romantic definition lies in the attempt to connect a bygone time with the very present that is flitting away from us. It is a legend, prolonging itself, from an epoch now gray in the distance down into our own broad day-light, and bringing with it some of its legendary mist" (14). White's novels have the nineteenth-century tone of a swirling authorial pres-ence, in which the various centres of intelligence seem not repre-sentations of a referential reality but representations of authorial desire. Wiebe's are more restrained, as shown in the historical claim in his rejected introduction to *Big Bear*, although once again the referential is de-emphasized in favour of a fictive psyche, repre-sented in the undefined racial consciousness of *Big Bear* and a defined version of the same in *Scorched-Wood*.

Harry Shaw's *The Forms of Historical Fiction* (1983) comments on "history as drama": "By setting a novel in the past, popular roman-cers from Ainsworth to the present have offered their readers a world in which life is more intense, passions simpler, men braver, women more beautiful than they appear to be today. This might be thought of as employing history as pastoral, too, but there is a difference between using history as a screen on which to project present con-cerns, and using history to intensify a fictional story's imaginative force" (82). To use Shaw's divisions, these historical texts, with the obvious exception of *My Lovely Enemy*, seldom make overt compar-isons to the present, and thus do not become Shaw's version of pastoral, nor do they fit that aspect of Hawthorne's definition of romance. They instead emphasize history as subject, elucidating the meaning of history. Yet there are many ways in which these texts turn to an approximation of "history as drama," particularly in their interest in mysticism, in their devotion to Hawthorne's "legendary mist." They are far from "simpler," or simplistically sexist, as Shaw's comments suggest. They are not examples of "the debased and escapist form" (82) which Shaw states is the primary medium in which history as drama usually appears today. They conform in that they present a realm "braver" and, most important, "more intense" than today. These polished representations of what is commonly considered a degenerate genre use historicist assumptions of the indigene as intense life to enhance claims for a symbiotic relation between spirit and nation.

To a degree even greater than that in most texts, mysticism can be seen in Wiebe and White as the lens through which all the other commodities are filtered. Dubbo's experience of nature is presented as essential but it is a psychological experience, "the hunting grounds of his imagination" (*Riders* 371):

Alf Dubbo now went bush, figuratively at least, and as far as other human beings were concerned. Never communicative, he retired into the scrub of half-thoughts, amongst the cruel rocks of obsession. (340)

In the same way as other texts, however, while the indigene is valorized as mystical nature, the corollary of natural mysticism cannot be denied. In each text the indigenes are established as "natural," in all of the senses usually applied, such as the "wholly natural" (377) Aborigines who come to Voss's cave. *Scorched-Wood* divides its application of the standard commodities of the indigene between the mystical leadership of Riel and the violent leadership of Gabriel Dumont, Riel's second-in-command. Falcon presents Dumont as aristocrat entwined with his realm:

> He never thought of how he looked either, never saw his own face like a cliff undercut by a prairie river from one year to the next; he and his brothers and their people were their own lords, their only rulers the sky and the long land and slow muddy loops of prairie rivers, and the buffalo, their true king and ruler who gave them everything for life and happiness. (11)

Even the black inside of the Indian lodge is a part of holistic nature in *Big Bear*: "darkness moving like raw yearling buffalo hung headless, turning in the complete circle of living and solid sweet immovable and ever changing Earth" (51).

Like the omnipresent buffalo in *Big Bear* and *Scorched-Wood*, many minor aspects defined elsewhere as prime signifiers of the natural are also employed in these texts. The Scottish name of the white initiate in *Big Bear*, Kitty McLean, is an historical fact, and thus is not a "textual choice" as an example of the British savage receptive to the native culture, but Ellen Roxburgh's emphatically Cornish background in *A Fringe of Leaves* is a very different matter. Miss Scrimshaw refers to Cornwall as "A *remote* county ... Of dark people" (7). When the shipwreck removes the facade of gentility Ellen had gained through her marriage "She would have got to her feet like any other beast of nature, steadying herself in the mud and trampled grass, had it been a field and not a waterlogged boat" (208).

The standard commodities similarly are products of a natural genesis, as in the sexuality of *Big Bear*: "mounting a woman kneeling as if he were a stallion" (56). Or in the violence of *Scorched-Wood*:

> Gabriel was dancing. On the hides, all alone, the fiddlers playing the power he churned in all of us, a magnificent male dance that frothed with Métis fighting spirit, wild and living and shaped in our people by our strong horses and the wide, wide earth we rode. (42)

Or in the orality of *Voss*:

> The singing, as monotonous as grey earth, as grey wood, rose in sudden
> spasms of passion, to die down, down, as the charcoal lying. The voices
> of dust would die right away. To rise and sing. One voice, alone, would
> put on the feathers of parakeets in gay tufts of song. The big, lumbering
> pelican voices would spread slower wings. (377)

Or the mysticism of *First and Vital Candle*:

> Then the missionary came and told us of Jesus and we listened and soon
> our old beliefs seemed of little use for us to live. We have lived this way
> most of my life, and every year the deer have been less. And our prayers
> to God do not bring them back. In the old days the shaman did. (82)

Or the sense of the prehistoric in Crowfoot, one of the "regal dead"
in Wiebe's play, *Far as the Eye Can See* (1977):

> The shining mountains, where the sun falls behind the sharp white teeth
> of the earth. From nowhere we came, to nowhere we go, we are the
> shadow that runs across the grass and is lost in the sunset. (9)

Yet the standard commodities in these texts seldom have the simplistic shape found in many other examples. The violence of the
treacherous redskin still represents fear but not a simple fear which
the agents of civilization must obliterate. Neither is the sexuality of
the Indian maiden a simple temptation with no embrace nor immediate destruction if the embrace is made. The commodities are primarily vehicles to provide mystical processes of indigenization for
white characters or for the texts themselves.

While sexuality is given a positive valorization in most of these
texts, it is not without ambivalence. In *Riders* Alf seems to be unusually attractive as a sexual object for both male and female whites,
but he is never able to become subject in control of that sexuality:

> At no time in his life was Alf Dubbo able to resist what must happen.
> He had, at least, to let it begin, for he was hypnotized by the many
> mysteries which his instinct sensed. (330)

From this mystically instinctive response to his guardian's homosexuality, he quickly moves to the heterosexual clutches of a female
derelict: "as they became possessed of the same daemon" (338).

One Indian in *Big Bear* makes his adolescent discovery of sex through playing with a mare (54). Later another character observes the soldiers' prostitutes and the way in which white sex denaturalizes the Indian object:

> I'll tell you. All summer they fight and in winter they have something like women in their camps. They have holes like women but they can't cook or have children. They just lie in their lodges and those soldiers stand in a line with presents to mount them. Then in summer they want to do the same with our real women. (60–1)

The process of indigenization for Kitty McLean is a holistic initiation, in which she responds to the suggestions of Big Bear. The latter suggests that she is "so much like a Person" (312), like a Cree, and she replies, "I want to be more like you. A Person." (313). She responds to his presence:

> He smelled of smoke and sweat, sharply sweet; she felt her legs, arms, outer and inner parts of her whole body loosening as if they were clothes being unhooked. (313)

The following scene is one of overwhelming sensuality and sexuality although there is no suggestion of intercourse. Big Bear dances and chants until he mystically raises her to a holistic plane beyond her powers of analysis:

> She never remembered a word of it, nor a situation ... "Remember," he said, and she had forgotten those words too. (314–315)

The process employed by Big Bear is an undefined native ritual but Kitty McLean's transformation is definitively orgasmic, as the earth does move:

> She felt herself becoming again, the farthest tips of her moving out towards fire until she knew herself too complete to comprehend, too enormous, each unknown part of her vastness she could not yet quite feel but which would certainly surround the whole earth bending back under her. (314)

When Big Bear is captured and brought to trial he attempts to communicate through sign language with Kitty. She is unable to understand him but he once again awakens her sexuality:

Her enormous certainties had somewhere leaked between her fingers, almost suddenly, she could not tell whether – she thought in a revelation it was the monthly blackness seeping through her and momentarily she would feel dampness, she was certain she felt it, once, and when she could look at herself there would be the dark worm crawling between the blackish hair inside her leg out of that unstoppable entrance into herself. (384)

In the case of *My Lovely Enemy*, the sexual urges of the metaphorically named James Dyck are more explicit, to the point at which his exploration of sexuality might seem indulgent self-absorption. Wiebe has noted that the connection between native religion and sexuality in *Big Bear* is part of his general attempt to overcome the split he perceives in our culture between body and soul. (Interview 1980) *My Lovely Enemy* turns to the Christian ultimate in such reconciliation, *The Song of Solomon*, and then proceeds to apparently indigenous manifestations of similar blendings. *My Lovely Enemy*'s connection of sexuality and religion employs not imminent but immanent Indians. The highlight of the sexual encounters between James and his graduate student, Gillian, is on the stone wheel, associated with both the great buffalo herds and Indian ritual (110–14). As they join, they conjoin the land, and the animal and human manifestations of that land. When Gillian feels James has not recognized the enormity of the event, she confronts him with her own vision of the act and of him:

Who is this man who searches out this forgotten, lost, ancient holy place, this worship at the bare elements of the universe? Who is this man? And you told me, you showed me, and when the spirit of that place gathered, wrapped us up into one with itself, what did you think we were doing, eh? *Fuck*ing? (153)

Here, as in their many other discussions of the subject, there is a recognition that sex must be a part of a mystical unity in order to be of value.

Sexuality is superficially limited in *Voss*. The small amount of personal contact between Laura and Voss has no apparent physical dimension. When their devotion to each other is explored, it seems to be a reflection not of a sexual bond but of an hermaphroditic unity. Laura's virginal motherhood seems to imply this when she acquires the illegitimate daughter of her dead maid and thus achieves procreation without sex or pregnancy. Elsewhere, however, there is a suggestion that just as Voss in his ignorance embraces all Australian knowledge, and Laura in her stasis embraces his journey, their asexuality includes an undefined sexuality, which Voss implies in his many comments about Laura as wife and the narration reflects in an observation on the Aboriginal women:

> The women were altogether hairless, for those other parts which should have been covered, had been exposed by plucking. By some perversity of innocence, however, it did seem to emphasize the modesty of those who had been plucked. (204)

A similar inverted modesty is found in the cave drawing which Jackie explains:

> "Kangaroo," said the boy. "Old man," he smiled, touching certain parts. These were very prominent, and befitting. (274)

Such innocent power is, however, quite beyond some whites:

> The simplicity and truthfulness of the symbols was at times terribly apparent, to the extent that each man interpreted them according to his own needs and level.
> So there was ribaldry rising out of Turner, who spat, and said:
> "There is no mistaking the old man kangaroo. They have seen to that."
> (279)

The attitude seems to reflect Gillian's comment in *My Lovely Enemy*. Turner would turn the Aboriginal sign into "fucking."

In *Of Grammatology*, Derrida considers many aspects of the approach/avoidance response to writing as a "supplement" to speech. In this context his discussion of Rousseau's comments on masturbation might shed some light on the praise for and yet fear of indigene sexuality: "The dangerous supplement, which Rousseau also calls a 'fatal advantage,' is properly *seductive*; it leads desire away from the good path, makes it err from natural ways, guides it toward its loss or fall and therefore it is a sort of lapse or scandal (*scandalon*)" (151). This reaction to masturbation is related by Derrida to a fear of castration but there is also a simpler implication. Masturbation gives a greater degree of control and thus supplements sexuality but at the same time represents a move "from natural ways," from procreation, and from the necessity of male-female bonding, confusing though the latter may be. Indigene sexuality in these texts is of course "wholly natural," but it is at the same time severely alien to the white text. The transfiguration by holistic sexuality in *Big Bear* is countered by a strangely underscored asexuality in *Voss* and an ardently embraced and yet confusing sexuality in *My Lovely Enemy*. In the latter, James notes, "To live genitally is a beginning, also an end" (132). Alpha and Omega but also birth and death.

Violence is a source of constant tension in Wiebe's texts, particularly in *Big Bear*. The other Indian leaders call for war against the white invaders, but while Big Bear accepts violence as intrinsic to his culture, he finds a justification for pacifism within an apparently indigenous mysticism:

> The Spirit must have sent these whites to us so we must find the way He wants us to live with them. We see we cannot fight them. Fighting is good in raids, and makes men, but we know it cannot be His way for us to do nothing but kill. (105)

In *My Lovely Enemy*, Maskepetoon is, in violence, as in so many other factors, on the border of history. The violence which makes him kill his wife defines him as the treacherous redskin who is then transformed by Christian pacifism. In *First and Vital Candle* Inuit violence is shown to be a response to natural experience. The madness of starvation leads to violence, to which the only response is more violence in order to maintain the community. When a visiting air force captain wants to talk to the Objiwa children, the teacher warns him that her pupils will be unable to understand military defense or the possibility of preparing to kill someone you do not hate:

> These children are simple. Even the oldest hasn't had much western history to – condition – them. They can't imagine anyone making plans to kill and doing so without any particular emotion. (234)

Pierre Falcon depicts the violence of the Métis as a necessary part of communication, a source of integration rather than the alienation produced by the white violence:

> Men who have felt their fists meet each other's faces can often endure each other's ideas much better than before – at least so the Métis have always believed or, in any case, behaved. (*Scorched*, 65–6)

The violence of *Riders* is limited to that alienation, almost always a white violence, which represents the failure of society at large to understand the visionary, whether black or white. When Alf becomes violent towards his sexual partners it does not seem a rebirth of the violence as communitas represented by Falcon. Alf's violence is either just a failed comprehension similar to that displayed by the whites or perhaps an inevitable product of the degradation of his situation. This is a familiar pattern in portraits of contemporary indigenes which represent them as post-lapsarian. A similar scenario is a major factor in *First and Vital Candle*. The young Ojibwa girl, Violet, is a typical object of the gaze of the trader: "There could be no question; this girl had been shaped in mind and body to comfort tormented man" (160). Her appeal is traditional but the result is not. She attracts her cousin, Alex, who is denied her by incest taboos but, because he has been deindigenized by education, he is unable to accept these limitations. When Alex tries to possess Violet with the assistance of "the pseudo-bravado of brew" (266) and the collective violence of his intoxicated friends, the possession is not the product of natural freedom but a reflection of deindigenized decadence:

> This was obscenity only the most drunken or perverted Indian would ever commit in private, leave alone before others reeling and laughing as they watched. (262)

All of these texts by both authors are concerned with suffering and the mystical vision which suffering can provide. Violence might be considered in the context of that suffering, as of value because of the value of the suffering. Wiebe's texts seldom present indigene violence as validated in this way. The suffering which ennobles Riel and Big Bear and Abe Ross is caused by either malevolent white violence or the unshapable violence of the land. *Riders* is quite similar. White's other texts present a more complicated valorization of violence, in which suffering predominates but the violence which produces that suffering is not the enemy of the sufferer but a part of him/her. The Aboriginal Jackie's killing of Voss is pure and even purification: "He must break the terrible magic that bound him remorselessly, endlessly, to the white men" (419). Yet the act proves to tie Jackie even more firmly to his "victim."

Cannibalism is used by both Wiebe and White, although by the former in only a very restrained way in *First and Vital Candle*. The sexual violence associated with the degraded Ojibwa at the end of the novel is paralleled by the cannibalism of the starving Inuit at the beginning, but the latter is similarly shown as destructive, here as part of madness:

> "Where are the chil — " I begin but Nukak jogs my arm, gesturing to the floor. There are so many split bones lying about that I stumbled coming

in. As I blink down at them now suddenly the woman laughs again. And in that shriek I understand. (75)

This enigmatic reference is never expanded but is left to resonate within or beneath the text. Here cannibalism replaces sexuality as Foucault's mentioned unmentionable.

Voss similarly presents cannibalism as a response to the famine which is a part of a harsh land, but the metaphysical resonances are more obvious. When the Aborigines kill the expedition's horses, they gorge themselves in an orgiastic fashion; "If they were beyond pardon, it was their lean lives that had damned them" (392). The demonic is demonically natural. Voss recognizes that this landscape of starvation makes cannibalism almost inevitable:

"If we are not devoured by blacks," Voss replied, "or the Great Snake, then we shall be eaten by somebody eventually." (379)

In the first part of Ellen Roxburgh's captivity in *A Fringe of Leaves*, she is obsessed with food; the Aborigines have little to eat and she has even less. Then she unwittingly comes upon a cannibal feast and picks up from the remnants the thigh bone of a girl:

Her stiffened body and almost audibly twangling nerves were warning her against what she was about to do, what she was, in fact, already doing. She had raised the bone, and was tearing at it with her teeth, spasmodically chewing, swallowing by great gulps which her throat threatened to return. But did not. She flung the bone away only after it was cleaned, and followed slowly in the wake of her cannibal mentors. She was less disgusted in retrospect by what she had done, than awed by the fact that she had been moved to do it. The exquisite innocence of this forest morning, its quiet broken by a single flute-note endlessly repeated, tempted her to believe that she had partaken of a sacrament. But there remained what amounted to an abomination of human behaviour, a headache, and the first signs of indigestion. In the light of Christian morality she must never think of the incident again. (248)

Cannibalism is not solely an Aboriginal factor in *A Fringe of Leaves*, as shown when Ellen confronts the other survivor from the shipwreck, Pilcher, the second mate:

"And what about your companions? Did they favour eating one another?" Mr. Pilcher swallowed. "Some of 'em was eaten." (347)

Marcus Clarke's *His Natural Life* (1870) provides a morbidly humorous account of the cannibalism of escaped convicts, with the following note:

> I would not have introduced so repulsive an incident as this cannibalism of escaping convicts, were not such incidents hideously frequent among absconders; and no writer, professing to give a truthful picture of the results of the old convict system, can afford to ignore them. (559)

Such claims for the novel as another version of the explorer's documentary "info-text" have little value in reference to *A Fringe of Leaves*, in which Aboriginal cannibalism quickly rises from the imperative of hunger to metaphysics. Anthropologists have constantly argued about the actual practice of cannibalism by Aboriginal societies, but it clearly has at least a metaphorical role in many. A.P. Elkin, in his classic study *Aboriginal Men of High Degree* (1945), compares such ritual cannibalism to transubstantiation (60). A similar parallel is drawn in the description of Mr. Roxburgh's reaction to the death of a shipmate named Spurgeon:

> As one who had hungered all his life after friendships which eluded him, Austin Roxburgh did luxuriate on losing a solitary allegiance. It stimulated his actual hunger until now dormant, and he fell to thinking how the steward, had he not been such an unappetizing morsel, might have contributed appreciably to an exhausted larder. At once Mr. Roxburgh's self-disgust knew no bounds. He was glad that night had fallen and that everyone around him was sleeping. Yet his thoughts were only cut to a traditional pattern, as Captain Purdew must have recognized, who now came stepping between the heads of the sleepers, to bend and whisper, *This is the body of Spurgeon which I have reserved for thee, take eat and give thanks for a boil which was spiritual matter* ... Austin Roxburgh was not only ravenous for the living flesh, but found himself anxiously licking the corners of his mouth to prevent any overflow of precious blood. (209–10)

Roxburgh's dream, stimulated by physical and spiritual hunger and the presence of the mad Captain, and "cut to a traditional pattern," might be seen to reverse Elkin's analogy. Ellen's response to an Aboriginal serpent dance continues the reverberations:

> She slapped and moaned, and was carried away. She might have been carried further still had it not been for the sudden vision of Mr. Roxburgh ... Her vision was making her cry out: one of his legs had been torn off

at the hip; she could smell the smell of crackled skin ... When at last she
sat up, her eyes were closed, her lips parted to receive – the burnt sacrifice?
the bread and wine? (258–9)

In *A Fringe of Leaves* cannibalism is still a sign of terrible indigene
violence, but relative theology links it to mystical Christianity which
then gives it a power of transformation analogous to the sexual
energies transmitted from Big Bear to Kitty. Ellen not only participates in the Aboriginal life, she partakes of the Aborigine. If the
theory is that the dead person's powers will be acquired by the eater,
the young girl is a perfect choice, established before as an "inex-
haustible" (230) symbol of youth and beauty. She is first noted diving
for lily roots, an activity which Ellen repeats when escaping with
the convict, Jack Chance: "When I rescued a lady," he shouted, "I
didn't bargain for a *lubra*" (290).

Ellen's adaptation to Aboriginal society is partly a reflection of her
own primitive Cornish sensibility. She replies to Jack's comment on
her indigenization, "Wouldn't go hungry, would ee?," her dialect
defining her allegiances. But it is also a comment on the distance of
the civilized English, shown in Austin's devotion to his Virgil:

> Soon after his arrival her own reasoning told her that books held more
> for Austin Roxburgh than the life around him. (43)

His choice of Virgil as literary inspiration is constantly re-empha-
sized, as when he looks at the island on which they are deserted:

> But of vegetation or shade there was little: nothing of that pastoral green
> Mr. Roxburgh had hoped to find, in which to re-live the pleasures of the
> Georgics. (186)

Of course, the latter pleasures cannot be "re-lived" because they
have never existed in the first life in other than Roxburgh's mind.
Derrida has claimed that there is nothing outside the text, but Roxburgh's experience suggests that there is nothing inside the text,
nothing of life. Roxburgh's obliteration of his diary from "guilt or
fears" (57) is followed by a similar reaction when Ellen examines the
diary in which her mother-in-law compelled her to write:

> As she rummaged, it became of increasing consequence to find, to read,
> to confirm that she had not written more of the truth than can bear looking
> at. (158)

This oralist fear of the supplement of writing can be linked to all aspects of their overdetermined dichotomous marriage. The separation between Austin's life in books and Ellen's life, reinforced by the assertions of her presence in dialect, are underscored by the difference in their sexuality:

> Just as she was to learn that death was for Mr. Roxburgh a 'literary conceit,' so she found that his approach to passion had its formal limits. (64)

In *Allegories of Reading*, (1979) Paul de Man suggests that "A literary text simultaneously asserts and denies the authority of its own rhetorical mode" (17). He calls this "an allegory of reading. As the report of the contradictory interference of truth and error in the process of understanding, the allegory would no longer be subject to the destructive power of this complication. To the extent that it is not itself demonstrably false, the allegory of the play of truth and falsehood would ground the stability of the text" (72). *A Fringe of Leaves* is less concerned with establishing the truth of orality than with questioning the truth of writing and reading. The assertions of Aboriginal truth in the novel are through dance and cannibalism. The sounds of the Aborigines are primarily "their customary wailing" (249), an ongoing statement of presence.

Voss provides similar claims for writing as falsehood. Judd, Voss's convict companion, fears "the great mystery of words":

> Words were not the servants of life, but life, rather, was the slave of words. So the black print of other people's books became a swarm of victorious ants that carried off a man's self-respect. (203)

The arid leaders of Sydney society are similarly opposed to books, but their antagonism comes in the form of contempt for Laura's absurd devotion to the useless practice of reading. The text's clear rejection of these socialites might lead the reader to expect the written word to be supported in opposition to the ignorance of Judd and the philistinism of Sydney. But even the best of such words are shown to be inadequate. The letters between Laura and Voss almost never reach their destination. The letters are validated not as communication but as a spur to mystical communion. The character most devoted to writing, Le Mesurier, is also the most tortured by failure, which even he realizes in his suicide: "This book no longer bore looking at, although his life was contained in its few pages" (380).

Unlike *A Fringe of Leaves*, however, the Aborigines of *Voss* assert a clear opposition, in both natural orality and aversion to writing. When the older guide, Dugald, departs from the white men, to fulfill the destiny of his Aboriginal prehistoricism and go away to die, Voss gives him a letter to Laura. Once Dugald finally gets away from "the conscience he had worn in the days of the whites" (219), he also discards the letter:

> These papers contained the thoughts of which the whites wished to be rid, explained the traveller, by inspiration: the sad thoughts, the bad, the thoughts that were too heavy, or in any way hurtful. These come out through the white man's writing-stick, down upon paper, and were sent away. (220)

Not unlike Ellen, Dugald recognizes writing as Derrida's "dangerous supplement."

Falcon similarly notes in *Scorched-Wood* that "letters are dangerous; I never knew a Métis except Riel who liked them" (170). Riel's supplement drives him yet also dooms him:

> And he was writing; words to fill the leather suitcase, to give his unwritten people a place on paper before the frozen earth closed them away one by one and no one would hear them, the words they cried to each other lost like the cry of gulls turning trackless over the river, words to be used against him, for every written word called to judgement. (245)

The oral is natural but impermanent, doomed by the commodity of the prehistoric indigene. The written is permanent but damning. Big Bear makes a similar judgment when he rejects Cree Syllabics: "I knew that once. But when I looked at the paper it always said only what the missionaries said, so I forgot them" (144). He offers the alternative of aural memory: "I will keep hearing every good word said here" (145). His own oratorical ability at producing such memories is remarked throughout the text and made explicit in his long speech when on trial for treason. One white official's report from the field moves from the confusions of newspaper clippings to a recognition of Big Bear as presence: "I believe now it is his voice, and his perception, which draws more and more people to him" (113). It might be the equivalent of the voice conjured by the narrator of Wiebe's story "Where is the Voice Coming From?" (1974). He stands looking at a museum case which holds remnants of the last battle of the Cree Almighty Voice with the Mounted Police:

And there is a voice. It is an incredible voice that rises from among the young poplars ripped of their spring bark ..., a voice so high and clear, so unbelievably high and strong in its unending wordless cry.

The voice of "Gitchie-Manitou Wayo" – interpreted as "voice of the Great Spirit" – that is, The Almighty Voice. His death chant no less incredible in its beauty than in its incomprehensible happiness.

I say "wordless cry" because that is the way it sounds to me. I could be more accurate if I had a reliable interpreter who would make a reliable interpretation. For I do not, of course, understand the Cree myself. (*Where*, 143)

The name of Almighty Voice becomes signifier for a presence of orality which mystically transcends historical presence, for which the valorization is greater because of the impossibility of linear comprehension.

Maskepetoon, in *My Lovely Enemy*, seems to hold more hope than Big Bear for the maintenance of Indian orality within the supplement of literacy. An undefined Indian narrator quotes Maskepetoon as saying, "The mystery of words and the world is revealed in the Book for those who truly want to know" (159). This narrator observes,

When we first saw words we could lift and put down with our hands, we thought such words would destroy both listening and memory alto-gether. However, after many long thoughts around a centre fire, we understood that this was not so. Rather, the knowledge of how to fix words in wood or leather or paper gave them their ultimate power: now one could handle them, make them and send them in silence, see them as well as hear and remember. (159)

But neither the text nor James seems similarly convinced of the superiority of this supplement:

I don't speak Cree, I should do this properly but I don't, in the oral tradition remembering the past date by date is no Indian tradition, how can a white man find any fact beyond the story memory of a language he doesn't talk unless he tries to trace say one name of one person through all the white documents he can find, letters, diaries, notes, travel books, white gossip in the unlikeliest places you can dig from the nineteenth century? (43–4)

James seems to provide a more complicated version of the reaction of Almighty Voice's "auditor." The passage suggests a surface acceptance of the Indian's oral presence over white writing but as well there is a morass of confusion about the speech/writing dichotomy, represented in the ambiguous references to "oral tradition," "Indian tradition," "story memory," and even "language." This might be part of the text's rejection of the naive belief in Book put forth by the Indian narrator. All the writing "remembered" in the university library is defeated by James's vision of Christ, who asserts,

> You are then forced to contemplate the creation of the world not as the act of physical birth out of God's womb, but rather as the act of being *spoken into existence by Words coming out of God's mouth.* (142)

This seems again a refinement, perhaps a Christianizing of the presence of Almighty Voice. The passage represents logos, the belief in the Word as essence, with a vengeance, but a logos very much removed from writing and very much convinced of the presence of speech.

Maskepetoon wraps up in himself most of these contradictions. Regardless of Big Bear's rejection of its potential for truth, the Cree syllabics which Maskepetoon reads are apparently closer to the oral than most writing. Much more than our nonphonetic English it is writing which claims to be speech. Yet this Book which claims to turn his oral signs into written ones is a white creation, made from outside his sign system. The text itself balances between that assertion of ignorance by James and assertions of indigenous semiosis such as the Indian consciousness or even Maskepetoon's name. At the beginning, James states that history records English, Cree, Blackfoot, and French names for the Indian leader, as well as anglicized French and various English transliterations of Indian names. The choice made by the text, however, is the most obviously "Indian," Maskepetoon.

This gesture towards an indigene semiosis might be compared to one in *A Fringe of Leaves*, in which the limitations of Ellen's centre of intelligence are reinforced by the absence from the text of Aboriginal names. Except for the other white blackfellow, Jack Chance, known as Ulappi, and an old "wise man": "'Turrwan,' as the others constantly referred to the magician" (260), the names, like the culture, remain of the Other. In *Voss*, the two Aboriginal guides are named Dugald and Jackie. The first seems absurdly elevated, the remnant of some strange christening by a Scot – or anti-Scot. "Jackie" is a station-black name of such frequency as to have become generic. Unlike Wiebe's novel, there is no suggestion of an alien naming system. Just as Jackie's legend remains outside the text, so does the Aboriginal semiosis.

Yet even after his ultimate visionary act of killing Voss, Jackie remains prey to limited white values. At the end of the novel, the mundane Colonel Hebden sends a letter to seek Jackie's help in the search for Voss. He asks that anyone seeing Jackie "send word to him" (417). After a novel in which writing has clearly failed and speech has been only slightly more successful, and the constant reiteration of the word, "word," has built a myriad of delusions, such a message seems doubly doomed.

In *Riders*, Alf responds to the Bible but only as a spur to his own dreams. As for most indigene figures, writing has little to offer him. He thinks of the library:

> All the readers had found what they had been looking for, the black man noticed with envy. But he was not altogether surprised; words had always been the natural weapons of whites. (342)

In *Riders* even logos offers little better than the word sent by Colonel Hebden. When the Jew, Himmelfarb, is let down from his mock crucifixion, the shawl and other articles of faith which the crucifiers had trampled are restored by Alf:

> The latter did not speak, though. He would not speak, now, or ever. His mouth could never offer passage to all that he knew to be inside him. (417)

Alf, of course, communicates primarily through his visionary paintings, but even they are insufficient to represent this sacrifice of Himmelfarb: "He would have liked to draw the touch of air. Once, though, he had attempted, and failed miserably to convey the skin of silence nailed to a tree" (434). In *Voss* the Aborigines are illiterate, and thus beyond the dangerous supplement of writing. When their signmaking is suggested in the cave drawings, it is immediately shown to be much more natural than white ways, represented by Turner's interpretation. Their "non-writing" is pure as is their sexuality. Yet the ultimate purity is the Aborigines' "arc of concentrated silence" (364), Jackie's legend beyond the text. *Voss* employs the standard commodity of orality in the indigene, particularly in its corollary of not-writing, only in order to surpass it through the embrace of a linked commodity, that of mysticism. The search continues to be for presence but for a presence of silence. As in White's other texts, no hope for logos remains. In Wiebe, however, although writing fails, the presence of the voice lives in wordless cry, but "lives" only as residue of the prehistoric. Although Crowfoot is joined in the "regal dead" by an Alberta premier, William Aberhart, and the namesake of the province, Princess Louise, it is Crowfoot who asserts their status as "shadow ... lost in the sunset" (9). To Falcon, the Métis are "unwritten people": "the frozen earth closed them away" (245). All they leave are the reverberations picked up in Bolt's play, *Gabe*, in which two contemporary Métis are doomed by their names, Louis and Gabriel, to look forever backward to the heroes, Riel and Dumont, never forward to any personal achievement. The historical damnation of Falcon's comment, in which the people are to be no more, is maintained by a play in which the present people are not present.

The commodity of the prehistoric is most directly presented in Wiebe in *First and Vital Candle*, in which the Inuit are a sign for death. Oolulik's *ubi sunt* chant: "*Where have gone the deer,/And the people of the deer?*" (82) is followed by the deaths by famine and the recognition that Oolulik has murdered, although in self-defense. In jail she hangs herself: "She too had gone away" (84). Among the Ojibwa there is death from the evil power of the liquor-selling trader, but the greater fear is deindigenization, in which "Pimadaziwin, the Good Life" is a thing only of remnant visions:

> Perhaps the child that had tugged the box over the foot-packed earth too had been dreaming about flying away where he would be forever child, an Indian child with sure knowledge of pimadaziwin – no – the children, if anyone, were becoming the most distinctly, most forcedly non-Indian. (220)

The hope for the child to remain the usual signifier of the child of human evolution fails as he is forced into white historicity, no longer the child of natural innocence but the child torn from all contact with the noumenal.

Ellen Roxburgh is clearly buffeted by history: married during the first splintering of the British class system, journeying to Australia when it was being opened to entrepreneurial capitalism, saved from the bush by the beginnings of convictism. But she herself is less convinced by history than by a prehistoric mysticism: "It was Ellen Gluyas's hope that she might eventually be sent a god. Out of Ireland, according to legend" (40). Her life with the Aborigines becomes itself a legend and she is "absorbed into tribal dreams" (226). In the dance "she bowed her head and swayed in time," (258) but she loses time, her vision wandering from the harvest dance of her youth through life with her husband in England through glimpses of an impossible future. She has entered something akin to the traces in

Alf Dubbo's mind when he watches an absurdly decadent dance by two "queans": "If there had been space, he, too, would have danced the figures he remembered from some forgotten time" (356). His memories of the forgotten, like the visions of Ellen in her Aboriginal captivity, and like Alf's dreams throughout, are suggestions of the indigenous noumenal, something far beyond the simple temporal assumptions of white Australia.

Voss and Laura "were writing their own legend" (367), but when he is lost and Laura is told that "Voss is already history," she replies, "But history is not acceptable until it is sifted for the truth" (413). Perhaps more truth is to be found in that unwritten legend of Jackie. He leaves "the country of the dead" but remains within it:

> Dugald had become so old he was again young, and he, Jackie, was weighed down with the wisdom of age ... Of the great country through which he travelled constantly, he was the shifting and troubled mind. His voice would issue out of his lungs, and wrestle with the rocks, until it was thrown back at him. He was always speaking with the souls of those who had died in the land, and was ready to translate their wishes into dialect. (420–1)

This ultimate Aboriginality voyages beyond time, to the dead, and beyond humanity, to the voice which wrestles the rock. Like the disembodied cry of an Almighty Voice or like the final sentence of *Big Bear*, when the latter lies down in the sand: "Slowly, slowly, all changed continually into indistinguishable, as it seemed, and everlasting, unchanging, rock" (415). Prehistoricity dooms the indigene as present figure but also establishes the indigene as unchanging presence, whether the voice sings in the air, wrestles with the rock, or is the rock itself.

The bifurcation of time in *My Lovely Enemy*, with the twentieth century looking back at the nineteenth, shapes the historicity of the text. The first-person narration increases the impression of presence in the text but that first person perceives the indigene only through writing, thus increasing the distance from both indigenous people and indigenous time. The opposite is the case in *A Fringe of Leaves* and *Voss*, which depict direct contact by Ellen and Voss with the Aborigines but in which the nineteenth-century tone of the narration establishes the temporal distance of the text from the reader. The Aborigines of *A Fringe of Leaves* and *Voss* remain somehow before time while in *My Lovely Enemy* Maskepetoon struggles on the cusp of chronology.

James undergoes a conscious use of the prehistoric and of histo-ricity in his indigenization. He asserts, "Nothing ever happens, the Indians say, but what has been already foretold" (114). The text thus explores James' visionary associations with Maskepetoon and with the Indianness of the place as a search for his own individuation, a seeking of future through past but, maintaining the standard com-modity of the prehistoric, a past which is never allowed to enter the present except through remnants of memory or, in the case of the stone wheel, the Indian rock which metaphorizes the transformation of Big Bear into rock. Metaphoric indigenization becomes most explicit in a scene which might be perceived as having an undertone of cannibalism because of the constant association of buffalo and Indian in Wiebe's texts and others. James journeys to a strange resort, a shrine of various signifiers of Albertan heritage, where he eats *"Bison in utero"* (202). The guests question whether it is an authentic Indian dish but the symbolism is none the less clear. Voss is born into Australia as he is eaten by the land. James in-corporates Canada as he swallows the land not-yet-born.

The distinction to be made between the texts of Wiebe and White and most of the others in this study is not one of essential difference but of a difference in sensitivity and tone, and, in the case of White, an assurance of distance. *A Fringe of Leaves* and *Voss* remain resolutely circumscribed by the semiotic field but the problematic of the texts is constantly asserted. Macherey's ideological horizon is reinscribed on every page, to be examined and considered. At the same time, the elements of fear in these texts, of an indigenization which leads to death in *Voss* and alienated exile in *A Fringe of Leaves*, allow the distance to be maintained. The ardent embrace which is the sign of indigenization in Wiebe's texts removes some of the distance and makes the horizon less a statement by the text than a statement of the text, a semiotic field which is revealed rather than displayed.

Yet such an assertion cannot be the final word on Wiebe's texts. Unlike many other contemporary white Canadians who depict native peoples in their texts, Wiebe is seldom if ever attacked by native people in public or in conversation. His texts combine careful scholarly research and extraordinary sensitivity to native cultures. This might then suggest that my methodology is in some way "unfair," that it results in nothing other than an impossible pros-cription, in which "even Rudy Wiebe" is unable to avoid transgres-sions. The issue goes beyond simple assertions of the difference between Wiebe's texts and Wiebe's intentions, as it is the texts as well as the author which have been accepted. If the white culture

has created a semiotic field of such power that no textual representation, very much including the study you are now reading, can
escape it, then semiosis has gone well beyond the level of "simple
signs" to be itself the trap which it represents. There seem three
possible responses. The first is to deny the conclusions of this study
and to accept the essential referentiality of at least "the best" of these
texts, such as those of Wiebe. The second is to accept the inevitability
of the semiotic field as an immutable product of the society. The
third is to establish an awareness of our semiotic snare and reverse
it so that it becomes a device of genealogy.

CHAPTER ELEVEN

A Polemical Conclusion

All of the assessments made in this study can be seen as reflections of the fear/temptation split manifested in the violence and sex commodities. The general sign of fear incorporates an indigenization which excludes the indigene. Temptation holds with it an indigenization by inclusion for the white who, one might say, "acquires Indian." Note that my word is "acquires," not "becomes." Some psychologists might diagnose this acquiring as a rejection of self for not-self which represents a significant degree of self-hate. The typical pattern of such narratives on the indigene must modify such an interpretation, however. The indigene is acquired, the white is not abandoned. The title character of Kroetsch's *Gone Indian* has quite clearly "gone" too far. The task is to go native, not to become gone native. *Gone Indian* captures the process in its reference to Grey Owl as "finest Indian of them all" (80). Grey Owl, the Englishman turned Indian who perfectly grasped that the signifiers of the indigene are the essence, not the signified, and most assuredly not the referent. He has many fictional brothers in the Canadian tradition and is a close relative of the various "white blackfellows" in the Australian, from Tucker's *Ralph Rashleigh* (1845?) to Jack Chance in White's *A Fringe of Leaves* (1976). The metaphorical attempt is to achieve roots in the new land but Grey Owl demonstrated that it is sufficient to acquire a veneer.

A central factor in all of the literature on the indigene is that his or her role is invariably that of the indigene. There are novels in which a woman is not Woman or a plumber is not Plumber but there are none in which an Indian is not INDIAN, or Maori not MAORI. Joan Clark's *Victory of Geraldine Gull* (1988) makes an observation which holds true for all texts, including her own:

You may not notice the lawyers, teachers and social workers in these cities, Indians who, when they wear suits and polished shoes, can walk past a doorman. (16)

They can also walk past a novel.

The situation is a still more extreme version of that noted by Teresa de Lauretis in *Alice Doesn't: Feminism, Semiotics, Cinema* (1984): "The relation between women as historical subjects and the notion of woman as it is produced by hegemonic discourses is neither a direct relation of identity, a one-to-one correspondence, nor a relation of simple implication. Like all other relations expressed in language, it is an arbitrary and symbolic one, that is to say, culturally set up" (5–6). The indigene as cultural item is similarly a result of hegemonic textualization. In Hilliard's *The Glory and the Dream*, the central white character observes, "The state of being Maori was never absent from their thinking; the state of being European was never present in his, except when he was with them" (110). The text seems to accept the accuracy of the comment but it fails to recognize the Foucauldian power of the gaze of the subject. The Maori are observed only through that gaze and thus they must be perceived by the gaze to be thinking Maori. Even in a text by a Maori, such as *Mutuwhenua: The Moon Sleeps* (1978) by Patricia Grace, they are valorized as Maori and must again be presented as thinking definitively Maori. Bishop Berkeley's "You are because I perceive you perceiving" is taken still another step. Hilliard's Maori enter the equation as "You are you because I perceive you perceiving as you."

The indigene field must be circumscribed in order to preserve its position as symbol of national essence. Roland Barthes has suggested that the Eiffel Tower is the ultimate signifier for things Parisian, an open symbol which has in itself no meaning and thus any meaning might be poured into it ("The Eiffel Tower"). How much more symbolic then is the Aborigine of Australia, the Maori of New Zealand, or the Indian or Inuk of Canada. Those of us who are white citizens of such countries often find that the indigenous culture is the only one of any interest to European observers. We might legitimately ask Europeans for consideration as at the very least the fruition of their invasions, the obverse of the Pakistani or Jamaican residents of England. We can say, "We're here because you were here." But they tend to dismiss us as less the cultivated plants grown from their ancestors' seeds than stale unfertilized pods, second-rate, second-hand Europeans, no matter how hard we try to convince them of the contrary. They would rather, like Grey Owl, look to the clearly shaped symbolic entity of the indigene.

In studies of this sort it is almost a commonplace to conclude with a discussion of the indigene writer's use of the image of the indigene. The desire for such texts is found throughout all three literatures. Moynihan's introduction to *The Feast of the Bunya* examines Aboriginal rituals and suggests, "There may be materials for an epic poem – which can never be written in the absence of an aboriginal genius" (14). At least recently, the search for "an aboriginal genius" is often a response to the stereotypes perceived in white texts: if the image is controlled by an indigene text, all will be well. But is it possible for the Maori writer to take a European form such as the novel and use it successfully to describe his or her own people? When this question has been addressed to me my usual reaction has been to attempt to deflect it. Regardless of Arnoldian claims for the freedom of the disinterested liberal critic, I question the right of any person to judge another's representation of his or her own culture. Thus, a reader will note that with very few, and usually very brief, exceptions, indigenous writers are not examined in this book.

The situation is not unlike that when whites comment on African literatures: it is not for them to tell the Africans whether or not they are getting it right. However, the African situation can also provide at least a tentative answer to the question which I am avoiding. Many African writers, among them Wole Soyinka and Chinua Achebe, have noted the extreme difficulties they have found in melding European literary forms and African culture, but they have also asserted the need to overcome this barrier in order to make use of the literary developments which would seem a major positive contribution of modern western culture. Native peoples in Canada, New Zealand, and Australia have not made as many attacks on that barrier as have Africans, but there are a number of noteworthy examples, such as the works of the Maori writer Witi Ihimaera and of the Aboriginal novelist Colin Johnson, whose novel *Doctor Wooreddy's Prescription for Enduring the End of the World* (1983) is, I think, a major landmark in Australian writing.

But if I examine them through the methodology established in this study, I perceive many of the same problems as in white texts. This could be simply the limitations of my centre as white Canadian reader, and I await the correctives which will no doubt come from critics who are able to write as Maori or Aboriginal readers. It could also, however, reflect the power of the semiotic field, as noted in connection with Wiebe, a white with a pronounced and considered commitment to native peoples. The epistemological assumptions in the indigene writer's "control" should be examined as well. No matter how much the object of a writing subject approximates the self, the object cannot be turned into subject. The writing subject no doubt has a number of unusual insights into that object, but the process of textual production creates inherent restrictions on the subject's liberation of the object. How much more so when the object is a long-established sign as rigid as the indigene. Eli Mandel captures the tendencies involved in "Chief Dan Kennedy" (1973), which describes an elderly Indian's attempts to explain his culture to the white poet:

> he showed me
> past
>   English journals
> with maps
> pictures of Indians. (*Stony*, 62)

This might be seen as an example of the inadequacy and decay of the indigenous culture because it lacks sign systems sufficient to display itself. Or it might be seen as a canny assessment of what the white poem requires. The indigene of the white text is the indigene for the white text.

The agenda of this study is, to use Terry Eagleton's term in *Literary Theory: An Introduction* (1983), "strategic" (210). The primary application of this strategy here is textual, and, to be still more restrictive, literary. But it can be of use in a much wider area. One example of such use is the following consideration of the "1887 One Hundredth Anniversary Collectors' Issue 1987" of *Saturday Night*, which claims in its advertising to be "Canada's Magazine." The cover of this issue is quite explicit, beginning with five words from the Canadian national anthem: "Our Home and Native Land: A celebration of people and places that make Canada a country unlike any other." However, inside the cover, the "Native," the people "that make Canada a country unlike any other," is very much an absent presence. The brief references to native peoples I have found in one hundred and ninety-two pages are as follows: Margaret Atwood's "True North" mentions one Indian from a novel and then notes "the natives" who guide American hunters to polar bears. Peter Foster's "The Destruction of Wealth," about oil exploration in the north, comments on "natives" as "polar-bear monitors" and then ends with the only individualized image of a native in the magazine: "In Tuktoyaktuk a moon-faced Inuvialuit child sits before the magic visions of a rock video" (164). The natural yet lunar and thus alien indigene defamiliarizes white technology into mysticism. Finally, in a specifically ethnic piece, Fil Fraser's "Black Like Me," which is very conscious of his unusual position as a fifty-four-year-old black born in Canada, there is no reference to the first "visible minority" except as a part of the melting-pot to the south: "Everyone – the Puerto Ricans, the Indians, the Mexicans, the various other Latinos – is 'American,' whether they like it or not" (184). Of course, I am assuming by context that this refers to Amerindians. Our imperial heritage makes many misreadings possible.

The editors of *Saturday Night* could respond that the magazine has done other pieces on native peoples – on the pope's planned visit to the north, on attempts to maintain native languages. They might also be able to refer to various assignments on the subject for the anniversary issue which "didn't pan out." Or they could claim that they simply failed to notice the implications of the title chosen for their cover. But, to slightly pervert Derrida's meaning, "There is nothing beyond the text."

Even this consideration of popular culture, of the wider realms of written culture, however, is a too limited view of the implications of this study. To return for a moment to Barthes, native peoples are of course not the Eiffel tower. As do any people, they have a dynamic which they shape and which is shaped for them. But so much of the shaping is produced by the role their image plays as Eiffel tower for Canada, Australia, or New Zealand, in any context. The article on native languages mentioned as a possible excuse for *Saturday Night*, "Beyond Words" by Ronald Wright, while a passionate call for native sovereignty, is a particularly extreme use of the standard commodities of orality, mysticism, and the prehistoric. Each representation in print journalism, in television, in films, in art, in conversation returns to the Image. As an almost perfect example of what Derrida claims to be the intended meaning of his famous phrase, they are part of a text. Derrida's "Racism's Last Word" emphasizes apartheid as "word." "Indian," "Maori," and "Aborigine" are words, although assuredly not "intention-laden" words such as apartheid is. Racism and apartheid seem intrinsically joined. Yet although there are many who use these indigene words without racist intent, the words exist only as signifiers, tied to the image of the indigene. That the valorization of this image begins with an ideology not unlike apartheid is represented in an editorial in *The Bulletin*, entitled "Our Black Brothers" (1883):

Gather them all together on an immense reserve in North-Western Australia, say; there is plenty of room there. Let them have no rum and no religion, but fight and frolic in their own way. And by the time the whites would be closing in on them, they would have reduced their own numbers so much by internal quarrels that the boundary line of their reservation could be shifted inwards far enough to allow of four or five "runs" in the space vacated. So the process of closing in could go on until the last survivors, two or three in number, were frozen out altogether. Some showman by that time would make a good thing of taking them around the other colonies and exhibiting them as curiosities. This is the way to let the black race die out easily and naturally. (6)

As the image is isolated, so should be the people. The violence would lead to the "natural" achievement of the prehistoric. The final remnants would be reduced to solely symbolic entities. Contemporary white reactions to native peoples are seldom as overtly racist, but they have a similar tendency to treat the indigene as object without recognizing the very textual position of that reification.

It is useful to look at the comments in various polemical texts presented by native peoples. *Beyond the Act* (1979), a confrontation with government policy in the Australian state of Queensland, published by the Foundation for Aboriginal and Islander Research Action, asserts "Aborigines must be allowed to become participants. They must not be forced to retain the status of recipients" (298). Henry Jack's "Native Alliance for Red Power" in *The Only Good Indian* (1970), edited by Waubageshig, asserts: "We will not be free until we are able to determine our destiny. Therefore, we want the power to determine the destiny of our reservations and communities, and power over our lives will entail the abolition of the Indian Act, and the destruction of the colonial office (Indian Affairs Branch)" (170). Donna Awatere's *Maori Sovereignty* (1984) takes the call one step further: "Maoris should have control of New Zealand because it is *our* country. Who the *hell* gave British and European immigrants the right to take over another place, whether it is Zimbabwe, Azania or Aotearoa" (15). These comments, arbitrarily selected, might be seen as reversing the general perception of the varying dimensions of the "native problem" in the three countries. Awatere's attack is made in New Zealand, usually regarded to have the "best" policies on native peoples. The section of *Beyond the Act* which includes this tentative expression of hope for Queensland Aborigines was written *for* the Aboriginal group by two white social workers, in a state which is regarded within Australia, the country with the "worst" record of the three considered in this study, as having a racist government. Another section of the book, similarly white-authored, attacks Queensland for being "out of step" (270) with Canada and New Zealand. Thus the text with the most anger is indigene-controlled, published in a society recognized as racially liberated. The text which hesitates to ask for the minimum is itself a part of a paternalistic system, published in a society where the white father is recognized to be never kin and always less than kind.

Many other texts could be as a basis for discussion of these issues. The various autobiographies of natives who have been politically active, such as Max Gros-Louis's *First Among the Hurons* (1974) or Charles Perkins's *A Bastard Like Me* (1975), or even the many magazine biographies of native leaders such as one by Nicola Legat in *Auckland Metro*: "Atareta Poananga and Te Ahi Kaa" (1986), with the telling subtitle: "What do Maori Nationalists Want?" are all possibilities. The careful polemic by Harold Cardinal, *The Rebirth of Canada's Indians* (1977), would be particularly relevant. Without the overt semiology used in this study, it traces many elements of Indian life in white society that reflect the standard commodities found in the literature. Cardinal's title reacts to both the general problem of assimilation and the commodity of the prehistoric which makes the indigene a sign of death: "In this rebirth, Indian people will undergo a process of de-brainwashing themselves from the stultifying century-long hold that the so-called Christian dominations have imposed upon them" (222). The reply of my study would be that the "hold" created by white society is more encompassing than the specifically religious.

Because it is so encompassing, the de-brainwashing cannot be limited to the indigenes. The shape and extent of the cultural conditioning in Canada, Australia, and New Zealand that consistently reifies the indigene, whether as object of fear or object of desire, must be universally recognized if the action necessary to oppose it is to be taken. In *Reading the Country*, Stephen Muecke notes: "Within the issue of Aboriginal sovereignty there is more at stake than the use of lands; there is the right to control the production of Australia's mythologies. Most importantly our conception of 'nationhood,' and it appears that Aboriginality is the commodity which is being bargained for in exchange for Aboriginal land and institutional power and control" (126). The attempt by indigenous peoples to seek sovereignty within white-dominated federal states has led me to believe that the impossibility of deviating from racial stereotypes must be recognized and then joined with the need to overcome the impossibility. The process of colonization has left us, as the white inheritors, with a legacy of untenable power structures in our societies. This analysis of the literary images which both reflect and mold those societies is part of aching toward a system which *is* tenable.

The literary process of attempting to hold the indigene within the white text and to create the indigene as subject liberated from past economies has thus far proven impossible. Perhaps it will continue to be impossible. But when white authors avoid considerations of native peoples they only create an emphatic absence which appears as a denial of the indigene's position in the writing of these countries. One white writer, after hearing me give a lecture, told me that she was about to complete a novel on an Indian topic and wanted me to examine the manuscript so she could "get rid of the problems." I replied that the problems cannot be dismissed. They will remain as Macherey's ideological horizon, the problematic which the text cannot hide.

Many political theorists believe native sovereignty is impossible. Yet Atareta Poananga easily embraces this impossible: "When we are all decolonised the rest will happen naturally." (Legat, 46) When Canada "brought home" the constitution, it removed the last residue of actual British control. Before this any structural change in federal-provincial relations had to be approved by the British privy council. A number of commentators suggested that the slim chance of provincial and federal governments agreeing sufficiently to create a proper petition for "patriation," for the delivery of the document from Britain, was reflected in the strangeness of the term. Canada sought not to repatriate something which had previously been part of itself as father but to patriate something, to make it anew as though it had been of the old. And patriation was accomplished (although through manipulations which many, most definitely including native peoples, found questionable). The impossible was made possible. Just as native sovereignty must be made possible. Just as the impossibility of seeing indigene as alien must be met by the impossibility of viewing white Canadians, Australians, and New Zealanders as not Canadian or not Australian or not New Zealanders, as not defineably within their own cultures. Thus the philosophical absurdities which arise in recognizing white views of indigenes as an apparently inevitable semiotic field and yet refusing to accept that inevitability.

Absurdities but necessities, necessities which some texts, such as those of Wiebe and especially White, recognize and attempt to deal with. White's texts in particular assert their position as ideological state apparatuses and demand the reader to examine them as such. If self can be viewed as a collective, as manifest nation, then the indigene at present is most assuredly not-self, politically, economically, ideologically. The indigene as not-self must become self if the country is to be won ideologically, if there is to be a completion to the need not only for individuation but for indigenization. Then the separation between "native" and "native Canadian," between "native" and "native Australian," between "native" and "native New Zealander," will not be erased – for it can never be erased – but will become a palimpsest of many meanings, no longer an obstacle but an enabling supplement.

Works Cited

Acheson, Frank O.V. *Plume of the Arawas*, Auckland: Whitcombe & Tombs, 1930.

Adam, G. Mercer, and A. Ethelwyn Wetherald. *An Algonquin Maiden: A Romance of the Early Days of Upper Canada*. Montreal: John Lovell & Son 1887.

Aikins, Carroll. *The God of Gods*. In *Canadian Plays from Hart House Theatre*, ed. Vincent Massey, vol. 2:1–67. Toronto: Macmillan 1927.

Aitchison, Raymond. *The Illegitimate*. Adelaide: Rigby 1964.

Alpha Crucis [Robert Dudley Sidney Powys Herbert]. "Trucanini's Dirge." In *The Song of the Stars: and Other Poems*, 142–4. London: Cassell, Petten, Galpin [1882].

Armstrong, L.O. *Hiawatha or Nanabozho*, N.p. 1984.

Armstrong, L.O., and W.D. Lighthall. *The Book of the Play of Hiawatha the Mohawk Depicting the Siege of Hochelaga and the Battle of Lake Champlain*. N.p. 1909.

Atwood, Margaret. *Surfacing*. Don Mills, Ontario: Paperjacks 1973.

– "True North." *Saturday Night*, Jan. 1987, 141–8.

Awatere, Donna. *Maori Sovereignty*. Auckland: Broadsheet 1984.

Bakhtin, Mikhail. *The Dialogic Imagination: Four Essays*. Trans. Caryl Emerson and Michael Holquist. Ed. Michael Holquist. Austin: University of Texas Press 1981.

Barker, Francis, Peter Hulme, Margaret Iverson, and Diana Loxley, eds. *Europe and Its Others*. 2 vols. Colchester: University of Essex Press 1985.

Barthes, Roland. "The Eiffel Tower." In *A Barthes Reader*, ed. Susan Sontag, 236–50. New York: Hill and Wang 1982.

Bartram, Grace. *Darker Grows the Valley*. Melbourne: Macmillan 1981.

Baume, F.E. *Half-Caste*. Sydney: Macquarie Head Press 1933.

Beilby, Richard. *The Brown Land Crying*. Sydney: Angus & Robertson 1975.

Bell, Alfred Bernie. *Wild Rocket and The Diamond of Glen Rock Australian Tales*. Brisbane: Black, Keid 1894.

Benterrak, Krim, Stephen Muecke, and Paddy Roe. *Reading the Country: Introduction to Nomadology*. Fremantle: Fremantle Arts Centre 1984.

Berger, John. *Ways of Seeing*. London: BBC 1972.

Berkhofer, Robert F. *The White Man's Indian: Images of the American Indian from Columbus to the Present*. New York: Vintage 1979.

Bett, S.G. *The Eyewash Indians*. *Curtain Call* 10, no. 4 (1939): 5–6.

Bhabha, Homi K. "Signs Taken for Wonders: Questions of Ambivalence and Authority Under a Tree Outside Delhi, May 1817." *Critical Inquiry* 12, no. 1 (1985): 144–65.

Bodsworth, Fred. *The Sparrow's Fall*. Toronto: Doubleday 1967.

– *The Strange One*. New York: Dodd, Mead 1959.

Bogatyrev, Petr. "Semiotics in the Folk Theatre." Trans. Bruce Kochis. In *Semiotics of Art: Prague School Contributions*, ed. Ladislav Matejka and Irwin R. Titunik, 33–50. Cambridge: MIT Press 1976.

Boldrewood, Rolf [Browne, T.A.]. *Robbery Under Arms: A Story of Life and Adventure in the Bush and in the Goldfields of Australia*. Melbourne: Macmillan 1968.

– *Old Melbourne Memories*. Sydney: George Robertson 1884.

Bolt, Carol. *Gabe*. Toronto: Playwrights Co-op 1974.

Bowering, George. *Burning Water*. Toronto: General 1983.

– "Indian Summer." In *Rocky Mountain Foot: A Lyric, A Memoir*, 75. Toronto: McClelland & Stewart 1968.

Boyd, A.J. *Old Colonials*. London: Gordon and Cotch 1882.

Bracken, Thomas. "The March of Te Rauparaha." In *Lays of the Land of the Maori and Moa*, 15–40. London: Sampson, Low, Marston, Searle & Rivington 1884.

Bridle, Augustus. *Hansen: A Novel of Canadianization*. Toronto: Macmillan 1924.

Broderick, Damien. *The Dreaming Dragons: A Time Opera*. Carlton, Victoria: Norstrilia Press 1980.

Broome, Charles. "The Blood of Marlee: A Romance of North Australian Wilds." *The Steering Wheel and Society and Home*, June 1939, 50–2; July 1939, 48–9; August 1939, 49–51; Sept. 1939, 47–9; Oct. 1939, 53–5; Nov. 1939, 52–4; Dec. 1939, 54–6; Jan. 1940, 50–2; Feb. 1940, 54–5; April 1940, 50–1; and May 1940, 48–50.

Brown, Max. *The Black Eureka*. Sydney: Australasian Book Society 1976.

– *The Jimberi Track*. Sydney: Australasian Book Society 1966.

Brown, Russell, and Donna Bennett. *An Anthology of Canadian Literature in English*. 2 vols. Toronto: Oxford University Press 1982–3.

Bruce, Mary Grant. *A Little Bush Maid*. London: Ward, Lock, [1910].

– *Norah of Billabong*. London: Ward, Lock, [1913].

– *Son of Billabong*. London: Ward, Lock, 1939.

Burnham, Hampden. *Jack Ralston or The Outbreak of the Nauscopees: A Tale of Life in the Far North-East of Canada*. London: Thomas Nelson & Sons 1902.

Buzo, Alexander. *Macquarie*. Sydney: Currency 1971.

E.L.C. [E.L. Cushing]. "The Indian Maid: A Traditionary Tale." *The Literary Garland*, May 1846, 193–205.

H.V.C. [Cheney, Harriet]. "Jacques Cartier and the Little Indian Girl." *The Literary Garland* and *British North American Magazine*, Oct. 1848, 461–8; Nov. 1848, 520–7; Dec. 1848, 561–71.

Campbell, Wilfred. *Daulac: An Historical Tragedy of French Canada in Five Acts*. In *Poetical Tragedies*, 127–200. Toronto: William Briggs 1908.

Cardinal, Harold. *The Rebirth of Canada's Indians*. Edmonton: Hurtig 1977.

Carlin, Norah. "Ireland and Natural Man in 1649." In *Europe and Its Others*, ed. Barker et al, vol. 2, 91–112. Colchester: University of Essex Press 1985.

Carr, Emily. *Klee Wyck*. Toronto: Clarke, Irwin 1971.

Casey, Gavin. *Snowball*. Sydney: Angus & Robertson 1958.

Cato, Nancy, and Vivienne Rae Ellis. *Queen Trucanini*. London: Heinemann 1976.

Cheney, Harriet. *See* H.V.C.

Child, Philip. *The Village of Souls*. Toronto: Ryerson 1933.

Clark, Joan, *The Victory of Geraldine Gull*. Toronto: Macmillan 1988.

Clarke, Marcus. *His Natural Life*. Ringwood, Victoria: Penguin 1970.

Coetzee, J.M. *Waiting for the Barbarians*. Harmondsworth, Middlesex: Penguin 1982.

Cohen, Leonard. *Beautiful Losers*. New York: Bantam 1967.

Connolly, Roy, *Southern Saga*. Sydney: Dymock's Book Arcade 1946.

Connor, Ralph [Charles W. Gordon]. *Corporal Cameron of the North West Mounted Police: A Tale of the Macleod Trail*. New York: Grosset & Dunlap 1912.

– *The Gaspards of Pine Croft: A Romance of the Windemere*. New York: George H. Doran 1923.

– *The Patrol of the Sundance Trail*. Toronto: Westminster 1914.

Conrad, Joseph. *Heart of Darkness*. Ed. Robert Kimbrough. New York: W.W. Norton 1963.

Cook, James and James King. *A Voyage to the Pacific Ocean: Undertaken by Command of his Majesty, for making Discoveries in the Northern Hemisphere: Performed under the Direction of Captains Cook, Clarke, and Gore, In the Years 1776, 1777, 1778, 1779, and 1780. Being a copious, comprehensive, and satisfactory Abridgement of the Voyage written by Captain James Cook and Captain James King*. 3 vols. London: John Stockdale, Scatcherd and Whitaker, John Fielding, and John Hardy 1784.

Cook, Kenneth. *Eliza Fraser*. Melbourne: Sun Books 1976.

Cook, Michael. *On the Rim of the Curve*. In *Three Plays*, 7–50. Portugal Cove, Newfoundland: Breakwater 1977.

Copway, George. *The Life, History, and Travels of Kah-ge-ga-gah-bowh (George Copway)*. Philadelphia: James Harmstead 1847.

Cornwallis, Kinahan. *Yarra Yarra: or, The Wandering Aborigine*. London: Ward & Lock 1858.

Cossins, George. *The Wings of Silence: An Australian Tale*. London: Gay & Bird 1899.

Coward, Rosalind and John Ellis. *Language and Materialism: Developments in Semiology and the Theory of the Subject*. London: Routledge & Kegan Paul 1977.

Crawford, Isabella Valancy. *The Collected Poems*. Toronto: University of Toronto Press 1972.

Cumming, R.D. *Paul Pero*. Toronto: Ryerson 1928.

Cushing, E.L. *See* E.L.C.

D.D.D. "The Last of the Indians." *The Literary Garland*, March 1846, 132.

Dagg, Mel. *Same Truck Different Driver*. Calgary: Westlands 1982.

Dampier, Alfred, and Garnet Walch, "Robbery Under Arms." [1890]. Manuscript. Hanger Collection. University of Queensland, Brisbane.

Dann, George Landen. *Fountains Beyond*. Sydney: Australasian Publishing 1944.

– "Rainbows Die at Sunset." [c. 1970?]. Typescript. Hanger Collection. University of Queensland, Brisbane.

– "In Beauty It Is Finished" [1931]. Typescript. Hanger Collection. University of Queensland, Brisbane.

Dark, Eleanor. *No Barrier*. London: Collins 1960.

– *Storm of Time*. Sydney: Collins 1948.

– *The Timeless Land*. London: Collins 1943.

Davies, Robertson, *Question Time*. Toronto: Macmillan 1975.

Dawe, W. Carleton. *The Golden Lake or The Marvellous History of a Journey Through the Great Lone Land of AUSTRALIA*. London: A.P. Marsden 1894.

Dawe, Tom. "In There Somewhere." In *31 Newfoundland Poets*. ed. Adrian Fowler and Al Pittman, 10–11. [St. John's]: Breakwater 1979.

Day, Frank Parker. *John Paul's Rock*. New York: Minton, Balch 1932.

Daymond, Douglas, and Leslie Monkman. *Literature in Canada*. 2 vols. Toronto: Gage 1978.

De Boos, Charles. *Fifty Years Ago: An Australian Tale*. Sydney: Gordon & Gotch 1867.

de la Roche, Mazo. *Possession*. Toronto: Macmillan 1923.

de Lauretis, Teresa. *Alice Doesn't: Feminism, Semiotics, Cinema*. Bloomington: Indiana University Press 1984.

de Man, Paul. *Allegories of Reading: Figural Language in Rousseau, Nietzsche, Rilke, and Proust*. New Haven: Yale University Press 1979.

Review of *De Roberval*. *The Toronto Mail*, 23 July 1888, 8.

Derrida, Jacques. *Of Grammatology*. Trans. Gayatri Chakravorty Spivak. Baltimore: Johns Hopkins Press 1976.

– "Racism's Last Word." Trans. Peggy Kamuf. *Critical Inquiry* 12, no. 1 (1985): 290–9.

Devaney, James. *The Vanished Tribes*. Sydney: Cornstalk 1929.

Devanny, Jean. *Lenore Divine*. London: Duckworth 1926.

Diamond, Richard. "In the Shade of the Coolibah Tree: A Musical Play." [c. 1950?]. Typescript. Hanger Collection. University of Queensland, Brisbane.

Dickson, Bassett. *Honi Heki, in Two Cantos: Warbeck, In Two Cantos: And Miscellaneous Pieces*. Launceston: Author 1847.

Domett, Alfred. *Ranolf and Amohia: A Dream of Two Lives*. 2 vols. London: Kegan Paul, Trench 1883.

Drake-Brockman, H. *Men Without Wives: and Other Plays*. Sydney: Angus & Robertson 1955.

Drew, Wayland. *The Wabeno Feast*. Toronto: Anansi 1973.

Drewe, Robert. *The Savage Crows*. Sydney: Collins 1976.

Dryden, John. *The Indian Emperour, or, The Conquest of Mexico by the Spaniards*. Vol. 9, *The Works of John Dryden*, 1–112. Ed. John Loftis. Berkeley: University of California 1967.

Dryden, John and Robert Howard. *The Indian Queen, A Tragedy*. Vol. 8, *The Works of John Dryden*, 181–231. Ed. John Harrington Smith and Dougald MacMillan. Berkeley: University of California Press 1967.

Dunlop, Eliza Hamilton. *The Aboriginal Mother and Other Poems*. Canberra: Mulini Press 1981.

Duvar, John Hunter. *See* Hunter Duvar.

Eagleton, Terry. *Literary Theory: An Introduction*. Oxford: Basil Blackwell 1983.

Elam, Keir. *The Semiotics of Theatre and Drama*. London: Methuen 1980.

Eliade, Mircea. *Shamanism: Archaic Techniques of Ecstasy*. Trans. Willard R. Trask. New York: Bollingen Foundation 1964.

Elkin, A.P. *Aboriginal Men of High Degree*. St.Lucia: University of Queensland Press 1977.

Elliott, Brian, ed. *The Jindyworobaks*. St. Lucia: University of Queensland Press 1979.

Esson, Louis. *Andeganora*. In *Best Australian One-Act Plays*, ed. William Moore and T. Inglis Moore, 1–12. Sydney: Angus & Robertson 1937.

Eugene [Douglas S. Huyghue]. *Argimou: A Legend of the Micmac*. Sackville, New Brunswick: R.P. Bell Library 1977.

Evans, Hubert. *Mist on the River*. Toronto: McClelland & Stewart 1973.

Eyre, Edward John. *Journals of Expeditions of Discovery into Central Australia, and Overland from Adelaide to King George's Sound, In the Years 1840–1: Sent by the Colonists of South Australia. With the Sanction and Support of the Government: including an Account of the Manners and Customs of the Aborigines and the State of their Relations with Europeans.* 2 vols. London: T. & W. Boone 1845.

Fabian, Johannes. *Time and the Other: How Anthropology Makes Its Object.* New York: Columbia University Press 1983.

Fairbairn, A.M.D. *Plays of the Pacific Coast.* Toronto: Samuel French 1935.

Fairchild, Hoxie. *The Noble Savage: A Study in Romantic Naturalism.* New York: Russell & Russell 1961.

Fanon, Frantz. *Black Skin White Masks.* Trans. Charles Lam Markmann. St. Albans, Herts: Paladin 1970.

– *The Wretched of the Earth.* Trans. Constance Farrington. New York: Grove 1968.

Ferguson, Dugald. "The Upper Darling." In *A Century of Australian Song,* ed. Douglas Sladen, 154. London: Walter Scott 1888.

Figes, Eva. *Tragedy and Social Evolution.* London: John Calder 1976.

Finlayson, Roderick. *Brown Man's Burden and Later Stories.* Ed. Bill Pearson. Auckland: Auckland University Press 1973.

Foster, Peter. "The Destruction of Wealth." *Saturday Night*, Jan. 1987, 160–4.

Foucault, Michel. *The History of Sexuality: An Introduction.* Trans. Robert Hurley. New York: Pantheon Books 1978.

– *Power/Knowledge: Selected Interviews and Other Writings 1972–1977).* Trans. Colin Gordon et al. Ed. Colin Gordon. New York: Pantheon Books 1980.

– "What is an Author?" In *Textual Strategies: Perspectives in Post-Structuralist Criticism,* ed. Josue V. Harara, 141–160. Ithaca: Cornell University Press 1979.

Foundation for Aboriginal and Islander Research Action. *Beyond the Act.* N.p. 1979.

Fraser, Fil. "Black Like Me." *Saturday Night*, Jan. 1987, 180–4.

Fraser, W.A. *The Blood Lilies.* Toronto: William Briggs 1903.

Fry, Alan. *Come a Long Journey.* Toronto: Doubleday 1971.

– *How a People Die.* Toronto: Doubleday 1970.

– *The Revenge of Annie Charlie.* Toronto: Doubleday 1973.

Frye, Northrop. "Canada and Its Poetry." In *The Bush Garden: Essays on the Canadian Imagination,* 129–43. Toronto: Anansi 1971.

– "Conclusion." In *The Literary History of Canada: Canadian Literature in English,* ed. Carl F. Klinck, 821–849. Toronto: University of Toronto Press 1965.

Gare, Nene. *Bend to the Wind*. Melbourne: Macmillan 1978.

– *The Fringe Dwellers*. Melbourne: Heinemann 1961.

Gilman, Sander L. "Black Bodies, White Bodies: Toward an Iconography of Female Sexuality in Late Nineteenth-Century Art, Medicine, and Literature." *Critical Inquiry* 12 (1985): 209–31.

– *Difference and Pathology: Stereotypes of Sexuality, Race and Madness*. Ithaca: Cornell University Press 1985.

Goldie, Terry. "Contemporary Views of an Aboriginal Past: Rudy Wiebe and Patrick White." *World Literature Written in English* 23 (1984): 429–39.

– "The Necessity of Nobility: Indigenous Peoples in Canadian and Australian Literature." *The Journal of Commonwealth Literature* 20 (1985): 131–47.

Goody, Jack. *The Domestication of the Savage Mind*. Cambridge: Cambridge University Press 1977.

Grace, Alfred, A. *Tales of a Dying Race*. London: Chatto & Windus 1901.

Grace, Patricia. *Mutuwhenua: The Moon Sleeps*. Auckland: Longman Paul 1978.

Grant, A.C. *Bush-Life in Queensland or John West's Colonial Experiences*. 2 vols. Edinburgh: William Blackwood and Sons 1881.

Gray, Oriel. "Had We But World Enough." [1950?]. Typescript. Hanger Collection. University of Queensland, Brisbane.

Gros-Louis, Max. *First Among the Hurons*. Trans. Sheila Fischman. Montreal: Harvest House 1974.

Gubar, Susan. "'The Blank Page' and the Issues of Female Creativity." In *The New Feminist Criticism: Essays on Women, Literature and Theory*, ed. Elaine Showalter, 292–313. New York: Pantheon 1985.

Gunn, Mrs. Aeneas. *We of the Never-Never*. London: Hutchinson 1954.

Gutterridge, Don. *Riel: A Poem for Voices*. Toronto: Van Nostrand Reinhold 1972.

Haggard, H. Rider. *She*. London: Hodder & Stoughton 1886.

Harpur, Charles. "The Creek of the Four Graves." In *The Bushrangers: A Play in Five Acts, and Other Poems*, 63–70. Sydney: W.R. Piddington 1853.

Harrison, Craig. *Broken October: New Zealand 1985*. A.H. & A.W. Reed 1976.

Hatfield, William. *Black Waterlily*. Sydney: Angus & Robertson 1935.

– *Desert Saga*. Sydney: Angus & Robertson 1933.

Hawthorne, Nathaniel. *The House of the Seven Gables and the Snow Image and Other Twice-Told Tales*. Boston: Houghton, Mifflin 1883.

Healy, J.J. *Literature and the Aborigine in Australia 1770–1975*. St.Lucia: University of Queensland Press, 1978.

– "The Lemurian Nineties." *Australian Literary Studies* 8, no. 3 (1978): 307–16.

Hearne, Samuel *A Journey from Prince of Wale's Fort in Hudson's Bay to the Northern Ocean Undertaken by Order of the Hudson's Bay Company for the Discovery of Copper Mines, A North West Passage &c. In the Years 1769, 1770, 1771, & 1772.* Edmonton: M.G. Hurtig 1971.

Herbert, Robert. *See* Alpha Crucis.

Herbert, Xavier. *Capricornia.* Sydney: Angus and Robertson 1972.

– *Poor Fellow My Country.* Sydney: Pan 1977.

Hibberd, Jack. "Captain Midnight V. C.: A Light Piece." [1972]. Typescript. Hanger Collection. University of Queensland, Brisbane.

Hilliard, Noel. *The Glory and the Dream.* Auckland: Heinemann 1978.

– *Maori Girl.* London: Heinemann 1960.

– *Maori Woman.* London: Robert Hale 1974.

– *A Night at Green River.* London: Robert Hale 1969.

Hodgman, Helen. *Blue Skies.* London: Duckworth 1976.

Hooker, John. *The Bush Soldiers.* Sydney: Collins 1984.

Honzl, Jindrich. "Dynamics of the Sign in the Theater." Trans. I.R. Titunik. In *Semiotics of Art: Prague School Contributions,* ed. Ladislav Matejka and Irwin R. Titunik, 74–93. Cambridge: MIT Press 1976.

Hori [W. Norman McCallum]. *Fill It Up Again.* Auckland: Sporting-Life [1964].

– *Flagon Fun.* Auckland: Sporting-Life [1966].

– *The Half-Gallon Jar.* Auckland: Sporting-Life [1960].

Houston, James. *Eagle Song: An Indian Saga Based on True Events.* New York: Harcourt Brace Jovanivich 1983.

– *Spirit Wrestler.* Toronto: McClelland & Stewart 1980.

Howe, Joseph. *Poems and Essays.* Toronto: University of Toronto Press 1973.

Howitt, Richard. *Australia: Historical, Descriptive, and Statistic: with an Account of A Four Years' Residence in that Colony: Notes of a Voyage Round the World: Australian Poems, etc.* London: Longman, Brown, Green and Longmans 1845.

Hudson, Helen. *Flames in the Wind.* London: Hodder & Stoughton [1918].

Hulme, Keri. *The Bone People.* Wellington: Spiral 1983.

Hulme, Peter. "Polytropic Man: Tropes of Sexuality and Mobility in Early Colonial Discourse." In *Europe and Its Others,* ed. Barker et al, vol. 2, 17–32.

Hungerford, T.A.G. "The Only One Who Forgot." In *Aliens in Their Land,* Rorabacher, 93–102.

Hunter Duvar, John. *De Roberval. A Drama.* Saint John, New Brunswick: J. & A. McMillan 1888.

Hutcheon, Linda. *A Theory of Parody: The Teachings of Twentieth-Century Art Forms.* London: Methuen 1985.

Huyghue, Douglas S. *See* Eugene.

Idriess, Ion L. *Nemarluk: King of the Wilds*. Sydney: Angus and Robertson 1941.

– *The Red Chief: As Told By the Last of His Tribe*. Sydney: Angus and Robertson 1953.

Ihimaera, Witi. *Pounamu Pounamu*. Auckland: Heinemann 1972.

– *Tangi*. Auckland: Heinemann 1973.

– *Whanau*. Auckland: Heineman 1974.

"The Indian's Dream" *The Literary Garland*, Jan. 1839, 61–4.

"The Indian Nurse's Death Song." *The Literary Garland and British North American Magazine*, March 1850, 106.

Ingamells, Rex. *Conditional Culture*. Adelaide: F.W. Preece 1938.

– *The Great South Land: An Epic Poem*. Melbourne: Georgian House 1951.

– *Of Us Now Living: A Novel of Australia*. Melbourne: Hallcraft 1952.

– *Selected Poems*. Melbourne: Georgian House 1944.

Ireland, David. *The Glass Canoe*. Melbourne: Macmillan 1976.

– *Image in the Clay*. St. Lucia: University of Queensland Press 1964.

Irvin, Eric. *Australian Melodrama: Eighty Years of Popular Theatre*. Sydney: Hale & Iremonger 1981.

G.J. "St. Lawrence." *The Literary Garland*, Nov. 1840, 529–33.

Jack, Henry. "Native Alliance for Red Power." In *The Only Good Indian*, ed. Waubageshig, 162–80. Toronto: New Press 1970.

JanMohammed, Abdul R. "The Economy of Manichean Allegory: The Function of Racial Difference in Colonialist Literature." *Critical Inquiry* 12, no. 1 (1985): 59–87.

Johnson, Collin. *Doctor Wooreddy's Prescription for Enduring the End of the World*. Melbourne: Hyland House 1983.

Johnson, E. Pauline. *Canadian Born*. Toronto: George N. Morang 1903.

– *Flint and Feather*. Toronto: Musson [1912].

– *The Moccasin Maker*. Toronto: William Briggs 1913.

– *The Shagganappi*. Toronto: Ryerson 1913.

Jones, Dorothy L.M. "The Treatment of the Aborigine in Australian Fiction." Master's thesis. University of Adelaide 1960.

Joyce, James. *Finnegans Wake*. New York: Viking 1974.

– *Ulysses*. New York: Modern Library 1946.

H.J.K. "Indian Address to the Mississippi." *The Literary Garland*, May 1846, 213.

Kearney, W.D. *The Open Hand: An Epic Poem Dealing With the Early Settlement of Maine and New Brunswick, Founded on Tradition*. Hartland, New Brunswick: Hartland 1981.

Kelly, John Liddell. *Heather and Fern: Songs of Scotland and Maoriland*. Wellington: New Zealand Times 1902.

Kelly, M.T. *A Dream Like Mine*. Toronto: Stoddart 1987.

Kelsey, Henry. *The Kelsey Papers*. Ottawa: Public Archives 1929.

Kendall, Henry. "Peter the Picaninny." In *The Poetical Works of Henry Kendall*, ed. T.T. Reed, 184–87. Adelaide: Libraries Board of South Australia 1966.

– *Leaves From Australian Forests*. Adelaide: Rigby 1975.

Keneally, Thomas. *Bullie's House*. Sydney: Currency 1981.

– *The Chant of Jimmie Blacksmith*. Ringwood, Victoria: Penguin 1973.

Kidd, Adam. *The Huron Chief, and Other Poems*. Montreal: The Herald and New Gazette 1830.

Kidman, Fiona. *Search for Sister Blue: A Play for Radio*. Wellington: A.H. & A.W. Reed 1975.

Kimber, Robert. "Run Run Away." [1979]. Typescript. Hanger Collection. University of Queensland, Brisbane.

King, Phillip P. *Narrative of a Survey of the Intertropical and Western Coasts of Australia Performed between the Years 1818 and 1822*. 2 vols. London: John Murray 1827.

Kinsella, W.P. *Born Indian*. [Ottawa]: Oberon 1981.

– *Dance Me Outside*. Ottawa: Oberon 1977.

– *The Moccasin Telegraph and Other Stories*. Toronto: Penguin 1983.

– *Scars*. [Ottawa]: Oberon 1978.

Klein, A.M. *Collected Poems*. Ed. Miriam Waddington. Toronto: McGraw-Hill Ryerson 1974.

Kovel, Joel. *White Racism: A Psychohistory*. New York: Pantheon 1970.

Kroetsch, Robert. *Badlands*. Don Mills, Ontario: New Press 1975.

– *Gone Indian*. Toronto: New Press 1973.

– *What the Crow Said*. Toronto: General 1983.

Lampman, Archibald. "At the Mermaid Inn." In *Archibald Lampman: Selected Prose*, ed. Barrie Davies, 55–80. Ottawa: Tecumseh 1975.

Lane, Patrick. *Beware the Months of Fire*. Toronto: Anansi 1974.

Lang, John Dunmore. "Australian Hymn." In *Aurora Australis: or Specimens of Sacred Poetry, for the Colonists of Australia*, 17–20. Sydney: G. Eagar 1826.

Laurence, Margaret. *The Diviners*. Toronto: Bantam 1975.

Lawson, Henry. "The Drover's Wife." In *Henry Lawson*, ed. Brian Kiernan, 96–103. St. Lucia: University of Queensland Press 1976.

Leacock, Stephen. "Mettawamkeag: An Indian Tragedy." *Over the Footlights*, 143–4. New York: Dodd, Mead 1923.

Lee, Dennis. *Savage Fields: An Essay in Literature and Cosmology*. Toronto: Anansi 1977.

Legat, Nicola. "Atareta Poananga and Te Ahi Kaa: What Do Maori Nationalists Want?" *Auckland Metro*, March 1986, 44–58.

Leigh, W.H. *The Emigrant: A Tale of Australia*. London: Simmonds and Ward 1847.

LeMay, Bonnie. "Hit and Run" [1967]. Typescript. MG 28I30, vol. 12. National Archives of Canada, Ottawa.

Leprohon, Rosanna E. *See* R.E.M..

Lescarbot, Marc. *Neptune's Theatre*, Trans. Edna B. Holman. New York: Samuel French 1927.

Lévi-Strauss, Claude. *The Raw and the Cooked: Introduction to a Science of Mythology: I*. Trans. John and Doreen Weightman. New York: Harper & Row 1969.

– *The Savage Mind*. London: Weidenfeld and Nicolson 1972.

Lighthall, W.D. *The Master of Life: A Romance of the Five Nations and of Prehistoric Montreal*. Toronto: Musson 1908.

Lowrey, Harold. *Indian Gold*. Toronto: Musson 1929.

Lumholtz, Carl. *Among Cannibals: An Account of Four Years' Travels in Australia and of Camp Life with the Aborigines of Queensland*. London: John Murray 1889.

M. [Henry Melville]. *The Bushrangers: or Norwood Vale, Hobart Town Magazine*, (April 1834): 82–6.

J.R.M. [J.R. McLachlan]. "Arabin, or Adventures of a Colonist. A Drama in Three Acts Freely Dramatized from Mr. McCombie's recent Popular Work" [1847]. Manuscript. Mitchell Library, State Library of New South Wales, Sydney.

R.E.M. [Rosanna E. Leprohon]. "The Huron Princess." *The Literary Garland and British North American Magazine*, Dec. 1850, 582.

Macherey, Pierre. *A Theory of Literary Production*. Trans. Geoffrey Wall. London: Routledge & Kegan Paul 1978.

MacKay, Isabel Ecclestone. *Indian Nights*. Toronto: McClelland & Stewart 1930.

Mackay, Kenneth. *A Bush Idyl*. Sydney: Edwards, Dunlop 1888.

Mackay, Kenneth and Alfred Dampier. "To the West" [1896]. Typescript. Hanger Collection. University of Queensland, Brisbane.

Mackenzie, Alexander. *Voyages from Montreal on the River St. Laurence through the Continent of North America to the Frozen and Pacific Oceans In the Years 1789 and 1793 with a Preliminary account of the Rise, Progress, and Present State of the Fur Trade of that Country*. Rutland, Vermont: Charles E. Tuttle 1971.

Mackenzie, J.B. *Thayendanegea: An Historico-Military Drama*. Toronto: The Author 1898.

Mair, Charles. *Dreamland and Other Poems/Tecumseh: A Drama*. Toronto: University of Toronto Press 1974.

Mandel, Eli. *Stony Plain*. Erin, Ontario: Press Porcepic 1973.

Manifold, John. *Six Sonnets on Human Ecology*. Brisbane: Communist Arts Group 1974.

Mann, Leonard. *Venus Half-Caste*. London: Hodder & Stoughton 1963.

Mannoni, O. *Prospero and Caliban: The Psychology of Colonialization*. Trans. Pamela Powesland. New York: Frederick A. Praeger 1964.

Maple, Eric. *The Domain of Devils*. London: Robert Hale 1966.

Marcuse, Herbert. *Eros and Civilization: A Philosophical Inquiry into Freud*. Boston: Beacon 1966.

– *Five Lectures: Psychoanalysis, Politics, and Utopia*. Trans. Jeremy J. Shapiro and Shierry M. Weber. Boston: Beacon 1970.

Maris, Hyllus and Sonia Borg. *Women of the Sun*. Sydney: Currency 1983.

Marshall, James Vance [Donald Gordon Payne]. *The Children*. London: Michael Joseph 1959.

Mason, Bruce. *The Pohutukawa Tree: A Play in Three Acts*. Wellington: Price Milburn 1960.

Mathew, John. *Australian Echoes Including The Corroboree and Other Poems*. Melbourne: Melville and Mullen 1902.

– *Ballads of Bush Life and Lyrics of Cheer*. Melbourne: Melville & Mullen 1914.

McCallum, Norman W. *See* Hori.

McCauley, Sue. *Other Halves*. Auckland: Hodder & Stoughton 1982.

McCombie, Thomas. *The Colonist in Australia; or, The Adventures of Godfrey Arabin*. London: George Slater 1850.

McCrae, George Gordon. *Mamba ("The Bright-Eyed"): An Aboriginal Reminiscence*. Melbourne: H.T. Dwight 1867.

– *The Story of Balla-deadro*. Melbourne: H.T. Dwight 1867.

McDonald, Roger. *1915*. St. Lucia: University of Queensland Press 1979.

McGarrity, John. *Once a Jolly Blackman*. Melbourne: Wren 1973.

McGee, Thomas D'Arcy. *The Poems of Thomas D'Arcy McGee*. London: D. & J. Sadlier 1870.

McKelvie, B.A. *The Black Canyon: A Story of '58*. Toronto: J.M. Dent 1927.

– *Huldowget: A Story of the North Pacific Coast*. Toronto: J.M. Dent 1926.

McLachlan, Alexander. "To an Indian Skull." In *The Poetical Works of Alexander McLachlan*, 69–71. Toronto: University of Toronto Press 1974.

McLachlan, J.R. *See* J.R.M.

McLean, Angus. *Lindigo, the White Woman, or, The Highland Girl's Captivity Among the Australian Blacks*. Melbourne: H.T. Dwight 1866.

Melville, Henry. *See* M.

Meredith, Louisa A. *A Tasmanian Memory of 1834. In Five Scenes*. Hobart Town: J. Walch & Sons 1869.

Meredith, P.R. "The Lost Tribe of Boonjie: A Romance of the Australian Wilds." *The Steering Wheel and Society and Home*, May 1940, 54–5, 80; June 1940, 51–3; July 1940, 47–9; Aug. 1940, 48–51, 80; Sept. 1940, 46–8; Oct. 1940, 44–5; Nov. 1940, 47–9; Dec. 1940, 48–9; and Jan. 1941, 45–7.

Milgate, Rodney. *A Refined Look at Existence*. London: Methuen 1968.

Miller, Nancy K. "Writing (from) the Feminine: George Sand and the Novel of Female Pastoral." In *The Representation of Women in Fiction*, ed. Carolyn G. Heilbrun and Margaret R. Higonnet, 124–151. Baltimore: Johns Hopkins University Press 1983.

Mitchell, T.L. *Three Expeditions into the Interior of Eastern Australia; With Descriptions of the Recently Explored Region of Australia Felix, and of the Present Colony of New South Wales*. 2 vols. London: T. & W. Boone 1839.

Mitchell, W.O. *The Vanishing Point*. Toronto: Macmillan 1975.

"Moan Bambi." *Lili-Illa: a Romance of the Australian Aborigines*. Sydney: Associated Printing and Publishing 1923.

Moncrieff, W.T. [W.T. Thomas]. *Van Diemen's Land: An Operatic Drama*. London: G.H. Davidson [1830s].

Monkman, Leslie. *A Native Heritage: Images of the Indian in English-Canadian Literature*. Toronto: University of Toronto Press 1981.

Moore, Brian. *Black Robe*. Toronto: McClelland & Stewart 1985.

Moorhouse, Frank. "Imogene Continued." *The Everlasting Secret Family*, 81–163. Melbourne: Angus and Robertson 1980.

Moynihan, Cornelius. *The Feast of the Bunya: An Aboriginal Ballad*. Brisbane: Gordon and Gotch 1901.

Muecke, Stephen, Krim Benterrak, and Paddy Roe. *Reading the Country. See* Benterrak.

Mudie, Ian. *The Australian Dream*. Adelaide: Jindyworobak 1944.

– *Corroboree to the Sun*. Melbourne: Hawthorn 1940.

Muller, Hugo. *Waswanipi: Songs of a Scattered People*. Toronto: Anglican Book Centre 1976.

Murray, Les. *The Boys Who Stole The Funeral: A Novel Sequence*. Sydney: Angus & Robertson 1980.

Musgrave, Susan. *The Charcoal Burners*. Toronto: McClelland & Stewart 1980.

Newland, Simpson. *Paving the Way: A Romance of the Australian Bush*. London: Gay and Hancock 1913.

Newlove, John. *The Fat Man: Selected Poems 1962–1972*. Toronto: McClelland & Stewart 1977.

Nicholas, John Liddiard. *Narrative of a Voyage to New Zealand, Performed in the Years 1814 and 1815, In Company with the Rev. Samuel Marsden*. 2 vols. London: James Black and Son 1817.

Nisbet, Hume. *The Rebel Chief: A Romance of New Zealand*. London: F.V. White 1896.

O'Grady, Frank. *Goonoo Goonoo*. London: Cassell 1956.

O'Grady, Standish. *The Emigrant, a Poem, in Four Cantos*. Montreal: Author 1841.

O'Hagan, Howard. *Tay John*. New York: Clarkson N. Potter 1960.

– *Wilderness Men*. Vancouver: Talonbooks 1978.

Ong, Walter J. *Orality and Literacy: The Technologizing of the Word*. London: Methuen 1982.

O'Reilly, John Boyle. *Moondyne: A Story of Life in West Australia*. Adelaide: Rigby 1975.

"Our Black Brothers." *The Bulletin*, 9 June 1883, 6.

O'Sullivan, E.W. "Coo-eè or Wild Days in the Bush." [1906]. Typescript. University of Queensland, Brisbane.

Palmer, Vance. *The Man Hamilton*. Adelaide: Rigby 1960.

– *Men Are Human*. London: Stanley Paul & Co. 1928.

Parker, Gilbert. "She of the Triple Chevron." *Pierre and His People: Tales of the Far North*, 74–126. Chicago: Stone & Kimball 1894.

– "A Prairie Vagabond." *Pierre and His People: Tales of the Far North*, 66–73. Chicago: Stone & Kimball 1894.

Parmenius, Stephen. "The Newfoundland Letter." In *The New Found Land of Stephen Parmenius: The life and writings of a Hungarian poet, drowned on a voyage from Newfoundland, 1583*, ed. David B. Quinn and Neil M. Cheshire, 167–85. Toronto: University of Toronto Press 1972.

Paterson, A.B. *The Collected Verse of A.B. Paterson*. Sydney: Angus and Robertson 1946.

Patrick, John. *Inapatua*. Melbourne: Cassell Australia 1966.

Payne, Donald Gordon. *See* Marshall, James Vance.

Pearson, Bill. "Attitudes to the Maori in Some Pakeha Fiction." *Fretful Sleepers and Other Essays*, 46–71. Auckland: Heinemann Educational Books 1974.

Perkins, Charles. *A Bastard Like Me*. Sydney: Ure Smith 1975.

Peterson, Leonard. *Almighty Voice*. Agincourt, Ontario: The Book Society of Canada 1974.

– *The Great Hunger*. Agincourt, Ontario: The Book Society of Canada 1967.

Pittman, Al. "Shanadithit." *Once When I Was Drowning*. [St. John's]: Breakwater 1978. 43–6.

Pollock, Sharon. *Walsh*. Vancouver: Talonbooks 1973.

Pope, Alexander. *An Essay on Man*. Menston, Yorkshire: Scolar 1969.

Popular Theatre Troupe. "The White Man's Mission." [1975]. Typescript. Hanger Collection. University of Queensland, Brisbane.

Praed, Mrs Campbell. *Fugitive Anne*. London: John Long [1903].

– *The Head Station*. 2 vols. Leipzig: Tauchnitz 1891.

Pratt, E.J. "Brébeuf and His Brethren." In *Selected Poems of E.J. Pratt*, ed. Peter Buitenhuis, 93–151. Toronto: Macmillan 1968.

Pratt, Mary Louise. "Scratches on the Face of the Country; or, What Mr. Barrow Saw in the Land of the Bushmen." *Critical Inquiry* 12, no. 1 (1985): 119–43.

Price, Theo. *God in the Sand: An Australian Mystical Romance*. Sydney: P.R. Stephensen 1934.

Prichard, Katharine Susannah. *Brumby Innes and Bid Me To Love*. Sydney: Currency 1974.

– *Coonardoo*. Sydney: Angus & Robertson 1975.

– "Happiness." In *Kiss on the Lips and Other Stories*, 107–132. London: Jonathan Cape 1932.

– "Happiness." In *The Penguin Book of Australian Short Stories*, ed. Harry Heseltine, 87–100. Ringwood, Victoria: Penguin 1976.

– *Winged Seeds*. Sydney: Australasian Publishing 1950.

Purdy, Al. *Being Alive: Poems 1958–78*. Toronto: McClelland & Stewart 1978.

– *North of Summer: Poems from Baffin Island*. Toronto: McClelland & Stewart 1967.

– "Sundance." *Sundance at Dusk*, 12–17. Toronto: McClelland & Stewart 1976.

– *Wild Grape Wine*. Toronto: McClelland & Stewart 1968.

Rayment, Tarlton. *The Valley of the Sky*. Sydney: Angus & Robertson 1937.

Redbird, Duke. *We Are Métis*. Willowdale, Ontario: Ontario Métis and Non-Status Indian Association 1980.

Reed, Bill. *Truganinni: 3 Workshop Plays*. Richmond, Victoria: Heinemann Educational 1977.

Reynolds, Henry. "Race and Class in Colonial Australia." In *Social Issues in the 1980s*, 11–16. Australian Studies Centre Occasional Papers 4, St. Lucia: University of Queensland 1984.

Richardson, John. *Wacousta or The Prophecy*. Toronto: McClelland & Stewart 1967.

Richardson, Henry Handel. *The Fortunes of Richard Mahony*. Collected edition. London: Heinemann 1930.

Richler, Mordecai. *The Incomparable Atuk*. Toronto: McClelland & Stewart 1963.

Richon, Olivier. "Representation, the Despot and the Harem: Some Questions Around an Academic Orientalist Painting by Lecomte-duNouy (1885)." In *Europe and Its Others*, ed. Barker et al, vol. 2, 91–112. Colchester: University of Essex Press 1985.

Ringwood, Gwen. *The Collected Plays of Gwen Pharis Ringwood*. Ed. Enid Delgatty Rutland. Ottawa: Borealis 1982.

Robinson, Bec. *Dark, Out There*. In *Australian One-Act Plays: Book Three*, ed. A. Musgrave Hornes, vol. 3, 74–95. Adelaide: Rigby 1967.

Robinson, Roland, *Aboriginal Myths and Legends*. Melbourne: Sun 1966.

– *Legend & Dreaming*. Sydney: Edwards & Shaw 1952.

Roddick, Amy Redpath. *The Seekers: An Indian Mystery Play*. Montreal: John Dougall & Son 1920.

Roe, Paddy. *See* Benterrak, Krim.

Rogers, Robert. *Ponteach: a Tragedy*. Ed. L. Allan Nevins 1914. New York: Bart Franklin 1971.

Roland, Betty. *Beyond Capricorn*. London: Collins 1976.

Ronan, Thomas. *Vision Splendid*. Melbourne: Cassell 1954.

Rorabacher, Louise E., ed. *Aliens in Their Land: The Aborigine in Australian Short Story*. Melbourne: F.W. Cheshire 1968.

Rose, Lyndon. *Country of the Dead*. Sydney: Angus & Robertson 1959.

Rowe, Frederick. *Extinction*. Toronto: McGraw-Hill Ryerson 1977.

Rowley, C.D. *Outcasts in White Australia*. Ringwood, Victoria: Penguin 1972.

Ruhen, Olaf. *Naked Under Capricorn*. London: Macdonald 1958.

[Rusden, G.W.] *Moyarra: An Australian Legend in Two Cantos*. Maitland: R. Jones "Mercury" Office 1851.

Ryan, Lyndall. *The Aboriginal Tasmanians*. St. Lucia: University of Queensland Press 1981.

Ryga, George. *The Ecstasy of Rita Joe*. Vancouver: Talonplays 1970.

Said, Edward. *Orientalism*. London: Routledge & Kegan Paul 1978.

– "Orentalism Reconsidered." In *Europe and Its Others*, ed. Barker et al, vol. 1, 14–27. Colchester: University of Essex Press 1985.

Sartre, Jean-Paul. *No Exit*. Trans. Stuart Gilbert. *No Exit and Three Other Plays*. New York: Vintage 1955.

Satchell, William. *The Greenstone Door*. Auckland: Whitcombe & Tombs 1950.

Saturday Night. Jan. 1987.

Sayce, Conrad. *Comboman: A Tale of Central Australia*. London: Hutchinson [1934].

– *The Splendid Savage: A Tale of the North Coast of Australia*. London: Thomas Nelson & Sons [1927].

Scott, Duncan Campbell. *The Administration of Indian Affairs in Canada*. N.p.: The Canadian Institute of International Affairs 1931.

– "Charcoal." In *Selected Stories of Duncan Campbell Scott*, ed. Glenn Clever, 41–49. Ottawa: University of Ottawa 1972.

– "Expiation." *The Witching of Elspie: A Book of Stories*, 101–111. New York: George H. Doran 1923.

– "Joy! Joy! Joy!" [1927]. Microfilm of Typescript. Metropolitan Library, Toronto.

– *Selected Poems of Duncan Campbell Scott*. Ed. E.K. Brown. Toronto: Ryerson 1951.

Scott, G.Firth. *The Last Lemurian: A Westralian Romance*. London: James Bowden 1898.

Searle, John. "The Logical Status of Fictional Discourse." *New Literary History* 6 (1975): 319–32.

Shakespeare, William. *All's Well That Ends Well*. Ed. George Lyman Kittredge. Waltham, Mass.: Blaisdell 1968.

Shaw, Harry E. *The Forms of Historical Fiction: Sir Walter Scott and His Successors*. Ithaca: Cornell 1983.

Shearer, Jill. *The Foreman*. In *Currency Double Bill*, 53–79. Woolahra, New South Wales: Currency 1977.

Sheppard, Trish. *Children of Blindness*. Sydney: Ure Smith 1976.

Sinclair, Keith. "Memorial to a Missionary." In *The Penguin Book of New Zealand Verse*, ed. Allen Curnow, 261–65. Auckland: Blackwood & Janet Paul 1966: 261–5.

Smith, A.J.M. *The Book of Canadian Prose: Early Beginnings to Confederation*. Toronto: Gage 1965.

Smith, Jo. "The Girl of the Never Never." [1912]. Typescript. Mitchell Library, State Library of New South Wales, Sydney.

Soyinka, Wole. *Myth, Literature and the African World*. Cambridge: Cambridge University Press 1978.

Spenser, Edmund. *A View of the Present State of Ireland*. Ed. W.L. Renwick. Oxford University Press 1970.

Spivak, Gayatri Chakravorty. *In Other Worlds: Essays in Cultural Politics*. New York: Methuen 1987.

– "Three Women's Texts and a Critique of Imperialism." *Critical Inquiry* 12, no. 1 (1985): 243–61.

Stellmach, Barbara. *Dark Heritage*. In *Four Australian Plays*, 1–65. St. Lucia: University of Queensland Press 1973.

Stephen, Sid. *Beothuck Poems*. [Ottawa]: Oberon 1976.

Stephens, James Brunton. *The Poetical Works of Brunton Stephens*. Sydney: Angus & Robertson 1902.

The Story of Louis Riel the Rebel Chief. Toronto: Coles 1970.

Stow, Randolph. *To the Islands*. London: Secker & Warburg 1982.

Stuart, Donald. *The Driven*. Melbourne: Georgian House 1961.

– *Ilbarana*. Melbourne: Georgian House 1971.

– *Malloonkai*. Melbourne: Georgian House 1976.

– *Yandy*. Melbourne: Georgian House 1959.

– *Yaralie*. Sydney: Australasian Book Society 1963.

Sturt, Charles. *Two Expeditions into the Interior of Southern Australia. During the Years 1828, 1829, 1830, and 1831: with Observations on the Soil, Climate, and General Resources of the Colony of New South Wales*. 2 vols. London: Smith, Elder 1833.

Such, Peter. *Riverrun*. Toronto: Clarke, Irwin 1975.

Terdiman, Richard. "Ideological Voyages: Concerning a Flaubertian Disorient-ation." In *Europe and Its Others*, ed. Barker et al, vol. 1, 28–40. Colchester: University of Essex Press 1985.

Thérien, Gilles, ed. *Les Figures de l'Indien*, Montreal: Les cahiers du département d'études littéraires Université du Québec à Montréal, 1988. No. 9.

Thomas, W.T. *See* Moncrieff, W.T.

Thompson, David. *David Thompson's Narrative of His Explorations in Western America 1784–1812*. Ed. J.B. Tyrrell. Toronto: The Champlain Society 1916.

Todorov, Tzvetan. *The Conquest of America: The Question of the Other*. Trans. Richard Howard. New York: Harper & Row 1984.

– *The Poetics of Prose*. Trans. Richard Howard. Ithaca: Cornell University 1977.

Townend, Christine. *Travels With Myself*. Sydney: Wild & Woolley 1976.

Traill, Catharine Parr. *The Canadian Crusoes: A Tale of the Rice Lake Plains*. Boston: Crosby, Nichols, Lee 1861.

Tucker, James. *Ralph Rashleigh*. Sydney: Angus & Robertson 1975.

Vogan, A.J. *The Black Police: A Story of Modern Australia*. London: Hutchinson [1890].

Walker, Joe. *No Sunlight Shining*. London: Hutchinson [1960].

Wallace, J.W. *Drift*. ([Geelong?]: n.p. [1882]).

Ward, Jill. "Patrick White's *A Fringe of Leaves*: History and Fiction." *Australian Literary Studies* 8(1978): 402–18.

Watson, Don. *Caledonia Australis: Scottish Highlanders on the Frontier of Australia*. Sydney: Collins 1984.

Watson, E.L. Grant. *The Desert Horizon*. New York: Alfred A. Knopf 1923.

Waubageshig, ed. *The Only Good Indian*. Toronto: New Press 1970.

Webb, Grahame. *Numunwari*. Sydney: Aurora 1980.

Weir, Peter. *The Last Wave* 1974.

White, Patrick. *A Fringe of Leaves*. New York: Avon 1978.

– *Riders in the Chariot*. Ringwood, Victoria: Penguin 1974.

– *The Twyborn Affair*. Ringwood, Victoria: Penguin 1981.

– *Voss*. Ringwood, Victoria: Penguin 1981.

Wiebe, Rudy. *The Blue Mountains of China*. Toronto: McClelland & Stewart 1975.

– *First and Vital Candle*. Toronto: McClelland & Stewart 1966.

– Interview [Februrary 1980]. Videocassette. Memorial University of Newfoundland, St. John's.

– *My Lovely Enemy*. Toronto: McClelland & Stewart 1983.

– "On the Trail of Big Bear." *Journal of Canadian Fiction*. 3, no. 2 (1974): 45–8.

– *The Scorched-Wood People*. Toronto: McClelland & Stewart 1977.

– *The Temptations of Big Bear*. Toronto: McClelland & Stewart 1976.

– *Where Is the Voice Coming From?* Toronto: McClelland & Stewart 1974.

Wiebe, Rudy and Theatre Passe Muraille. *Far as the Eye Can See*. Edmonton: NeWest 1977.

Wilcox, Dora. "At Onawe." In *The Jubilee Book of Canterbury Rhymes*, ed. O.T.J. Alpers, 137–8. Christchurch: Whitcombe & Tombs 1900.

Wilks, William. *The Raid of the Aborigines*. Transactions of the Bibliographical Society of Queensland, 2d ser., vol. 1. Brisbane 1936.

Williams, Margaret. *Australia on the Popular Stage: 1829–1929*. Melbourne: Oxford University Press 1983.

Willshire, W.H. *The Land of the Dawning: Being Facts Gleaned from Cannibals in the Australian Stone Age*. Adelaide: W.K. Thomas 1896.

Wolf, Eric R. *Europe and the People Without History*. Berkeley: University of California Press 1982.

Wongar, Birimbir. *The Trackers: A Novel*. Collingwood, Victoria: Outback 1975.

– *The Track to Bralgu*. London: Jonathan Cape 1978.

Wright, Ronald. "Beyond Words." *Saturday Night*, April 1987, 38–46.

Wrightson, Patricia. *The Bunyip Hole*. Sydney: Angus & Robertson 1957.

– *The Ice is Coming*. London: Hutchinson 1977.

– *The Nargun and the Stars*. Ringwood, Victoria: Penguin 1975.

– *The Rocks of Honey*. Sydney: Angus & Robertson 1960.

Yeats, W.B. "The Second Coming." *The Collected Works of W.B. Yeats*, 210–211. London: Macmillan 1952.

Young, Egerton, R. *Children of the Forest: A Story of Indian Love*. Toronto: Fleming H. Revell 1904.

– *Winter Adventures of Three Boys in the Great Lone Land*. New York: Eaton & Mains 1899.

Young, T.F. "The Indian." *Canada, and Other Poems*, 57–9. Toronto: Hunter, Rose & Company 1887.

Zahar, Renate. *Frantz Fanon: Colonialism and Alienation*. Trans. Willfried F. Fewser. New York: Monthly Review 1974.

Index

"Aboriginal Love-letter" (Mathew), 59
Aboriginal Men of High Degree (Elkin), 204
Aboriginal Myths and Legends (Robinson), 152, 161
Aboriginal Tasmanians, The (Ryan), 154
Absence, 14–15, 109, 158, 169
"Acadia" (Howe), viii, 28, 34–5, 49–50, 90, 130
Achebe, Chinua, 217
Acheson, Frank, 140
Adam, G. Mercer, 69, 71
Administration of Indian Affairs in Canada, The (D.C. Scott), 166
Advertising, 3, 17, 150
Africa, 46, 82, 107, 166, 220
African literature, vii, 14, 217
Aikins, Carroll, 177, 181, 186
Aitchison, Raymond, 105
Alberta, 211, 213
Alcheringa, 23, 101, 132
Alcohol, 83, 98–9, 167, 202
Algeria, 151, 155. *See also* Fanon, Frantz
Algonquin, 153
Algonquin Maiden: A Romance of the Early Days of Upper Canada, An (Adam and Wetherald), 69, 71
Alice Doesn't: Feminism, Semiotics, Cinema (de Lauretis), 216
Allegories of Reading: Figural Language in Rousseau, Nietzsche, Rilke, and Proust (de Man), 206
All's Well That Ends Well (Shakespeare), 171
Almighty Voice, 180, 207–8, 212
Almighty Voice (Peterson), 180–1
Alpha Crucis [pseud. of Robert Herbert], 159
American literature, viii, 14
Amerindian, 6, 219
Among Cannibals: An Account of Four Years' Travels in Australia and of Camp Life with the Aborigines of Queensland (Lumholtz), 42–3, 96

Andeganora (Esson), 177, 179–80
Animal, indigene as, 25–6, 29–30, 45, 101
Animism, 133–4
Anthology of Canadian Literature in English, An (R. Brown and Bennett), 46
Apartheid, 219
"Arabin, or Adventures of a Colonist. A Drama in Three Acts Freely Dramatized from Mr. Mc-Combie's recent Popular Work" (J.R. McLachlan), 174–5
Arcadia, 23, 30
"Arctic Indian's Faith, The" (McGee), 131
Argimou: A Legend of the Micmac (Huyghue), 93
Armstrong, L.O., 187
Arnold, Matthew, 217
Art, 21, 22–3, 38, 47, 123–4, 162–3, 168, 184, 200, 210
"Art According to Artaud" (Todorov), 4, 184–5
Artaud, 4, 181, 183, 184–5
Assyrian, indigene as, 152
"Atareta Poananga and Te Ahi Kaa: What Do Maori Nationalists Want?" (Legat), 221, 222
"At Onawe" (Wilcox), 154
"At the Mermaid Inn" (Lampman), 62
"Attitudes to the Maori in Some Pakeha Fiction" (Pearson), 13
Atwood, Margaret, 37, 47, 123–4, 146, 168, 218
Australia on the Popular Stage: 1829–1929 (Williams), 176
Australian Dream, The (Mudie), 122
"Australian Hymn" (Lang), 150–1
Australian Melodrama: Eighty Years of Popular Theatre (Irvin), 187
Author, 189, 192, 213, 222; indigene author, 217, 220–1
Autobiographies, 221
Awatere, Donna, 220

Bacchae, 183
Badlands (Kroetsch), 74–6, 123, 162
Bakhtin, Mikhail, 52–6, 187–8, 190
Barthes, Roland, 216, 219
Bartram, Grace, 76–7, 86, 103, 141
Bastard Like Me, A (Perkins), 221
Baume, F.E., 69, 70, 72
Beautiful Losers (Cohen), 77–8, 110, 114, 131, 134, 141–2, 152, 156, 158, 160
Beilby, Richard, 37, 78, 168
Bell, Alfred Bernie, 50
Bend to the Wind (Gare), 135
Bennett, Donna, 46
Bennilong, 172, 175, 183–4
Benterrak, Krim, 39. See also *Reading the Country*

Bentham, Jeremy, 44
"Beothuck Indian Skeleton in Glass Case" (Purdy), 61
Beothuck Poems (Stephen), 126, 156
Beothuk, 5, 122, 126, 154–8, 169, 183
Berger, John, 4, 65, 71, 81, 150
Berkeley, Bishop, 45, 216
Berkhofer, Robert F., 14
Bett, S.G., 174
Beyond Capricorn (Roland), 77, 90
Beyond the Act, 220–1
"Beyond Words" (Wright), 219
Bhabha, Homi K., 121
Bible, 120–1, 209-10
Big Bear. *See Temptations of Big Bear, The*
"Black Bodies, White Bodies: Toward an Iconography of Female Sexuality in Late Nineteenth-Century Art, Medicine, and Literature" (Gilman), 67–8
Black Canyon: A Story of '58, The (McKelvie), 96
Black Eureka, The (M. Brown), 40
Black-face, American, 175–7
Blackfoot, 209
"Black Like Me" (F. Fraser), 218–9
Black Police: A Story of Modern Australia, The (Vogan), 99, 101
Black Robe (Moore), 71, 119–20, 133–4, 148–9, 153
Black Skin White Masks (Fanon), 12, 107
Black Troopers, 104–5
Black Velvet, 66–7
Black Waterlily (Hatfield), 30, 69, 73, 114
"'Blank Page' and the Issues of Female Creativity, The" (Gubar), 84
Blank Verse, 173
Blood, 29, 85, 89, 93, 94, 95, 100, 106
Blood Lilies, The (Fraser), 105, 143
Blood of Marlee: A Romance of North Australian Wilds, The" (Broome), 75
Blue Mountains of China, The (Wiebe), 191
Blue Skies (Hodgman), 158
Bodsworth, Fred, 21, 26, 37, 69, 95, 118, 133, 134, 137
Bogatyrev, Petr, 170–1
Boldrewood, Rolf [pseud. of T.A. Browne], 90, 108, 153, 176
Bolt, Carol, 177, 211
Bone People, The (Hulme), 22, 47, 137
Book, 120–2, 208–9
Book of Canadian Prose: Early Beginnings to Confederation, The (A.J.M. Smith), 46
Book of the Play of Hiawatha the Mohawk Depicting the Siege of Hochelaga and the Battle of Lake Champlain, The (Armstrong and Lighthall), 187
Borg, Sonia, 40

Born Indian (Kinsella), 51, 104
Bowering, George, 28, 47, 64, 96, 101, 120–1, 123, 139–40, 158
Boxing, 104–5
Boyd, A.J. 88
Boys Who Stole The Funeral: A Novel Sequence, The (Murray), 60, 122, 137
Bracken, Thomas, 25, 32, 87
Brant, Joseph, 33–4. *See also Thayendanegea: An Historico-Military Drama* (Mackenzie)
"Brébeuf and His Brethren" (Pratt), 93–4
Brecht, 179, 185
Bridle, Augustus, 72–3, 96
Briton, indigene as ancient, 152–3
Broderick, Damien, 47, 143, 162
Broken October: New Zealand 1985 (Harrison), 103
Broome, Charles, 75
Brown, Max, 37, 40
Brown, Russell, 46
Brown Land Crying, The (Beilby), 37, 78, 168
Brown Man's Burden and Later Stories (Finlayson), 11, 53
Browne, T.A. *See* Boldrewood, Rolf
Bruce, Mary Grant, 108
Brumby Innes (Prichard), 177, 179–80
Buffalo, 26, 48, 160, 193, 196, 199, 213
Bulletin, The, 14, 219–20
Bullie's House (Keneally), 78–9, 185–90
Bunyip Hole, The (Wrightson), 136
Burnham, Hampden, 114
Burning Water (Bowering), 28, 47, 64, 96, 101, 120–1, 123, 139–40
Bush ballad, 59, 108
Bush Idyl, A (Mackay), 60
Bush-Life in Queensland or John West's Colonial Experiences (Grant), 85–6
Bush Soldiers, The (Hooker), 103
"Bushrangers; or Norwood Vale, The" (Melville), 175, 176
Buzo, Alexander, 183–4

Caledonia Australis: Scottish Highlanders on the Frontier of Australia (Watson), 26–7, 137
Campbell, Wilfred, 90
"Canada and Its Poetry" (Frye), 39–40
Canadian Crusoes: A Tale of the Rice Lake Plains, The (Traill), 58, 95, 137
Cannibalism, 26, 96–7, 108, 202–6, 213
Canoe, 21–2, 49
"Canoe" (Carr), 22
Capricornia (X. Herbert), 69, 135–6, 160
"Captain Midnight V.C.: A Light Piece" (Hibberd), 79, 80, 81, 155, 184–5, 188

"Caraway" (Kinsella), 136
Cardinal, Harold, 221
Carlin, Norah, 26
Carr, Emily, 22, 123
Casey, Gavin, 105
Cato, Nancy, 77, 140, 162
Celtic savage, 26–7, 70, 101–2, 122, 137, 140, 141, 196, 205, 209, 211
Centre, critical, 7–9, 85, 217–8
Chant of Jimmie Blacksmith, The (Keneally), 29, 64, 66, 78, 79, 103–4, 106, 123, 135, 138, 164
"Charcoal" (D.C. Scott), 104, 114
Charcoal Burners, The (Musgrave), 26, 78–9, 80–1, 86–7, 160
Cheney, Harriet, 21, 28, 118, 131
"Chief Dan Kennedy" (Mandel), 218
Child, indigene as, 28, 99, 103, 107–8, 166, 211
Child, Philip, 22, 33, 39, 131, 143
Children, The (Marshall), 57
Children of Blindness (Sheppard), 25–6, 53, 80–2, 83, 166
Children of the Forest (Egerton Young), 87
Chippewa, 95
Christianity, 16, 86, 88, 95, 103, 118–9, 120–1, 128–35, 139, 156, 183, 194, 197, 199, 201, 204–5, 209, 210, 221
Chronopolitics, 152–3, 168–9. *See also* Fabian, Johannes
Clark, Joan, 215–6
Clarke, Marcus, 204
Class, 24, 101–2, 211
Coetzee, J. M., 14
Cohen, Leonard, 77–8, 110, 114, 131, 134, 141–2, 152, 156, 158, 160
Colonist in Australia: or, The Adventures of Godfrey Arabin, The (McCombie), 174–5
Columbus, 20
Comboman: A Tale of Central Australia (Sayce), 75, 105–6, 116, 138–9
Come a Long Journey (Fry), 22, 51–2, 95, 112, 136, 152
Conditional Culture (Ingamells), 13
"Confession of the Flesh, The" (Foucault), 89
Connolly, Roy, 104
Connor, Ralph [pseud. of Charles W. Gordon], 23, 27, 72, 90, 110–1, 119, 129, 135, 141
Conquest of America: The Question of the Other, The (Todorov), 20, 43, 56, 86, 100, 134
Conrad, Joseph, 46
"Contemporary Views of an Aboriginal Past: Rudy Wiebe and Patrick White" (Goldie), 96
Convictism. *See* Convicts
Convicts, 24, 101–2, 105, 204, 211

"Coo-ee or Wild Days in the Bush" (O'Sullivan), 175
Cook, James, 27, 96
Cook, Kenneth, 47, 79
Cook, Michael, 156, 183
Coonardoo (Prichard), 54–6, 73–5, 160–1
"Coppermine Massacre" (Hearne), 43–6. *See also*
    Hearne, Samuel
Copway, George, 129
Cornish. *See* Celtic savage
Cornwallis, Kinahan, 48
*Corporal Cameron of the North West Mounted Police: A
    Tale of the Macleod Trail* (Connor), 27
Corroboree, 78, 106, 179–80, 181
Cossins, George, 50
Country of the Dead (Rose), 23, 38, 113, 160, 168
Coward, Rosalind, 7, 80–1
Craig, Edward Gordon, 181–2
Crawford, Isabella Valancy, 22, 50, 60
Cree, 96, 198, 207–9
"Creek of the Four Graves, The" (Harpur), 89
Crowfoot, 197, 210–11
"Culture" (Muller), 167
Cumming, R.D., 92
Cushing, E.L., 71

D.D.D., 159
Dagg, Mel, 125, 151–2
Dampier, Alfred, 175, 176–7
Dance, 30, 77, 95–96, 106, 141, 159, 163, 181, 196,
    198, 204, 206, 211–12
Dance Me Outside (Kinsella), 51, 78, 136
Dann, George Landen, 170, 177, 178, 179, 181
Dark, Eleanor, 73, 76, 117, 123, 149, 152, 160, 166
Dark Heritage (Stellmach), 177, 178
Dark, Out There (B. Robinson), 177
Darker Grows the Valley (Bartram), 76–7, 86, 103, 141
"Daulac: An Historical Tragedy of French Canada in
    Five Acts" (Campbell), 90
*David Thompson's Narrative of His Explorations in West-
    ern America 1784–1812*, 91, 110, 120–1, 128, 137,
    140
Davies, Robertson, 96, 182
Dawe, Tom, 169
Dawe, W. Carlton, 34
Day, Frank Parker, 27
Daymond, Douglas, 46
Death of the indigene, 37, 43–4, 46, 67, 73, 85, 114,
    137, 138, 153–60, 180, 211, 212, 213, 221
De Boos, Charles, 32–3
Defamiliarization, 16, 55–7, 186, 218
Deindigenization, 38, 47, 132, 165–6, 167–8, 181,
    188–9, 202, 211

Deixis, 185, 187–8
de la roche, Mazo, 64, 73–5, 81
de Lauretis, Teresa, 216
de Man, Paul, 206
Demonic indigene, 87–8, 94, 96–7, 99–100, 105, 203
De Roberval, A Drama (Hunter Duvar), 173, 177
Derrida, Jacques, 6, 85, 108, 200, 205, 207, 219
Desert Horizon, The (E.L. Watson), 29
Desert Saga (Hatfield), 131, 152
"Destruction of Wealth, The" (Foster), 218
Detribalized indigene, 37, 165–6, 168, 188–9. *See also* Deindigenized
Devaney, James, 160
Devanny, Jean, 31
Diachrony, ix, 6, 148, 150, 152, 163–4, 167–8
Dialogic, 54–6
Diamond, Richard, 177
Diamond of Glen Rock, The (Bell), 50
Dickson, Bassett, 48, 94, 103, 130, 152
Difference and Pathology: Stereotypes of Sexuality, Race and Madness (Gilman), 11, 15, 142, 166
"Discourse in the Novel" (Bakhtin), 54
Diviners, The (Laurence), 78, 80–81, 104, 112, 123, 137–8, 160
Doctor Wooreddy's Prescription for Enduring the End of the World (C. Johnson), 217
Domain of Devils, The (Maple), 97
Domestication of the Savage Mind, The (Goody), 9, 36, 108–9, 116, 119, 127, 130
Domett, Alfred, 23, 30, 35, 67, 68, 70, 71, 89, 93, 121, 122, 141, 159, 172
Drake-Brockman, H., 78, 177, 179–80
"Drama and the African World-view" (Soyinka), 185
Dream, 43, 58, 142–5, 167, 169, 211–12
Dreaming Dragons: A Time Opera, The (Broderick), 47, 143, 162
Dream Like Mine, A (M.T. Kelly), 37, 42–3, 104, 143, 144
Dreamtime, 142–3, 161–2, 167
Drew, Wayland, 37, 47, 118, 135, 160, 167–8
Drewe, Robert, 26, 77, 116, 162
Drift (Wallace), 176
Driven, The (Stuart), 57, 124
"Drover's Wife, The" (Lawson), 34
Druid, 153, 166. *See also* Briton, indigene as ancient
Drum, 111, 114, 123, 180
Dryden, John, 171
Dumont, Gabriel, 196, 211
Dunlop, Eliza Hamilton, 58, 61
"Dynamics of the Sign in the Theater" (Honzl), 189–90

"Eagle Chief, The" (Dunlop), 58

Eagle Song: An Indian Saga Based on True Events (Houston), 123
Eagleton, Terry, 218
Ebb-Tide (Fairbairn), 177
Ecology, *See* Environmentalism
"Economy of Manichean Allegory: The Function of Racial Difference in Colonialist Literature, The" (JanMohammed), 10, 88
Ecstasy of Rita Joe, The (Ryga), 30, 185–90
Eden, 161, 162
Egyptian, indigene as, 152
"Eiffel Tower, The" (Barthes), 216, 219
Elam, Keir, 170, 171, 178–9, 180, 183, 185, 187–8, 189
Eliade, Mircea, 129, 132, 135, 137, 138, 141–2, 144, 145–6
Eliza Fraser (Cook), 47, 79
Elkin, A.P., 204
Elliott, Brian, 13, 50–1
Ellis, John, 7, 80–1
Ellis, Vivienne Rae, 77, 140, 162
Emigrant, a Poem, in Four Cantos, The (S. O'Grady), 28, 110
Emigrant: A Tale of Australia, The (Leigh), 31
Environmentalism, 35–8, 160
Epic, 48–50, 58–61
Epic theatre, 179
Episteme, viii, 8–9, 16, 110, 122, 125–6, 139–40, 142, 152, 217–18
Eros and Civilization: A Philosophical Inguiry into Freud (Marcuse), 88
Essay on Man, An (Pope), 3
Esson, Louis, 177, 179
Ethnography, 53, 55–8, 155
Eugene [pseud. of Douglas S. Huyghue], 93
Europe and The People Without History (Wolf), 5, 154–5, 158
Evans, Hubert, 22, 25, 124, 168
"Expiation" (D.C. Scott), 141
Explorer's narratives, 14–15, 20, 27–8, 41–6, 56, 64, 66, 101, 110–11, 128, 140, 165, 171. *See also* individual names, e.g., Eyre
Expressionism, 185
Extinction (Rowe), 154
"Eye of Power, The" (Foucault), 44, 203
Eyewash Indians, The (Bett), 174
Eyre, Edward John, 27, 45, 66

Fabian, Johannes, 152–3, 164, 169
Fairbairn, A.M.D., 71–2, 177, 180, 182
Fairchild, Hoxie, 20, 31
Falcon, Pierre, 193–4, 196, 207

Fanon, Frantz, 12, 86, 88, 94–5, 102–3, 107, 126, 129, 136, 146–7, 151, 155, 183

Far as the Eye Can See (Wiebe & Theatre Passe Muraille), 197, 210–11

Feast of the Bunya: An Aboriginal Ballad, The (Moynihan), 9, 217

Feminist approaches, 9, 64–5, 74–5, 80–2, 84, 215–6

Ferguson, Dugald, 23

Fertility, 78–9

Fifty Years Ago: An Australian Tale (De Boos), 32–3

Figes, Eva, 49

Figures de l'Indien, Les (Thérien), 14

Fill It Up Again (McCallum), 53, 97, 98

Finlayson, Roderick, 11, 53

Finnegans Wake (Joyce), 122

First Among the Hurons (Gros-Louis), 221

First and Vital Candle (Wiebe), 193, 197, 201, 202–3, 211

"First Approach of Civilization to Australia Felix" (Howitt), 162

Five Lectures: Psychoanalysis, Politics, and Utopia (Marcuse), 100

Flagon Fun (McCallum), 53, 98

Flames in the Wind (Hudson), 96

Foreman, The (Shearer), 167, 177

Form, 42–62, 116

Forms of Historical Fiction: Sir Walter Scott and His Successors, The (Shaw), 195

"Forms of Time and the Chronotope in the Novel" (Bakhtin), 52

"Forsaken, The" (D.C. Scott), 95

"For Simon Fraser" (Lane), 28

Fortunes of Richard Mahony, The (H.H. Richardson), 14, 17

Foster, Peter, 218

Foucault, Michel, viii, 6, 7, 9–10, 17, 63–4, 66, 71, 79, 85, 89, 125, 156–7, 183, 188, 192, 216

Foundation for Aboriginal and Islander Research Action, 220

Fountains Beyond (Dann), 177, 179, 181

Frantz Fanon: Colonialism and Alienation (Zahar), 88

Fraser, Fil, 218–19

Fraser, W.A., 105, 143

Freudian approaches, 23, 25, 63–4, 77, 88. *See also* Psychological approaches

Fringe Dwellers, The (Gare), 53, 98

Fringe of Leaves, A (White), 192, 194, 196, 203–6, 207, 209, 211–12, 213, 215

Fry, Alan, 22, 51–2, 55, 78, 83, 95, 99, 112, 135, 136, 152, 160

Frye, Northrop, 39, 42

Fugitive Anne (Praed), 33, 65, 79, 81, 128–9, 135, 141

Gabe (Bolt), 177, 211
"Gangrened People, The" (Ingamells), 36
Gare, Nene, 53, 98, 135
Gaspards of Pine Croft: A Romance of the Windemere, The (Connor), 72, 141
Gaze, 15, 42, 44–5, 65–6, 71, 73, 216
Genealogies, 85, 214
George, Chief Dan, 189–90
Gilman, Sander L., 11, 15, 67–8, 142, 166
"Girl of the Never Never, The" (J. Smith), 35, 176
Glass Canoe, The (Ireland), 56, 98, 102
Glory and the Dream, The (Hilliard), 120, 163, 216
Glossaries, 56–7
"Goarang, the Anteater" (Wongar), 135
God in the Sand: An Australian Mystical Romance (Price), 30–1, 33, 143
God of Gods, The (Aikins), 177, 181–2, 186
Golden age, 17, 161, 162
Golden Lake or The Marvellous History of a Journey Through the Great Lone Land of AUSTRALIA, The (W.C. Dawe), 34
Goldie, Terry, 33, 96
Gone Indian (Kroetsch), 26, 47, 144–5, 191, 215
Goody, Jack, 9, 36, 108–9, 116, 119, 127, 130
Goonoo, Goonoo (O'Grady), 99, 141, 158, 159
Gordon, Charles W. *See* Connor, Ralph
Grace, Alfred A., 96, 160
Grace, Patricia, 216
Grant, A.C., 85–6
Gray, Oriel, 177
Great Hunger, The (Peterson), 182
Great South Land: An Epic Poem, The (Ingamells), 29, 60, 101, 102
Greeks, indigenes as, 152
Greenstone Door, The (Satchell), 38, 58, 95, 112, 114
Grey Owl, 144–5, 215, 217
Gros-Louis, Max, 221
Gubar, Susan, 84
Gunn, Mrs. Aeneas, 114
Gutteridge, Don, 70

"Had We But World Enough" (Gray), 177
Haggard, H. Rider, 46
Haida, 180
"Half-Breed Girl, The" (D.C. Scott), 70
Half-Caste (Baume), 69–70, 72
Half-Gallon Jar, The (McCallum), 53, 97, 98
Hansen: A Novel of Canadianization (Bridle), 72–3, 96
"Happiness" (Prichard), 55–6
Harpur, Charles, 89

Harrison, Craig, 103
Hatfield, William, 30, 69, 73, 114, 131, 152, 161
Hawthorne, Nathaniel, 194–5
Head Station, The (Praed), 112–13, 124
Healy, J.J., 13, 33
Hearne, Samuel, 20, 38–9, 43–6, 54, 64, 128, 140
Heart of Darkness (Conrad), 46
Hegel, 166
Hegemonic discourse, 216
"Height of Land, The" (D.C. Scott), 114, 118
Herbert, Robert, *See* Alpha Crucis
Herbert, Xavier, 27, 30, 35, 69, 71, 78, 79, 95, 105, 111, 114, 119, 122, 124, 134, 135, 136, 138, 144, 153, 160, 191
Heroic tragedies, 32, 48–50, 173–4, 177
Hiawatha, 94, 112
Hiawatha (Longfellow), 112, 174, 187
Hiawatha or Nanabozho (Armstrong), 187
Hibberd, Jack, 79, 80, 81, 155, 184–5, 188
Hilliard, Noel, 24, 55, 78, 80, 83, 90, 97–8, 120, 162, 163, 216
His Natural Life (Clarke), 204
Historical romance, 49, 149–50, 194–5
Historicity, 28, 45–6, 103, 109, 132, 133, 148–69, 186, 192, 194–5, 211–13
History of Sexuality: An Introduction, The (Foucault), 63, 66, 71, 79, 125, 157
"Hit and Run" (LeMay), 177–8
Hodgman, Helen, 158
Holistic indigene, 36, 79, 133–5, 139, 146, 196, 198, 200–1
Homosexuality, 64, 197, 212
Honi Heki, in Two Cantos (Dickson), 48, 94, 103, 130, 152
Honzl, Jindrich, 189–90
Hooker, John, 103
Hori [pseud. of W. Norman McCallum], 53, 55, 97
"Horseman of Agawa, The" (Purdy), 123
House of the Seven Gables and the Snow Image and Other Twice-Told Tales, The (Hawthorne), 194–5
Houston, James, 22, 112, 119, 123
How a People Die (Fry), 55, 83, 99, 135, 160
Howard, Robert, 171
Howe, Joseph, viii, 28, 34–5, 49–50, 90, 99, 130
Howitt, Richard, 162
Hudson, Helen, 96
Huldowget: A Story of the North Pacific Coast (McKelvie), 153
Hulme, Keri, 22, 47, 137
Hulme, Peter, 42
Hungerford, T.A.G., 39
Hunter Duvar, John, 173

Huron Chief and Other Poems, The (Kidd), 49, 99, 161, 166
"Huron Princess, The" (Leprohon), 131
Hutcheon, Linda, 47–8
Huyghue, Douglas S. *See* Eugene

Ice is Coming, The (Wrightson), 136
"Ideological Voyages: Concerning a Flaubertian Dis-
   orientation" (Terdiman), 15
Ideology of the text, 5, 8, 14, 62, 85, 136, 183–4, 185,
   213, 219, 222
Idriess, Ion L, 139, 161, 166
Igloo, 182
Ignoble savage, 59, 98
Ihimaera, Witi, 217
Ilbarana (Stuart), 57–8, 93
Illegitimate, The (Aitchison), 105
Illiteracy, 108–10, 112–13. *See also* Orality
Image, 5–7
Image in the Clay (Ireland), 94, 177, 182
"Imogene Continued" (Moorhouse), 82–3
Imperialism, 5, 10, 12, 16, 34, 46, 65, 71, 86, 100–2,
   106, 121, 152, 220–3
Inapatua (Patrick), 21, 78, 81–2, 125, 141, 165
"In Beauty It Is Finished" (Dann), 177
Incomparable Atuk, The (Richler), 51
Incubus, 40, 81, 84, 137
India, 12, 16, 121
"Indian, The" (T.F. Young), 122
"Indian Address to the Mississippi" (H.J.K.), 35–6
*Indian Emperour, or, The Conquest of Mexico by the Span-
   iards, The* (Dryden), 171
Indian Gold (Lowrey), 33
"Indian Maid: A Traditionary Tale, The" (Cushing),
   71
Indian Nights (I. E. MacKay), 51, 112
"Indian Nurse's Death Song, The" 130
Indian Queen, A Tragedy, The (Dryden and Howard),
   171
"Indian Reservation" (Klein), 114
"Indian Struck" (Kinsella), 80
"Indian Summer" (Bowering), 158
Indianisms. *See* Indigenisms
"Indian's Dream, The" 31
Indigene maiden, 44, 61, 68–77, 84, 87, 89, 90–1, 105,
   114, 173
Indigene writers, 217–18
Indigenisms, 10, 33, 50, 59–60, 87, 98–9, 172
Indigenization, 13–17, 46–7, 49–50, 146, 157–8, 213,
   214, 223
Individuation, 46–7, 193, 213, 223

Ingamells, Rex, 13, 28, 36, 60, 83–4, 101, 102, 149, 152
"In Maoriland" (J.L. Kelly), 69–70
Interview (Wiebe), 199
"In There Somewhere" (Dawe), 169
In the Shade of the Coolibah Tree: A Musical Play" (Diamond), 177
"Introduction to Verisimilitude, An" (Todorov), 52
"Inuit" (Purdy), 162–3
"Ireland and Natural Man in 1649" (Carlin), 26
Ireland, David, 56, 94, 98, 102, 177, 182
"I Remember Houses" (Kinsella), 104
Irish. See Celtic savage
Irony, 58–9, 67, 179
Iroquois, 78, 92
"Iroquois at the Stake, The" (Mair), 92, 94
Irvin, Eric, 187

G.J., 153
Jack, Henry, 220
Jack Ralston or The Outbreak of the Nauscopees: A Tale of Life in the Far North-East of Canada (Burnham), 114
"Jacques Cartier and the Child" (McGee), 131
"Jacques Cartier and the Little Indian Girl" (Cheney), 21, 28, 118, 131
JanMohammed, Abdul R., 10, 88
Jesuit, 71, 93–4, 119. See also Missionary
Jimberi Track, The (M. Brown), 37
Jindyworobak Review, 112
Jindyworobaks, 13, 15, 29, 50, 112, 144, 149
Jindyworobaks, The (Elliott), 13, 50
John Paul's Rock (Day), 27
Johnson, Colin, 217
Johnson, E. Pauline, 61
Jones, Dorothy L. M., 13
Journals of Expeditions of Discovery into Central Australia, and Overland from Adelaide to King George's Sound, In the Years 1840–1; Sent by the Colonists of South Australia, With The Sanction and Support of the Government: including an Account of the Manners and Customs of the Aborigines and the State of their Relations with Europeans (Eyre), 27, 45, 66
Journey from Prince of Wale's Fort in Hudson's Bay to the Northern Ocean Undertaken by Order of the Hudson's Bay Company for the Discovery of Copper Mines, A North West Passage &c. In the Years 1769, 1770, 1771, & 1772, A (Hearne) 20, 38, 39, 43–6, 64, 128, 140
"Joy! Joy! Joy!" (D.C. Scott) 182
Joyce, James, 9, 122
Judaism, 122, 134, 210

Jung, 96, 142, 143

H.J.K., 35–6
Kanaka, 183
Kayak, 22. *See also* Canoe
Kearney, W.D., 90, 154
Kelly, John Liddell, 69–70
Kelly, M.T., 37, 42–3, 104, 143, 144
Kelsey, Henry, 111
Kelsey Papers, The, 111
Kendall, Henry, 48, 59
Keneally, Thomas, 29, 64, 66, 78–9, 103–4, 106, 123,
     135, 138, 164, 185–90
"The Kid in the Stove" (Kinsella), 51
Kidd, Adam, 49, 99, 161, 166
Kidman, Fiona, 177
Kimber, Robert, 181
King, James, 27
King, Phillip P, 10
Kinsella, W.P., 51–3, 55, 62, 78, 80, 83, 97–8, 104,
     105, 135–6
Klee Wyck (Carr), 22, 123
Klein, A. M., 114
Koonapippi, 114
Kovel, Joel, 25, 36, 77, 97, 119, 145
Kroetsch, Robert, 26, 47, 74–6, 123, 144–5, 162, 168,
     191, 215

Lacanian approaches, 80–1, 145
Lament, 48, 159
Lament for Harmonica (Maya), The (Ringwood), 177
Lampman, Archibald, 62
*Land of the Dawning: Being Facts Gleaned from Cannibals
     in the Australian Stone Age, The* (Willshire), 66–7,
     104
Land rights, 136, 155, 192, 220–3
Lane, Patrick, 28
Lang, John Dunmore, 150–1, 152
"Language and Literature" (Todorov), 53
*Language and Materialism: Developments in Semiology
     and the Theory of the Subject* (Coward and Ellis), 7,
     80–1
Language, indigenous, 117–20, 178
Lanney, William, 122, 156, 162
"Last Bison, The" (Mair), 26, 48, 159–60
Last Lemurian: A Westralian Romance, The (G.F. Scott),
     28, 161
"Last of His Tribe, The" (Kendall), 48, 59, 159–60
"Last of the Indians, The" (D.D.D.), 159
Last Wave, The (Weir), 168
Laurence, Margaret, 78, 80–1, 104, 112, 123, 137–8,
     160

Law, 91–2, 95
Lawson, Henry, 34–5
Leacock, Stephen, 173
Lee, Dennis, 19, 36
Legat, Nicola, 221, 222
Legend & Dreaming (Robinson), 112
"Legend of Chileeli, The" (Mair), 90–1
Legends, 112, 125, 152, 159, 194
Leichhardt, Ludwig, 193
Leigh, W.H., 31
LeMay, Bonnie, 177–8
"Lemurian Nineties, The" (Healy), 33
Lenore Divine (Devanny), 31
Leprohon, Rosanna E. *See* R. E. M.
Lescarbot, Marc, 186–7
Lévi-Strauss, Claude, 8, 9, 10, 20, 118, 126, 133, 135, 139, 148, 159, 163, 164–5, 167
Liberation, indigene as 15, 23–5, 81, 88, 97–8, 101
Life, History and Travels of Kah-ge-ga-gahbowh (George Copway), The, 129
Lighthall, W.D., 94, 124, 131, 143, 150
Lili-Illa: a Romance of the Australian Aborigines ("Moan Bambi"), 130
"Lilliri" (Ingamells), 83–4
Lindigo, the White Woman, or, The Highland Girl's Captivity Among the Australian Blacks (McLean), 70, 137
Literariness, 41–2
Literary Garland, The, 31, 35, 61, 71, 130, 135, 153, 159
Literary Theory: An Introduction (Eagleton), 218
Literature and the Aborigine in Australia 1770–1975 (Healy), 13
Literature in Canada (Daymond and Monkman), 46
Little Big Man, 189
"Logical Status of Fictional Discourse, The" (Searle), 178
Logos, 209
Longfellow. *See Hiawatha*
Lost tribe novels, 33–4, 46, 161
"Lost Tribe of Boonjie: A Romance of the Australian Wilds, The" (P.R. Meredith), 69, 99, 161
Lowrey, Harold, 33
Lumholtz, Carl, 42–3, 96

M. [pseud. of Henry Melville], 175, 176
J.R.M. [pseud. of J.R. McLachlan], 174
R.E.M. [pseud. of Rosanna E. Leprohon], 131
Macherey, Pierre, 8, 213, 222
MacKay, Isabel Ecclestone, 51, 112
Mackay, Kenneth, 60, 175
Mackenzie, Alexander, 66
Mackenzie, J.B., 32–4, 48–50, 172–3
Macquarie (Buzo), 183–4

Mair, Charles, 26, 32–4, 48–50, 70, 90–1, 92, 103, 117, 122, 131, 139, 159–60, 172, 174, 175, 177

"Malcolm's Katie" (Crawford), 22, 50, 60

Malloonkai (Stuart), 57–8

Mamba ("The Bright-Eyed"): An Aboriginal Reminiscence (McCrae), 48, 177

Man Hamilton, The (Palmer), 71–2, 75

Mandel, Eli, 218

Manichean, 10, 25, 88, 95, 100, 142

Manifold, John, 28

"Manitou Motors" (Kinsella), 105

Mann, Leonard, 70, 83, 105

Mannoni, O., 23, 64–5, 163

Maori Sovereignty (Awatere), 220

Maori Woman (Hilliard), 78, 80, 98, 162

Maple, Eric, 97

Maquinna, 139

"March of Te Rauparaha, The" (Bracken), 25, 32, 87

Marcuse, Herbert, 88, 100

Maris, Hyllus, 40

Marshall, James Vance [pseud. of Donald Gordon Payne], 57

Mask, 99, 182

Maskepetoon, 208–9, 212

Mason, Bruce, 94, 160, 168, 177, 180, 181, 186

Massacre, 3, 43–6, 89–90, 100

Master of Life: A Romance of the Five Nations and of Pre-historic Montreal, The (Lighthall), 94, 124, 131, 143, 150

Material culture, 20–3, 181–2, *See also* Art

Mathew, John, 59, 79, 99

Maza, Bob, 188–9

McCallum, Norman W. *See* Hori

McCauley, Sue, 80–1, 87

McCombie, Thomas, 174

McCrae, George Gordon, 48, 96, 149–50, 177

McDonald, Roger, 76–7

McGarrity, John, 83, 99, 102, 105, 122, 166

McGee, Thomas D'Arcy, 131

McKelvie, B.A., 96, 153

McLachlan, Alexander, 94

McLachlan, J.R. *See* J.R.M.

McLean, Angus, 70, 137

Medicine wheel, 182

Melville, Henry. *See* M.

"Memorial to a Missionary" (Sinclair), 77

Men Are Human (Palmer), 55, 72, 75, 76, 87

Mennonites, 191

Men Without Wives (Drake-Brockman), 78, 177, 179–80

Meredith, Louisa A, 89–90, 154

Meredith, P.R., 69, 99, 161

Métis, 37, 69, 70, 80, 104, 137–8, 160, 193–4, 201, 207, 211. *See also* Mixed-race
"Mettawamkeag: An Indian Tragedy" (Leacock), 173
Micmac, 157
Milgate, Rodney, 182–3
Miller, Nancy K., 74–5
"Miringu, The" (Wongar), 92
Miscegenation, 54, 57, 58, 64–84, 87, 106. *See also* Mixed-race; Sex
Missionary, 71, 87, 130, 197, 207. *See also* Jesuit
Mist on the River (Evans), 22, 25, 124
Mitchell, T.L., 87, 101, 171–2
Mitchell, W.O., 24–5, 77, 92, 119, 141
Mixed-race, 27, 29, 69–70, 105, 106, 140–1, 178, 184
"Moan Bambi," 130
"Moccasin Telegraph, The" (Kinsella), 104
Moccasin Telegraph and Other Stories, The (Kinsella), 51, 52, 104, 136
Moncrieff, W.T. [pseud. of W. T. Thomas], 115, 172
Monkman, Leslie, 13, 46
Moondyne: A Story of Life in West Australia (O'Reilly), 24, 33, 115, 141
Moore, Brian, 71, 119–20, 133, 148–9
Moorhouse, Frank, 82–3
"Morning" (Mudie), 144
Moyarra: An Australian Legend in Two Cantos (Rusden), 48
Moynihan, Cornelius, 9, 217
Mudie, Ian, 122, 132, 144, 145
Muecke, Stephen, 39, 113, 115, 121, 125, 161–2, 221
Muller, Hugo, 167
Murray, Les, 60, 122, 137
"Museum of Man, The" (Dagg), 151–2
Musgrave, Susan, 26, 78–9, 80–1, 86–7, 160
Music, 118, 175, 179–80. *See also* Drum
Mutuwhenua: The Moon Sleeps (P. Grace), 216
My Lovely Enemy (Wiebe), 193, 195, 199, 200, 201, 208–9, 212–13
"Myal Creek" (Mathew), 99
Mysticism, 16, 31, 36, 40, 50, 51–2, 78, 91, 96, 101, 111, 118, 126, 127–47, 162, 182, 185–6, 192–213, 218, 219
Myth, Literature and the African World (Soyinka), 49, 185

Naked Under Capricorn (Ruhen), 76
Naming, 115–17, 209
"Nannish" (Muller), 167
Nargun and the Stars, The (Wrightson), 136
Narration, forms of, 44–5, 51–6, 60–1, 112, 193–5, 212

Narrative of a Survey of the Intertropical and Western Coasts of Australia Performed between the Years 1818 and 1822 (P. King), 10

Narrative of a Voyage to New Zealand, Performed in the Years 1814 and 1815, In Company with the Rev. Samuel Marsden (Nicholas), 15, 38

"Native Alliance for Red Power" (Jack), 220

Native Heritage: Images of the Indian in English-Canadian Literature, A (Monkman), 13

Native sovereignty, 221–2

Nature, 14–15, 19–40, 73–4, 77–8, 113–14, 117, 123, 133, 136, 166, 181, 182, 196–7, 213

"Necessity of Nobility: Indigenous Peoples in Canadian and Australian Literature, The" (Goldie), 33

Nemarluk: King of the Wilds (Idriess), 139, 166

Neptune's Theatre (Lescarbot), 186–7

Newfoundland, 154, 157. *See also* Beothuk

"Newfoundland Letter, The" (Parmenius), 43

Newland, Simpson, 167

Newlove, John, 60–1

Nicholas, John Liddiard, 15, 38

"Nigger," indigene as, 59, 116

Night at Green River, A (Hilliard), 24, 55, 90, 97–8

Night Thoughts (Edward Young), 38

1915 (McDonald), 76–7

Nisbet, Hume, 152

No Barrier (Dark), 76, 123, 149

Noble savage, 31–4, 49, 51, 94, 187, 189

Noble Savage: A Study in Romantic Naturalism, The (Fairchild), 20, 31

No Exit (Sartre), 185

Nomads, 39

No Sunlight Shining (Walker), 53, 69, 83

Numunwari (Webb), 37

Nymph, indigene as, 59, 61–2, 159

Object. *See* Subject/object relations

Of Grammatology (Derrida), 205

Of Us Now Living: A Novel of Australia (Ingamells), 149

O'Grady, Frank, 99, 141, 158

O'Grady, Standish, 28, 110

O'Hagan, Howard, 30, 90, 117, 140, 162

Ojibwa, 95, 118, 123, 133, 143, 201, 202, 211

Old Colonials (Boyd), 88

Old Melbourne Memories (Boldrewood), 153

Once a Jolly Blackman (McGarrity), 83, 99, 102, 105, 122, 166

Ong, Walter J., 107–26, 127, 151, 159, 163, 164

Only Good Indian, The (Waubageshig), 220

"Only One Who Forgot, The" (Hungerford), 39

"Onondaga Madonna, The" (D.C. Scott), 62

On the Rim of the Curve (M. Cook), 156, 183
"On the Trail of Big Bear" (Wiebe), 192
Open Hand: An Epic Poem Dealing With the Early Settlement of Maine and New Brunswick, Founded on Tradition, The (Kearney), 90, 154
Orality, 16, 36, 90–1, 96, 107–26, 127, 136, 138, 151–2, 159–60, 161–62, 163, 173–4, 180, 186, 197, 205–9, 212, 219
Orality and Literacy: The Technologizing of the Word (Ong), 107–26, 127, 159, 163
Orator, indigene as, 110–11, 173
O'Reilly, John Boyle, 24, 33, 115, 141
Orientalism, 5, 8, 10–11, 16
"Orientalism Reconsidered" (Said), 8
Orientalism (Said), 4–5, 6, 10–11, 15
Ossian, 111
Ostension, 171, 179, 185, 187
O'Sullivan, E.W., 175
Other. *See* Self and Other
Other Halves (McCauley), 80–1, 87
"Our Black Brothers," 219–20
Outcasts in White Australia (Rowley), 69

Pacific Coast Tragedy, A (Fairbairn), 71–2, 177
Pakeha, 11
Palmer, Vance, 55, 71–2, 75, 76, 81, 87
Pantheism, 11, 133–6
Parker, Gilbert, 79, 120–1, 124
Parmenius, Stephen, 43
Parody, 3, 47–8, 60, 67, 115
"Parts of the Eagle" (Kinsella), 52, 136
Paterson, A.B., 122, 177
Patriarchy, 65, 185. *See also* Feminist approaches
Patriation, 222
Patrick, John, 21, 78, 81–2, 125, 141, 165
"Patrick White's *A Fringe of Leaves*: History and Fiction" (Ward), 192–3
Patrol of the Sundance Trail, The (Connor), 23, 110–11, 119
Paul Pero (Cumming), 92
Paving the Way: A Romance of the Australian Bush (Newland), 167
Payne, Donald Gordon. *See* Marshall, James Vance
Pearson, Bill, 11, 13, 53
Penguin Book of Australian Short Stories, The (Heseltine), 56
Periodicals, indigenes in, 218, 221
Perkins, Charles, 221
"Peter the Picaninny" (Kendall), 59
Peterson, Leonard, 180, 181, 182
Phenomenology, 107–8, 110, 124

Photograph, 123
"Piccaninny, A" (Stephens), 59
Pittman, Al, 61, 156, 157, 158
Plume of the Arawas (Acheson), 140
Poananga, Atareta, 222
Poet, indigene as, 90–1, 111. *See also* Orator, indigene
    as
"Poetics and Criticism" (Todorov), 41
Poetics of Prose, The (Todorov), 4
Pohutukawa Tree: A Play in Three Acts, The (Mason),
    94, 160, 168, 177, 180, 181, 182, 186
Pollock, Sharon, 182
"Polytropic Man: Tropes of Sexuality and Mobility in
    Early Colonial Discourse" (Hulme), 42
Ponteach: A Tragedy (Rogers), 32–4, 111, 174, 175,
    179
Poor Fellow My Country (Herbert), 27, 30, 35, 69, 71,
    78, 79, 95, 105, 111, 114, 119, 122, 124, 134, 136,
    138, 144, 153, 191
Pope, Alexander, 3
Popular Theatre Troupe, 156, 183
Possession (de la Roche), 64, 73–5, 81
"Powassan's Drum" (D.C. Scott), 114, 123
Praed, Mrs. Campbell, 33, 65, 79, 81, 90, 112–13, 124,
    128–9, 135, 141
"Prairie Vagabond, A" (Parker), 120–1
Pratt, E.J., 93–4
Pratt, Mary Louise, 42, 44
Prehistoric, 17, 48, 49, 99, 108, 111, 137, 138, 143,
    149, 151–3, 155, 159, 162, 164, 166–8, 197, 207, 212–
    13, 219, 220, 221
Presence, 4, 5, 14, 108–15, 124, 126, 138, 186, 189,
    208, 210
Price, Theo, 30–1, 33, 143
Prichard, Katharine Susannah, 54–6, 73–5, 132, 149,
    160–1, 177, 179
"Pride, The" (Newlove), 60–1
Primitivism, 11, 29–34, 90–1, 93, 95, 125–6, 151
"Prison Talk" (Foucault), 7
Problematic, 62, 185, 213, 222. *See also* Ideology
Props, 182
Prospero and Caliban: The Psychology of Colonialization
    (Mannoni), 23, 64–5, 163
Psychological approaches, 23, 25, 33, 36, 40, 46, 63–4,
    77, 80–1, 88, 97, 107–8, 141–2, 143–6, 215
Publishing, 53
Purdy, Al, 26, 61, 123–4, 162

Quadra, Bodega Y, 139
Queensland, 220–1
Queen Trucanini (Cato and Ellis), 77, 140, 162
Question Time (Davies), 96, 182

"Race and Class in Colonial Australia" (Reynolds), 100
Racism, 6–7, 219, 220, 221
"Racism's Last Word" (Derrida), 6, 219
Raid of the Aborigines, The (Wilks), 58, 97
"Rainbows Die at Sunset" (Dann), 170, 177, 178, 179
Ralph Rashleigh (Tucker), 24, 140, 215
Ranga, 186, 188–9
Ranolf and Amohia: A Dream of Two Lives (Domett), 23,
    30, 35, 67, 68, 70, 71, 89, 93, 121, 141, 159, 172
Rape, 76–7, 82–3, 86, 141
*Raw and the Cooked: Introduction to a Science of Mythol-
    ogy: I* (Lévi-Strauss), 164–5
Rayment, Tralton, 27
Reading the Country: Introduction to Nomadology
    (Benterrak, Muecke and Roe), 39, 113–14, 115, 125,
    161–2, 221
Realism, 7, 41–2, 53–8, 83, 177–8, 181–2, 185, 186,
    192. *See also* Verisimilitude
Rebel Chief: A Romance of New Zealand, The (Nisbet),
    152
Rebirth of Canada's Indians, The (Cardinal), 221
Redbird, Duke, 69
Red Chief As Told By the Last of His Tribe, The (Idriess),
    161
Red Revolutionary, The (Mair), 174. *See also Tecumseh*
Red Tory, 34
Reed, Bill, 99, 155–6, 180
Referent, 4, 62, 184, 214
Refined Look at Existence, A (Milgate), 182–3
Reification, 5, 25, 57, 65, 80, 88, 148, 158, 220
Representation, 1, 4, 11, 17, 52, 113, 116, 170–5,
    178–9, 185–90
"Representation, the Despot and the Harem: Some
    Questions Around an Academic Orientalist Paint-
    ing by Lecomte-duNouy (1885)" (Richon), 11–12
Repression, 63–5, 81, 83–4, 88–9
Revenge of Annie Charlie, The (Fry), 78
Revolution, 103–4
Reynolds, Henry, 100
Richardson, Henry Handel, 14, 17
Richardson, John, 15, 27, 70–1, 87, 124, 148–9
Richler, Mordecai, 51
Richon, Olivier, 11–12
Riders in the Chariot (White), 193, 194, 195, 197, 201,
    210
Riel, 70, 106, 192, 194, 196, 202, 207, 211
Riel: A Poem for Voices (Gutteridge), 70
Ringwood, Gwen, 177
Riverrun (Such), 21, 122, 169
*Robbery Under Arms: A Story of Life and Adventure in
    the Bush and in the Goldfields of Australia* (Boldre-
    wood), 176

"Robbery Under Arms" (Dampier and Walch), 176
Robinson, Bec, 177
Robinson, George, 77, 116, 140
Robinson, Roland, 50–1, 112, 152, 161
Rock paintings, 47, 123–4, 168, 200, 210. *See also* Art
Rocks of Honey, The (Wrightson), 29
Roddick, Amy Redpath, 30, 61
Roe, Paddy, 39, 113, 115. *See also Reading the Country*
Rogers, Robert, 32–4, 111, 174, 175, 177
Roland, Betty, 77, 90
Ronan, Thomas, 70
Rose, Lyndon, 23, 38, 113, 160, 168
Rousseau, Jean Jacques, 38, 200
Rowe, Frederic, 154
Rowley, C.D., 69
Ruhen, Olaf, 76
"Run Run Away" (Kimber), 181
Rusden, G.W., 48
Ryan, Lyndall, 154
Ryga, George, 30, 185–90

Said, Edward, viii, 4–5, 6, 10–11, 15
"St. Lawrence" (G.J.), 153
Sartre, Jean-Paul, 94, 98, 185
Satchell, William, 38, 58, 95, 112, 113
Saturday Night, 218–19
Savage Crows, The (Drewe), 26, 77, 116, 122, 162
Savage Fields: An Essay in Literature and Cosmology
    (Lee), 19, 36
Savage Mind, The (Lévi-Strauss), 8, 10, 20, 118, 133,
    148, 159, 163, 164, 167
Saxon, indigene as, 153
Sayce, Conrad, 75, 105–6, 116, 138–9, 166
Scars (Kinsella), 51, 105
Scatology, 24–5, 77, 119–20
Schoolcraft, 90
Scientia sexualis, 79
Scorched-Wood People, The (Wiebe), 193–4, 195, 196,
    201, 207
Scot. *See* Celtic savage
Scott, Duncan Campbell, 61–2, 70, 93, 95, 104, 114,
    118, 123, 141, 166, 182
Scott, G. Firth, 28, 161
"Scratches on the Face of the Country; or, What Mr.
    Barrow Saw in the Land of the Bushmen" (Pratt),
    42, 44
Search for Sister Blue: A Play for Radio (Kidman), 177
Searle, John, 178
"Second Coming, The" (Yeats), 8
Seekers: An Indian Mystery Play, The (Roddick), 30
Self and Other, 11–14, 16, 21, 54–6, 106, 124, 126,
    127–8, 138, 142, 146, 150, 164–5, 170, 190

Semiotic field, 9–16, 19, 52, 62, 190, 214
"Semiotics in the Folk Theatre" (Bogatyrev), 171
Sets, Theatrical, 181–2
Sex, 15, 23, 36, 40, 44, 49, 51, 63–84, 86–7, 88, 91,
    102, 134, 141, 162, 167, 175, 179, 184, 186, 196–201,
    203, 205, 206, 215; male indigene, 79–83, 86–7,
    119–20, 196–8; white female, 79–83; white male,
    78–80. *See also* Homosexuality
Shakespeare, William, 171
Shakespearean forms, 48–50, 173–4
Shaman, 96, 129, 135, 137–9, 141–6, 160, 182, 197
Shamanism: Archaic Techniques of Ecstasy (Eliade), 129,
    132, 135, 137, 138, 141–2, 144, 145–6
"Shanadithit" (Pittman), 61, 156
Shaw, Harry E., 195
Shawnandithit, 126, 156–7
She (Haggard), 46
Shearer, Jill, 167, 177
"She of the Triple Chevron" (Parker), 79
Sheppard, Trish, 25–6, 53, 80–2, 83, 166
"She Says Goodbye to Mr. Cormack" (Stephen), 126,
    156
Showboat, 177
"Signs Taken for Wonders: Questions of Ambiva-
    lence and Authority Under a Tree Outside Delhi,
    May 1817" (Bhabha), 121
Silence, 124–6, 127, 210
Sinclair, Keith, 77
Six Sonnets on Human Ecology (Manifold), 28
Sketch, 53
Smith, A.J.M., 46
Smith, Jo, 35, 176
Snowball (Casey), 104
Social problem, indigene as, 53, 83, 136, 178
Song, 116, 172–3, 180, 197
Song of Solomon, 199
"Song of the Black Captor" (Mathew), 79
Sonnet, 61–2
South Africa, 219
South African literature, 14
South America, 107
South American literature, 14
Southern Saga (Connolly), 104
Soyinka, Wole, 49, 185, 217
Sparrow's Fall, The (Bodsworth), 95, 118, 133, 134
Spartan, indigene as, 152
Spear, 182
Spenser, Edmund, 26
Spirit Wrestler (Houston), 22, 119
Spivak, Gayatri Chakravorty, viii, 12, 16
*Splendid Savage: A Tale of the North Coast of Australia,
    The* (Sayce), 166

Squatter novels, 83, 90, 99, 108, 112–13, 153
Squaw, 71–6
Stage conventions, 175–6, 184–6
Standard commodities, 15–18, 19, 23, 148, 162, 179
Stellmach, Barbara, 177, 178
Stephen, Sid, 126, 156
Stephens, James Brunton, 59, 108
Stoicism, 92–5
Stony, 25
Storm of Time (Dark), 117
Story of Balla-deadro, The (McCrae), 48, 96, 149–50, 177
Story of Louis Riel the Rebel Chief, 106
Stow, Randolph, 95, 134, 140, 144, 160
Strange One, The (Bodsworth), 21, 26, 37, 69, 137
Stuart, Donald, 57–8, 70, 93, 122, 124, 161
Sturt, Charles, 64
Subject/object relations, 45, 53–4, 60–1, 80–1, 158–9,
    182, 217–18
Succubus, 76, 81, 84
Such, Peter, 21, 122, 169
Suffering, 202
"Sundance" (Purdy), 26
"Sunday Evening on Axe Flats" (Dagg), 125
Supplement, 200, 206–10, 223
Surfacing (Atwood), 37, 47, 123–4, 146, 168
Synchronic method, ix, 5–6, 165

Tales of a Dying Race (Grace), 96, 160
Tasmania. *See* Tasmanian Aborigines
Tasmanian Aborigines, 77, 122, 153–9
Tasmanian Memory of 1834. In Five Scenes, A (Mere-
    dith), 89, 154
Tattooing, 38
Tay John (O'Hagan), 30, 117, 140
Technology, white, 20–4, 28, 35–8, 102, 118, 126, 131,
    133, 135, 143, 146, 165, 218. *For indigene technology,
    see* Art; Material culture. *See also* Environmentalism
Tecumseh: A Drama (Mair), 32–4, 48–50, 70, 73, 92, 94,
    103, 117, 122, 131, 139, 172, 174, 175
Tekakwitha, Catherine, 78, 134. *See also Beautiful Los-
    ers*
Television. *See* Advertising
Temptations of Big Bear, The (Wiebe), 191, 192, 193,
    195, 196, 198–9, 200–1, 207, 213
Terdiman, Richard, 15
Thayendanegea: An Historico-Military Drama (Macken-
    zie), 32–4, 172–3, 179
Theatre, 17, 41, 99, 114, 115, 170–90
Theatre Passe Muraille. *See Far as the Eye Can See*
Theory of Literary Production, A (Macherey), 8, 213, 222
*Theory of Parody: The Teachings of Twentieth Century Art
    Forms, A* (Hutcheon), 47

Thérien, Gilles, 14

Thomas, W.T. *See* W.T. Moncrieff

Thompson, David, 91, 110, 120–1, 128, 137, 140

Three Expeditions into the Interior of Eastern Australia; With Descriptions of the Recently Explored Region of Australia Felix, and of the Present Colony of New South Wales. (T.L. Mitchell), 87, 101, 171–2

"Three Women's Texts and a Critique of Imperialism" (Spivak), 12, 16

Time and the Other: How Anthropology Makes Its Object (Fabian), 152–3, 164, 169

Timeless, indigene as, 143, 151, 161–7, 212. *See also* Prehistoric

Timeless Land, The (Dark), 73, 149, 160, 166

"To an Indian Skull" (McLachlan), 94

Todorov, Tzvetan, 4, 12, 20, 40, 42, 52–4, 86, 100, 134, 184–5

Torture, 92–4

To the Islands (Stow), 95, 134, 140, 144, 160

"To the West" (MacKay and Dampier), 175, 177

Townend, Christine, 28, 80–2

"Tracker, The" (Wongar), 92

Trackers: A Novel, The (Wongar), 47, 113

Tragedy and Social Evolution (Figes), 49

Traill, Catharine Parr, 58, 95, 137

Transubstantiation, cannibalism as, 204

Travels With Myself (Townend), 28, 80–2

"Treatment of the Aborigine in Australian Fiction, The" (Jones), 13

"Trucanini's Dirge" (R. Herbert), 159

"True North" (Atwood), 218

Truganini, 77, 116, 140, 155–7, 159. *See also Truganinni: 3 Workshop Plays* (Reed); *Queen Trucanini* (Cato and Ellis); *Savage Crows* (Drewe)

Truganinni: 3 Workshop Plays (Reed), 99, 180

"Truth and Power" (Foucault), 7, 85

Tucker, James, 24, 140, 214

Tuktoyaktuk, 218

Two Expeditions into the Interior of Southern Australia, During the Years 1828, 1829, 1830, and 1831: with Observations on the Soil, Climate, and General Resources of the Colony of New South Wales (Sturt), 64

"Two Lectures" (Foucault), 9–10, 188

Twyborn Affair, The (White), 192

Ubi sunt, 48, 60, 159–60, 211

Ulysses (Joyce), 9

"Underground" (Mudie), 132

"Upper Darling, The" (Ferguson), 23

Valley of the Sky, The (Rayment), 27

Vancouver, George, 96, 139

Van Diemen's Land: An Operatic Drama (Thomas), 115, 172

Vanished Tribes, The (Devaney), 160

Vanishing Point, The (W.O. Mitchell), 24–5, 77, 92, 119, 141

Venus Half-Caste (Mann), 70, 83, 105

Verisimilitude, 7, 43, 51–8, 62, 171–2, 178–81, 184–90

Victory of Geraldine Gull, The (Clark), 215–16

View of the Present State of Ireland, A (Spenser), 26

Village of Souls, The (Child), 22, 33, 39, 131, 143

Violence, 15, 17, 23, 26, 37, 44–5, 51, 67, 76–7, 85–106, 179, 182, 186, 196, 197, 201–5, 210, 215

Virgil, 205

Vision Splendid (Ronan), 70

Vogan, A.J., 99, 101

Voss (White), 191, 193, 196, 197, 199–200, 201, 202, 203, 206–7, 209–10, 212, 213

Voyage to the Pacific Ocean; Undertaken by Command of his Majesty, for making Discoveries in the Northern Hemisphere: Performed under the Direction of Captains Cook, Clarke, and Gore, In the Years 1776, 1777, 1778, 1779, and 1780. Being a copious, comprehensive, and satisfactory Abridgement of the Voyage written by Captain James Cook and Captain James King, A, 27

Voyages from Montreal on the River St.Laurence Through the Continent of North America to the Frozen and Pacific Oceans In the Years 1789 and 1793 with a Preliminary account of the Rise, Progress, and Present State of the Fur Trade of that Country (A. Mackenzie), 66

Wabeno Feast, The (Drew), 37, 47, 118, 135, 160, 167–8

Wacousta or The prophecy (J. Richardson), 15, 27, 70–1, 73, 87, 124, 148–9

Waiting for the Barbarians (Coetzee), 14

Walch, Garnet, 176

Walker, Joe, 53, 69, 83

Wallace, J.W., 176

Walsh (Pollock), 182

"Waltzing Matilda" (Paterson), 122–3, 177

Ward, Jill, 192–3

Wardrums of Skedans, The (Fairbairn), 180

"Watkwenies" (D.C. Scott), 62, 93

Watson, Don, 26, 137

Watson, E.L. Grant, 29

Waubageshig, 220

Ways of Seeing (Berger), 4, 65, 71, 150

We Are Métis (Redbird), 69

Webb, Grahame, 37

Weir, Peter, 168

We of the Never-Never (Gunn), 114

Wetherald, A. Ethelwyn, 69, 71

"What is an Author?" (Foucault), 192

What the Crow Said (Kroetsch), 123, 168

"Where Is the Voice Coming From?" (Wiebe), 207–8

"White blackfellow", 24, 209, 215

"White Captive, The" (Mathew), 79

White god, 140–1

White Man's Indian: Images of the American Indian from Columbus to the Present, The (Berkhofer), 14

"White Man's Mission, The" (Popular Theatre Troupe), 156, 183

White, Patrick, 17–18, 97, 215, 222

White Racism: A Psychohistory (Kovel), 25, 36, 77, 145

Whitworth, Robert P., 187

Wiebe, Rudy, 17–18, 97, 191–214, 222

Wilcox, Dora, 154

Wilderness Men (O'Hagan), 162

Wilks, William, 58, 97

Williams, Margaret, 176

Willshire, W. H., 66–7, 105

Winged Seeds (Prichard), 132, 149

Wings of Silence: An Australian Tale, The (Cossins), 51

Winter Adventures of Three Boys in the Great Lone Land (Egerton Young), 128–9, 134, 135

Wolf, Eric R., 5, 154, 158

Women of the Sun (Maris and Borg), 40

Wongar, Birimbir, 47, 92, 113, 135

Wretched of the Earth, The (Fanon), 86, 88, 94, 98, 102–3, 129, 151, 155, 156

Wright, Ronald, 219

Wrightson, Patricia, 29, 136

Writing. *See* orality

"Writing (from) the Feminine: George Sand and the Novel of Female Pastoral" (Miller), 74–5

Yandy (Stuart), 57, 161

Yaralie (Stuart), 57, 70, 122

Yarra Yarra: or, The Wandering Aborigine (Cornwallis), 48

Yeats, W.B., 8

Young, Edward, 38, 39

Young, Egerton R., 87, 128–9, 131, 134, 135

Young, T.F., 122

Zahar, Renate, 88